PRESIDENT DONALD TRUMP AND HIS POLITICAL DISCOURSE

President Donald Trump and His Political Discourse brings together a diverse collection of perspectives on President Trump's Twitter rhetoric. Truly unique in its in-depth exploration, the volume demonstrates the ways in which international and U.S. relations, media and "fake news," and marginalized groups, among other things, have been the subject of President Trump's tweets. It also features qualitative–quantitative analyses, evaluating tweet patterns, broader language shifts, and the psychology of President Trump's Twitter voice. The purpose of this collection is not only to analyze the language used but also to consider the ramifications of the various messages on both individual and global levels, for which Trump is both celebrated and criticized. Interdisciplinary in approach, this collection is a useful resource for students in political rhetoric and communication, international relations, linguistics, journalism, leadership studies, and more.

Michele Lockhart, PhD, is a faculty member in the School of Arts, Technology, and Emerging Communication at The University of Texas at Dallas and serves as the Director of Programs and Accreditation for Academic Affairs and Office of the Provost. Her recent publications, co-edited with Kathleen Mollick, include *Political Women: Language and Leadership* (2013), *Global Women Leaders: Studies in Feminist Political Rhetoric* (2014), and *Hillary Rodham Clinton and the 2016 Election: Her Political and Social Discourse* (2015).

PRESIDENT DONALD TRUMP AND HIS POLITICAL DISCOURSE

Ramifications of Rhetoric via Twitter

Edited by Michele Lockhart

Routledge
Taylor & Francis Group

NEW YORK AND LONDON

First published 2019
by Routledge
711 Third Avenue, New York, NY 10017

and by Routledge
2 Park Square, Milton Park, Abingdon, Oxon, OX14 4RN

Routledge is an imprint of the Taylor & Francis Group, an informa business

© 2019 Taylor & Francis

Library of Congress Cataloging-in-Publication Data
Names: Lockhart, Michele, author of introduction.
Title: President Donald Trump and his political discourse: ramifications of rhetoric via Twitter / [introduction by] Michele Lockhart.
Description: New York, NY: Routledge, 2019.
Identifiers: LCCN 2018020910 | ISBN 9781138489059 (hardback) | ISBN 9781138489066 (pbk.)
Subjects: LCSH: Trump, Donald, 1946—Language. | Communication in politics—United States—History—21st century. | Rhetoric—Political aspects—United States—History—21st century. | Microblogs—Political aspects—United States. | Twitter.
Classification: LCC E913.3 .P74 2018 | DDC 973.933092—dc23
LC record available at https://lccn.loc.gov/2018020910

ISBN: 978-1-138-48905-9 (hbk)
ISBN: 978-1-138-48906-6 (pbk)
ISBN: 978-1-351-03878-2 (ebk)

Typeset in Bembo
by codeMantra

CONTENTS

CONTRIBUTORS

Christopher Carter is a Professor of English at the University of Cincinnati, where he teaches courses in writing theory, activist rhetoric, and visual culture while serving as Composition Director. He is an author of *Rhetoric and Resistance in the Corporate Academy* (Hampton Press, 2008), *Rhetorical Exposures: Confrontation and Contradiction in US Social Documentary Photography* (University of Alabama Press, 2015), and *Metafilm: Materialist Rhetoric and Reflexive Cinema* (Ohio State University Press, 2018).

Rod Carveth is an Associate Professor of Journalism in the School of Global Journalism and Communication at Morgan State University in Baltimore, MD. He also serves as the Director of Graduate Studies for the School. Rod teaches courses in digital media, financial journalism, and media economics. His current research examines Donald Trump's use of social media and how it impacts contemporary journalism.

Dawn F. Colley teaches in the Program for Writing and Rhetoric at the University of Colorado at Boulder, where she earned her doctorate in English. Her current research interests include animal rhetorics, the rhetoric of Big Data, and new media rhetorics. She is presently at work on an examination of how moral authority is established and maintained in new media platforms.

Lance Cummings teaches professional writing courses in the English Department at University of North Carolina Wilmington. His research has focused on comparative rhetoric and translingual histories of writing instruction, specifically in the early twentieth-century Young Men's Christian Association (YMCA), leading him to his current explorations of ethos, religion, and professional writing.

Anish Dave is an Associate Professor of English at Georgia Southwestern State University in Americus, GA. He has a PhD in Rhetoric and Professional Communication from Iowa State University and an MFA in Creative Writing (Fiction) from the University of Nevada, Las Vegas. His articles have appeared in journals such as *Technical Communication Quarterly*, *Research in the Teaching of English*, and *Business Communication Quarterly*.

Dorian Hunter Davis is an Adjunct Instructor and a doctoral candidate in communication at American University in Washington, DC. He has taught journalism at Marymount Manhattan College and Seton Hall University, and talked politics and popular culture on TV and radio. He holds an MA from The City University of New York (CUNY) Graduate School of Journalism and a BFA from New York University (NYU).

J. Brian Houston, PhD, is an Associate Professor and Chair in the Department of Communication at the University of Missouri and is a Director for the Disaster and Community Crisis Center at the University of Missouri. Houston's research focuses on communication at all phases of disasters and on the mental health effects and political consequences of community crises.

Michele Lockhart, PhD, is a faculty member in the School of Arts, Technology, and Emerging Communication at The University of Texas at Dallas and serves as the Director of Programs and Accreditation for Academic Affairs and Office of the Provost. She is the co-editor, along with Kathleen Mollick, of *Political Women: Language and Leadership* (2013), *Global Women Leaders: Studies in Feminist Political Rhetoric* (2014), and *Hillary Rodham Clinton and the 2016 Election: Her Political and Social Discourse* (2015).

Javier Lorenzo Rodríguez is an Assistant Professor of Political Science in the Department of Social Sciences at Universidad Carlos III de Madrid. He has been a visiting researcher in several academic institutions (SMaPP Lab at New York University (NYU), State University of New York (SUNY) Binghamton University, and Università Roma III, among others). His research interests and recent publications revolve around the analysis of elites' political behavior in social media as well as the impact of Information and Communication Technologies (ICTs) in electoral campaigns in the United States and the European Union.

Bryan A. Lutz is a Visiting Professor of Writing at Grand Valley State University. His research examines digital activism or how activist organizations use technology to construct an identity, argue, and advocate to solve problems. His teaching incorporates digital activism into academic writing and professional writing courses. Bryan's published scholarship appears in *Computers and Composition Online* and *The Journal of Critical Thought and Praxis*.

Francisco Seoane Pérez is an Assistant Professor of Journalism Studies in the Department of Journalism and Film Studies at Universidad Carlos III de Madrid. From 2010 to 2015, he was a Lecturer in Political Communication at the University of Castilla-La Mancha. He is the co-editor, along with Katharine Sarikakis from the University of Vienna, of the *International Journal of Media & Cultural Politics*. His latest book is *Political Communication in Europe: The Cultural and Structural Limits of the European Public Sphere* (Palgrave Macmillan, 2013).

Irene Asiaín Román is an MA candidate at the Spanish School of Diplomacy and a graduate in Journalism from the Universidad Carlos III de Madrid. She has worked in the Economy section of *El Mundo* (2016) and has contributed online to the Telecinco News and Cuatro News (2017). She will be presenting at the 68th International Communication Association (ICA) conference in 2018 in Prague.

Aram Sinnreich is an Associate Professor and Chair of Communication Studies at American University in Washington, DC. He is the author of *Mashed Up* (2010) and *The Piracy Crusade* (2013). He holds a Masters Degree from the Columbia University School of Journalism and a doctorate from the Annenberg School for Communication at the University of Southern California.

Erec Smith is an Associate Professor of Rhetoric at York College of Pennsylvania. He has published on the rhetorics of politics, size acceptance, Buddhist philosophy, and disciplinarity.

Sarah Smith-Frigerio is a doctoral student in the Department of Communication at the University of Missouri. Her research focus involves the ways in which mental health concerns are represented in entertainment and news media as well as the personal and political implications of such representations.

INTRODUCTION

Michele Lockhart

In his most recent venture, as President of the United States, his first political, elected position, Donald J. Trump gives rise to intense feelings about him, both at home and abroad, through his use of presidential rhetoric. Trump, the 45th President of the United States (Trump 2018), has used technology, the Internet, and social media to take control of his voice and message via Twitter, the online news and social networking platform. While a business person, a television show creator, and a published author of dozens of books over several decades, such as *Great Again: How to Fix Our Crippled America* (2015), *Think Big: Make It Happen in Business and in Life* (2007), *Trump: Surviving at the Top* (1990), and *Trump: The Art of the Deal* (1987), he has demonstrated his power of persuasion in those arenas.

The purpose of this collection is not only to analyze the language used but also to consider the ramifications of the various messages on both individual and global levels, for which people seem to either love him or hate him. As this collection goes to press, Trump is situated in his second year and first term in office—the collection serves as a snapshot and an early look at the man, the message, and the medium that this president uses to communicate with both friends and foes. Trump continues to be vocal with his tweets, despite having a team of White House staffers. Questions surrounding which forum and which voice is the official message from the White House, private opinion versus public opinion, have surfaced along with concerns of the content of some of the Twitter messages themselves. While the number of tweets published from the @realDonaldTrump Twitter account since the publication of this collection will be manifold, no doubt, and could serve as research and tangible evidence for scholars for years to come, this collection provides a foundation of the development of Trump's tweets and the scope of his messages.[1]

With my collaborator, Kathleen Mollick, and other colleagues in political rhetoric, our research and publications were geared toward the language women use in politics and leadership positions (*Political Women: Language and Leadership*, 2013; *Global Women Leaders: Studies in Feminist Political Rhetoric*, 2014; *Hillary Rodham Clinton and the 2016 Election: Her Political and Social Discourse*, 2015).[2] While still investigating the power of language, my scholarship has shifted from the rhetoric women use in leadership and political positions to one particular case study of the opposite gender. This shift was generated by the power of rhetoric itself: The Commander-in-Chief's use of language on Twitter was a rhetoric event that was urgent, regardless of gender.

The Language of Presidents: Attributes and Qualities

The language and communication styles of U.S. Presidents have been a source of scholarship since the first president of the United States; much of the scholarship often includes presidential leadership styles (Gergen 2001; Greenstein 2004; Edwards and Wayne 2006). And Trump is no exception.

Early twenty-first-century research laid a foundation of key presidential attributes and qualities. In *Presidential Leadership: Politics and Policy Making*, the authors examine the presidency through two lenses: the president as "director of change" (19) and "facilitator of change" (20). Another example is found with *The Presidential Difference: Leadership Style from FDR to George W. Bush*. Greenstein examines twelve presidencies and how they relate to "Effectiveness as a Public Communicator" (217), "Organizational Capacity" (218), "Political Skill" (219), "Vision" (220), "Cognitive Style" (220), and "Emotional intelligence" (221). "Beware the presidential contender who lacks emotional intelligence. In its absence all else may turn to ashes" (223). A final example is found in *Eyewitness to Power: The Essence of Leadership: Nixon to Clinton*, where Gergen takes the reader inside several presidential administrations and points to seven necessary attributes needed for effective and successful leadership: "Leadership Starts from Within," "A Central, Compelling Purpose," "A Capacity to Persuade," "An Ability to Work within the System," "A Sure, Quick Start," "Strong, Prudent Advisers," and "Inspiring Others to Carry On the Mission" (345–51). Considering such scholarship and the acknowledged importance of key attributes and qualities, one sees the research trend continue with more recent scholarship.

Analyzing the realities and ramifications when key attributes and qualities are weak or fail is the focus in "The Contemporary Presidency: Organizing the Trump Presidency" (2018). Pfiffner examines Trump's first nine months as President and the manner in which he organized and managed his White House teams. "His approach to his White House and cabinet differed significantly from his predecessors. Despite his protestations, his White House was characterized by the lack of a coherent policy process, infighting among factions of his staff, and conflict between Trump and his national security cabinet" (164). Interestingly, at the time of editing this collection, Trump had fired six members of his administration, including Secretary of State, Rex Tillerson, and FBI Director, James Comey, and sixteen members had resigned, including Press Secretary, Sean Spicer, and National Security Adviser, Michael T. Flynn (Berke); in consistent form, Trump has tweeted about such ongoings (Trump May 10, 2017; December 2, 2017; March 13, 2018).

The "Forum on the 2016 Presidential Primary: Rhetoric, Identity, and Presidentiality in the Post-Obama Era" (2017), which originated at the 2016 Rhetoric Society of America Conference (489), brings five scholars, including Karrin Vasby Anderson and Mary E. Stuckey, together to investigate "how (if at all) rhetorics of presidentiality have changed in the post-Obama era" (489) and "scholars reflect on rhetoric, identity, and change as manifested in the 2016 presidential primary" (490); the contributors argue that "[t]he post-racial, post-feminist, postpartisan political culture that some hoped would be forged during Obama's tenure did not materialize. That is, contributors to this forum would agree, for the best. Race, gender justice, and diversity of political opinion are not things that citizens in a diverse democracy should strive to move beyond" (492). Moving forward from the "Post-Obama Era" to the "Trump Era" proper brings seven scholars together in a "Politics Spotlight" with their attention drawn to language itself in "Contentious Politics in the Trump Era" (2018). The focus is on key terms and a "uniform vocabulary that can be used to describe instances of unjust treatment or control by the government" (17). The contributors also compare "Trump's administration to other authoritarian regimes" (17), "the degree to which Trump's administration has adopted authoritarian styles of rule" (17), and "specific human rights threats" (17), among other things. Interestingly, both the "Forum" and the "Spotlight" with its multiple contributors take an early and immediate look toward the future and what is needed: "rhetorical resources that foster ethical citizenship amid the chaos" (2017, 492) and "offer activists suggestions for real-world action" (2018, 17). And with the list of attributes and qualities deemed by presidential scholars to be most desirable and important, one can easily situate Trump somewhere else altogether based on his use of language, which echo his actions or serve as a warning for those actions yet to come.

The Voice of a President

> My use of social media is not Presidential – it's MODERN DAY PRESIDENTIAL. Make American Great Again!
>
> ~*Trump July 1, 2017*

Research surrounding U.S. Presidents also considers the voice of the president versus the speechwriter (Ritter and Medhurst 2004), and in most modern times, who is the writer behind a particular Twitter handle, such as @realDonaldTrump. And what power do presidential words entail (Campbell and Jamieson 2008).

For example, in *Presidents Creating the Presidency: Deeds Done in Words*, Campbell and Jamieson explicate the various rhetorical strategies implemented by presidents, illustrating how one can or cannot re-create a presidency (with words) in conjunction with the other branches of government (6–7). In "Disruption, Demonization, Deliverance, and Norm Destruction: The Rhetorical Signature of Donald J. Trump," Jamieson and Taussig (2017) note the "rhetorical signature" that Trump established before taking the Oath of Office and within his first one hundred days (619), which "includes seeming spontaneity laced with Manichean, evidence-flouting, accountability-dodging, and institution-disdaining claims. By offering apparently impromptu messaging in scriptless speeches and tweets at unusual hours [...]" (620). And it is that "rhetorical signature" that serves as tangible evidence for rhetoricians, psychologists, and presidential scholars, among others, to work toward an answer as to how and why Trump's language, attributes, and qualities vary from others before him. In "The Exception or the Rule: Using Words to Assess Analytic Thinking, Donald Trump, and the American Presidency" (2017), U.S. Presidents are ranked based on their use of language and analytic score (313). While considering trends, findings show that "Donald Trump is by far the least analytic President in history, but the same could have been said about Barack Obama 8 years ago" (314). "[...] the trends in presidential politics may continue to select Trump-like individuals for many elections to come" (315). And with such trends and predictions, examining and learning more about the voice of a president is at the forefront.

Organization of the Book

Part I: The Campaign, the Twittersphere, and the "New Age" of Rhetoric: Truth versus Reality

> A man must know the truth about all the particular things of which he speaks or writes[...].
>
> ~*Plato, Phaedrus, 167*

Part I begins with the 2016 U.S. Presidential Campaign, lays a foundation of all things Twitter, and prepares the reader for the "New Age" of Rhetoric. In Chapter 1, "Seizing the Populist Rhetorical Toolkit: A Comparative Analysis of Trump and Clinton's Discourse on Twitter during the 2016 U.S. Presidential Campaign," Francisco Seoane Pérez, Irene Asiaín Román, and Javier Lorenzo Rodríguez conduct a content analysis to characterize the populist features of Trump's rhetoric on Twitter and compare it to the opposing candidate, Hillary Clinton. The most recurrent rhetorical figures are examined to determine which discursive tropes and fallacies are tied to online populism. Among the findings in this chapter, Trump is twice as likely to question the truthfulness of a source. Dawn F. Colley explores the relationship between Trump's language, his use of Twitter, and the illusory truth effect to understand how Trump successfully and continually gains the support of his followers—even when his tweets are proven to be entirely false. In Chapter 2, "Of Twit-storms and Demagogues: Trump, Illusory Truths of Patriotism, and the Language of the Twittersphere," Colley contends that the way the brain processes language has a direct and fundamental connection to the determination of "truth value," and that everyone—independent of political ideology—is susceptible to falling victim to these innate processes that Trump, knowingly or not, exploits to his benefit. In Chapter 3, "The Dark Alchemy of Donald Trump: Re-inventing Presidential Rhetorics through Christian and 'New Age' Discourses," Lance Cummings argues the importance of the alchemy between "New Age" and Christian rhetorics to understanding Trump's persona and use of Twitter; the power of language to change the self is the same power Trump relies on to change political realities. This chapter will help scholars of contemporary rhetoric understand Trump's rhetoric and use of Twitter through his connection with "New Age" and Christian rhetorics not generally associated with the Trump movement.

Part II: Power and Abuse Abroad and at Home: Foreign Policy via Twitterverse, "Bullshit," and "Nut Job"

> We shall learn the qualities of governments in the same way as we learn the qualities of individuals, since they are revealed in their deliberate acts of choice; and these are determined by the end that inspires them.
>
> ~*Aristotle, Rhetoric, 197*

Part II of the book examines Trump's presidential rhetoric that engenders intense feelings, both positive and negative. In Chapter 4, "President Trump's Tweets on the Middle East, North Korea, and Russia: The Constructive and the Unconstructive," Anish Dave analyzes Trump's foreign policy tweets surrounding the Middle East, North Korea, and Russia from January 20, 2017 through January 4, 2018. The analysis surrounding Trump's tweets enlightens the reader about his foreign policy priorities and the manner in which he works on foreign policy issues. In "The Paradox of Dissent: Bullshit and the Twitter Presidency," Chapter 5, Christopher Carter examines Trump's attitude toward truth, which Harry Frankfurt suggests, ranges from negation (or deceit) to disregard (or bullshit). While Carter's chapter reaffirms inquiries into the general operation of bullshit, it focuses on the concept's specific importance to the Twitter presidency, describing a communicative process that commonly unfolds in three stages. Sarah Smith-Frigerio and J. Brian Houston explore Trump's media and Twitter discourse referencing mental health concerns in Chapter 6, "Crazy, Insane, Nut Job, Wacko, Basket Case, and Psycho: Donald Trump's Tweets Surrounding Mental Health Issues and Attacks on Media Personalities." Findings show that those with whom Trump disagrees are overtly attacked by construing them as possessing a mental health issue. This appears to be part of an effort to discredit and disparage them as opponents and individuals. Additionally, Trump links mental health concerns to personal shortcomings and failings, instead of attributing mental health concerns to biological causes or the experience of traumatic events. This is in direct conflict with the discourses used in effective anti-stigma messaging campaigns and educational workshops. In Chapter 7, "Habitat for Inhumanity: How Trolls Set the Stage for @realDonaldTrump," Erec Smith explores the relationship of Trump to the culture of trolling while explaining the rhetoric, ideology, and ritualistic actions of trolling, the possible influences of postmodern thought and media mistrust on the rise of trolling, and how Trump continues to attract more and more followers within a habitus of trolls in the environment which he feel most at home—the "Twitterverse."

Part III: "Fake News" and Madness: Read, Re-tweet, and Teach All about It

> For purposes of proof, however, the material at the orator's disposal is twofold, one kind made up of things which are not thought out by himself, but depend upon the circumstances and are dealt with by rule, [...]: the other kind is founded entirely on the orator's reasoned argument.
>
> ~Cicero, De Oratore, 324

Part III investigates "Fake News" and its maddening effects. Dorian Hunter Davis and Aram Sinnreich examine Trump's use of "fake news" as a rhetorical device to discredit unfavorable news coverage, in Chapter 8, "Tweet the Press: Effects of Donald Trump's 'Fake News!' Epithet on Civics and Popular Culture." More than 1,000 @realDonaldTrump tweets from Trump's first six months in office are examined: this chapter demonstrates that Trump used "fake news" more often as a reputation management tactic than he did to call out inaccurate reporting or distinguish between his own news values and those of the mainstream media. Davis and Sinnreich identify several consequences for civics and popular culture of Trump's "fake news" epithet. In Chapter 9, "Setting the 'Fake News' Agenda: Trump's Use of Twitter and the Agenda-building Effect," Rod Carveth explores how Trump has used social media to build an agenda for his presidency, one of which reflects what Richard Hofstadter referred to as a "paranoid style." The chapter reviews some of the evidence of Trump's feelings of persecution and engaging in conspiracy theories and examines the genesis and outcome of Trump's "ultimate alternative fact" of his being wiretapped. In Chapter 10, "Digital Sophistry: Trump, Twitter, and Teaching about Fake News," Bryan A. Lutz distinguishes fake news from other forms of misinformation by comparing two prolific fake news stories to earlier forms of tabloid media. The concept of sophistry is used to catalog the deceptive tactics of fake news sites and their relationship to social media: the blending of sophistic rhetoric with an understanding of digital literacy culminates into a concept called "Digital Sophistry." This chapter demonstrates how instructors may make old theories new, combining the sophistic tradition with digital literacy, and demonstrating how instructor and student can use digital sophistry as a concept for identifying and assessing fake news.

A Final Word

I thank my mentor of eleven years (and counting), Hugh Burns[3]: his invaluable insight and thoughtful talks while working through various iterations of this introduction are ones which I am indebted.

And I thank you, the readers, for your interest in this collection. After you read these chapters, my hope is that you will have a better perspective and understanding of the ramifications of one person's language via Twitter. Again, the purpose of the collection is not only to analyze the language used but also to consider the messages on both individual and global levels, for which Trump is both celebrated and criticized.

While Trump's actions do remind us of other presidential histories, intense political debates, nasty campaigns, and unpresidential acts of the past, at times, it is his use of social media—to tweet publicly—to declare, defend, or demean, as necessary, based on his agenda. It is his unrelenting private voice in a public forum and use of political rhetoric that is our present as this collection is sent to press. The research surrounding Trump's language is important not only in present day but also for our future. Throughout this collection, many angles have been examined. Examples of some of Trump's tweets that have been proven to be entirely false: we must question what is [T]ruth, false, and "fake" and how do we determine the difference. The plethora of personal attacks on individuals and populations of people, as explicated throughout this collection, raises the question: when am I next?

And even though the topic and focus of this collection has shifted from my previous publications, Trump's tweets and the research surrounding them serve as an energizer and motivator for women, among others, to seek positions in leadership and politics: Trump's language via Twitter has encouraged the Other to organize and resist.

It is unknown how, when, and why the next president will choose to communicate with the people and the press. Time will tell. But those words will give insight to the character and mind of the individual, whether those words are delivered via Twitter or not. The world will be watching and listening.

Notes

1 All Tweets contained within this collection are quoted verbatim, including original punctuation, spacing, and capitalization. [...] has been added (within quotation marks) to indicate that the tweet contained additional language, either before and/or after the provided text.
2 Lockhart, Michele and Kathleen Mollick (Eds.). Lanham, MD: Lexington Books.
3 Hugh Burns, Ph.D., Professor Emeritus (Texas Woman's University).

Bibliography

Anderson, Karrin Vasby. "Forum on the 2016 Presidential Primary: Rhetoric, Identity, and Presidentiality in the Post-Obama Era." [Special Section]. *Rhetoric & Public Affairs* 20, no. 3 (2017): 489–92.

Aristotle. "Rhetoric." In *The Rhetorical Tradition: Readings from Classical Times to the Present.* 2nd ed. Eds. Patricia Bizzell and Bruce Herzberg. New York: Bedford/St. Martin's, 2000, 179–240.

Berke, Jeremy. "VA Secretary Shulkin is Out—Here are All the Casualties of the Trump Administration So Far." *Business Insider* online, last modified March 28, 2018, www.businessinsider.com/who-has-trump-fired-so-far-james-comey-sean-spicer-michael-flynn-2017-7

Campbell, Karlyn Kohrs and Kathleen Hall Jamieson. *Presidents Creating the Presidency: Deeds Done in Words.* Chicago, IL: U of Chicago P, 2008.

Cicero. "De Oratore." In *The Rhetorical Tradition: Readings from Classical Times to the Present.* 2nd ed. Eds. Patricia Bizzell and Bruce Herzberg. New York: Bedford/St. Martin's, 2000, 289–339.

Crabtree, Charles and Christian Davenport. "Contentious Politics in the Trump Era." Politics Spotlight. *PS, Political Science & Politics* 51, no. 1 (2018): 17–25.

Edwards III, George C. and Stephen J. Wayne. *Presidential Leadership: Politics and Policy Making.* Belmont, MA: Thomas Wadsworth, 2006.

Gergen, David. *Eyewitness to Power: The Essence of Leadership: Nixon to Clinton.* New York: Touchstone, 2001.

Greenstein, Fred. *The Presidential Difference: Leadership Style from FDR to George W. Bush.* Princeton, NJ: Princeton UP, 2004.

Jamieson, Kathleen Hall and Doron Taussig. "Disruption, Demonization, Deliverance, and Norm Destruction: The Rhetorical Signature of Donald J. Trump." *Political Science Quarterly* 132, no. 4 (2017): 619–50.

Jordan, Kayla N. and James W. Pennebaker. "The Exception or the Rule: Using Words to Assess Analytic Thinking, Donald Trump, and the American Presidency." *Translational Issues in Psychological* Science 3, no. 3 (2017): 312–16.

Pfiffner, James P. "The Contemporary Presidency: Organizing the Trump Presidency." *Presidential Studies Quarterly* 48, no. 1 (2018): 153–67.

Plato. *Phaedrus.* In *The Rhetorical Tradition: Readings from Classical Times to the Present.* 2nd ed. Eds. Patricia Bizzell and Bruce Herzberg, 138–68. New York: Bedford/St. Martin's, 2000.

Ritter, Kurt and Martin J. Medhurst. *Presidential Speechwriting: From the New Deal to the Reagan Revolution and Beyond.* College Station, TX: Texas A&M UP, 2004.

Trump, Donald. "Donald J. Trump," assessed February 24, 2018. www.donaldjtrump.com/about/

Trump, Donald. Twitter Post. December 2, 2017. 9:14 A.M. https://twitter.com/realdonaldtrump/status/937007006526959618

Trump, Donald. Twitter Post. July 1, 2017, 3:41 P.M. https://twitter.com/realdonaldtrump/status/881281755017355264

Trump, Donald. Twitter Post. March 13, 2018, 5:44 A.M. https://twitter.com/realdonaldtrump/status/973540316656623616

Trump, Donald. Twitter Post. May 10, 2017. 4:19 A.M. https://twitter.com/realdonaldtrump/status/862265729718128641

Trump, Donald and Bill Zanker. *Think Big: Make It Happen in Business and in Life.* New York: HarperCollins Publishers, 2007.

Trump, Donald J. *Great Again: How to Fix Our Crippled America.* New York: Threshold Editions, 2015.

Trump, Donald J. and Charles Leerhsen. *Trump: Surviving at the Top.* New York: Random House, 1990.

Trump, Donald J. and Tony Schwartz. *Trump: The Art of the Deal.* New York: Random House, 1987.

PART I

The Campaign, the Twittersphere, and the "New Age" of Rhetoric

Truth versus Reality

1

SEIZING THE POPULIST RHETORICAL TOOLKIT

A Comparative Analysis of Trump and Clinton's Discourse on Twitter during the 2016 U.S. Presidential Campaign

Francisco Seoane Pérez, Irene Asiaín Román, and Javier Lorenzo Rodríguez

A Postmodern Campaign

The 2016 presidential campaign might be remembered as the one in which populism met digital social media. The "insulting" rhetoric of the then real estate tycoon and reality TV celebrity Donald Trump, and who Korostelina (2017, 50) describes as "The Great Insulter", catalyzed the anger of a frustrated electorate, especially in those counties "with more economic distress, worse health, higher drug, alcohol and suicide mortality rates, lower educational attainment, and higher marital separation/divorce rates" (Monnat and Brown 2017, 228). Although Facebook might have been more effective in spreading tailored political advertisements and in raising micro-donations, Twitter became the social medium of choice for influencing the journalistic agenda. Hillary Clinton announced her candidacy on this social network, but it would be her eventual rival who would keep journalists and the public abreast with his tweets.

The 2016 election was in many ways a showcase of digital politics' darkest features, such as uncivil language, polarization, disinformation, rumors, and lies (Collanyi et al. 2016; Owen 2018; Shanahan 2018). Trump's own victory as presidential candidate was for commentators like journalist Jeet Heer the confirmation of postmodernism's wildest predictions. We would be entering a world "where media overload is destroying a sense of a shared reality" (Heer 2017, para. 2). Trump would have been rewarded, in pure postmodernist fashion, for his performance, not for the truthfulness of what he is, a dubious real estate mogul, or what he says: His claim about Obama's birth outside the United States being the first of his many conspiracy theories (Uscinski 2016). Trump's reliance on his own celebrity vindicates Daniel J. Boorstin's early insight that modern fame and name recognition are not grounded on any objective merit but on one's constant presence in the media spotlight (Boorstin [1962] 2012). Following postmodernist authors like Frederic Jameson or Jean Baudrillard, Heer deems Trump "unreal," a "simulacra businessman" (Heer 2017, para. 7).

The relevance of social media such as Facebook or Twitter as a source of campaign information was certified by a Pew Research Center report (2016). Nearly half (44%) of U.S. adults followed campaign news on social media and one-fourth (24%) said they read posts from Trump and Clinton (2016). As Williams underscores, the percentage of the American population following the campaign via social media is larger than the proportion of citizens reading either local or national newspapers (Williams 2017).

It is Donald Trump himself who has, in his traditional hyperbolic tone, stated the relevance of social media, and particularly Twitter, for his campaign. Without Twitter, he claimed, he would not have become the President (Baynes 2017). As of Election Day, November 8, 2016, Trump had reached 12.9 million followers, two million more than Clinton (10.2 million followers). The difference in levels of engagement was even higher, both on Twitter and Facebook: In a study that analyzed three weeks during May 2016, the Pew Research Center (2016) revealed that Trump tweeted or posted on Facebook with a similar frequency as Clinton or Sanders, but that Trump received much more attention from users. Trump's tweets were five times more likely to be retweeted than Clinton's, and the number of shares on Facebook was eight times higher for Trump than for Clinton. While some argue that Trump did not do well during the televised debates (Decker 2016) and missed the editorial endorsement of traditional pro-Republican newspapers, his Twitter account continued to grow with supporters and engagement. According to a comparative study of the Twitter accounts of Trump and Clinton by Darwish et al. (2017), the Republican candidate beat his Democratic rival on several measures: Trump's campaign slogan, "Make America Great Again" resonated much more than Clinton's "Stronger Together." The second most frequent category of hashtags benefitting Clinton was about attacking Trump (e.g. #TrumpTapes, #TangerineNightmare, and #InterrogateTrump), which led these researchers to affirm that Clinton "was framed in reference to her rival" (Darwish et al. 2017, 156). Trump was also more effective in promoting campaign activities in swing states (153).

Twitter and social media were instrumental for Trump on several grounds. First, they allowed him to subvert the agenda-setting power of mainstream news media. His Twitter statements and his own celebrity status granted him $3 billion in free media coverage (Higgins 2016). Second, his campaign reliance on Facebook for targeted advertising helped Trump avoid expenditure on cable TV, saving funds and competing effectively with a much more experienced and financially resourced rival like Clinton (Allison et al. 2016).

Going Low

However sage, Trump's online campaigning was marred by its unfair play on two dimensions: the circulation of conspiracy theories and the use of an extremely uncivil tone that received accusations of racism and sexism (Korostelina 2017).

Twitter is well known for its propensity to be a platform for astroturfing, by which fake accounts simulate a widely popular uproar for or against a candidate. There is even a black market of fake Twitter accounts that can be used to create false trending topics. The hashtag #HillaryDown was among those promoted by an army of Twitter bots (Shane 2017). In an article entitled "Trump vs. Hillary: What went Viral during the 2016 U.S. Presidential Election," Kareem Darwish et al. (2017) found that 60% of the shared links in retweets during the campaign included attacks on Clinton, and that half of those linked to sites of mixed credibility. Among such sites, one was created in June 2016 by Russian intelligence: DC Leaks. It was used as a platform to publish hacked emails from notable Democratic donors, such as financier George Soros, as well as other materials from a former North Atlantic Treaty Organization (NATO) commander and Democratic and Republican party staffers. This site was promoted online from several fake Twitter accounts simulating average U.S. citizens, including pictures of individuals and their families in their profiles to make their claims more credible and difficult to trace back to their actual Russian origin (Shane).

Misinformation was used strategically by Trump, according to linguist George Lakoff (2017). When pressured to explain his connections with Russia, the Republican candidate diverted attention by accusing Obama of wire-tapping the Trump Tower. Lakoff used this tweet to illustrate four typical strategies in Trump's tweets: "pre-emptive framing" (para. 7), creating a new scandal with no evidence; "deflection" (para. 8), putting the burden of proof on Obama; "diversion" (para. 9), Trump goes away with his false accusations, diverting attention from his Russian links; and "trial balloons" (para. 10), testing whether this conspiracy theory is believable enough to be used as an effective distraction.

The most memorable speech of the 2016 campaign did not belong to any of the rival candidates, but to the then First Lady, Michelle Obama. During the Democratic National Convention in Philadelphia on July 25, 2016, Obama lent Clinton what could be considered the Democratic motto of the campaign: "When they go low, we go high" (Washington Post Staff, July 26, 2016). Just a few days before, the Clinton campaign had aired a TV advertisement with children watching a selection of Donald Trump's most derisive statements, warning about the dangers of taking such an unconventional candidate as a role model.

Ad hominem attacks, traditionally avoided by presidential candidates, were one of Trump's rhetorical marks (Jamieson and Taussig 2017). Winberg (2017) uses the term "insult politics" to define "a certain campaign rhetoric that is centered not on criticism per se, but on *ad hominem attacks of a disparaging nature aimed at an individual or group*" (3; emphasis in original). The insults drew not only media coverage but also editorial criticism and rejection from classic Republicans. So salient was Trump's disdainful language that *The New York Times* made a count of the number of people the Republican candidate had "insulted" on Twitter before Election Day. Of the 8,000 tweets Trump published during the campaign, 12.5% were considered "insulting" by *The New York Times* (Lee and Quealy 2016). These were targeted at 300 individuals. Examples include attacks on Republican rivals such as Ted Cruz: "[...] not very presidential. [...]" (Trump May 3, 2016); the mainstream media: "[...] the dishonest media [...]" (July 25, 2016); foreign executives: "Mexico's totally corrupt gov't [...]" (July 13, 2015); and international trade agreements, such as the North American Free Trade Agreement (NAFTA): "[...] the worst economic deal in U.S. history [...]" (May 17, 2016).

The linguistic anthropologist Adam Hodges has identified two roles that Trump would be adopting when insulting and exaggerating: the "schoolyard bully" and the "snake oil salesman" (207). "Insults, by their very nature, accord with the schoolyard bully persona, but those tweets also epitomize the rhetorical moves of the snake oil salesman –the language of advertising at its slimiest" (207). Hodges finds in Trump's own concept of "truthful hyperbole," defined by the candidate himself as "an innocent form of exaggeration" (Trump and Schwartz [1987] 2015, 58), the evidence of Trump's own self-consciousness as a charlatan.

Inductively, Hodges (2017) extracts from the careful reading of Trump's tweets a formula, a method for producing tweets the Trump way: write a *derogatory noun* (e.g. "clown"), add a *gratuitous modifier* (e.g. "stupid") and a *vacuous intensifier* (e.g. "really"). The formulaic Trump tweet ("really stupid clown") is there. Examples include calling Bloomberg's journalist Tim O'Brien a "[...] really stupid talking head[s] [...]" (Trump July 23, 2015) or naming Fox News Channel Chris Stirewalt a "[...] really dumb puppet[s] [...]" (October 15, 2015).

Such was the success of Trump's insult politics during the Republican primaries that rival candidate Marco Rubio tried to imitate Trump's disrespectful language, to no avail. The defensive reaction by the mainstream media and the Republic establishment to Trump's disrespectful language were turned into a virtue: This reinforced Trump's image of an outsider candidate, reinforcing his claim of authenticity (Enli 2017).

Trump broke the norms of presidential oratory, disrupting "the sanitized, prepackaged rhetoric of his predecessors" (Jamieson and Taussig 2017, 620). Although this has brought him notoriety, it has had a negative impact as well: 70% of the general electorate disapproved of him during the campaign (Clement 2016); he won the election with one of the lowest popular votes in history (Kentish 2016), and he had the lowest approval rate of any president when he took the oath of office in January 2017 (Farber 2017). The strategy of rumors and insults is not one without side effects, but it proved effective, perhaps because of the extraordinary polarization of the electorate. Polarization in U.S. society runs so high that any fact-checking revelations are filtered through ideological blinkers, preventing any agreement on the possibility of unbiased evidence (Tharoor 2017).

Although electorally successful, Trump's insult politics may have alienated many Americans: A poll by Quinnipiac University reported that 64% of U.S. citizens wanted the president to close his account on Twitter (Lui 2017). But authors like Kreis (2017) see a danger of "normalization of right-wing populist discourses" due to Trump's status as president. A report by the Data & Society Institute has alerted the use of humor, irony, and ambiguity by the so-called 'alt-right' to make its racist and sexist discourse more palatable (Wilson 2017).

Personal Connection

When invited to give her account on the 2016 presidential campaign to the Shorenstein Center at Harvard University, *The Atlantic*'s political correspondent Molly Ball confessed she had been impressed by the "sports-like connection" between Trump and his followers (Shorenstein Center 2016). When recalling a rally in South Carolina, Ball said,

> It felt joyful, there was a profound catharsis, there was a profound emotional connection that the people in the crowd were making to this performer up on the stage…they were connecting on an emotional level, on a level of identity, in a way that I have rarely seen in politics. I think that's why people who hard core support Donald Trump cannot be moved off of that, no matter what policy flip-flops he makes or offensive statements…because they're connected not in the way that people connect with a boring Jeb Bush policy paper that they've read on a website, but in the way that they connect with their sports team…they really feel like members of a group, like their voice is being heard in a way that it hasn't before.
>
> *(2016)*

Ball was tapping the power of populist rhetoric, the sensation of that personal connection between the political leader and the mass of followers. Although authors like Hawkins (2010) see populism as a "thin ideology" defined by some recurrent traits, such as opposition to elites, willing to overhaul the establishment, or preference for a perceived legitimacy over the codified legality, other authors like Winberg (2017) claim that "populism is not defined by ideology but by rhetoric" (4): The orator presents her/himself as an everyday person against the establishment, embodying the virtues of the nation against an 'other' that is constructed as an existential threat to the traditional community. For Jagers and Walgrave (2007), populism can be described as a "political communication style" that could be "thin," if it merely makes constant references to 'the people,' or "thick," if it goes against political and media elites, or if it discriminates against an ethnicity or set of the population (322). For Laclau (2005), populism is a rhetorical strategy to assemble diverse popular demands into a single, sweeping nationwide neo-identity under empty signifiers, which may be expressions, such as "Crooked Hillary," by which the anger toward the rival is codified into a catchy slogan, or the populist leader himself, who will embody the idea of a systemic change.

Populism may be blamed for democracy's bad press for millennia. The first skeptics of democracy were found in classical Athens, with Plato warning of the dangers of mob rule after the death sentence of his master Socrates. The Late Roman Republic limited democracy to the Senate, where the so-called *populares* claimed to be acting on behalf of the people (Strauss 2016). It was not until the American and French Revolutions, where democracy was enhanced by nationalism yet tamed by liberalism and is protection of individual rights, that liberal or constitutional democracy became a desirable standard of governance. This is why some authors like Cas Mudde (April 2002) claim that populism can be thought of as a hypertrophy of democracy, whereby majority rule becomes illiberal, sidelining the rule of law and the protection of minorities.

Trump may be deemed as the latest example of a tradition of populism in the United States that began with the People's Party (also known as Populist Party) in the late nineteenth century and its ideal of agrarian democracy (Berlet and Lyons 2000). Cowls (2017) finds in Charles Coughlin, a Roman Catholic priest who runs a series of popular radio seminars in the 1930s, a clear precedent of Trump's "paranoid populism" (11). Winberg (2017) cites Coughlin along with Louisiana governor and U.S. Senator Huey Long as initial supporters and eventual critics of Franklin Delano Roosevelt's New Deal. The governmental interventionism of the 1930s would prove pivotal to the emergence of right-wing populism in the post-World War II United States. Senators Joseph McCarthy and Robert A. Taft are cited by Winberg (2017) as prime populist figures in the 1940s and 1950s. They were supported by figures like Robert Welch, a retired candy maker who founded in 1958 the John Birch Society, an anti-Communist organization that circulated conspiracy theories that fed the so-called red scare during the Cold War (Micklethwait and Wooldrige 2004).

The 1960 decade would be marked by Alabama governor George Wallace's vociferous calls for segregation, whose incendiary rhetoric, like Trump's, would draw national media attention. The Southern uneasiness with the Civil Rights Act of 1964 fueled the campaign of Barry Goldwater, who despite losing the Presidential election against Lyndon Johnson by a record margin is still remembered by his daring rhetoric, a feature that relates him to Trump. The arrival of television would bring an audio-visual version of Coughlin's radio sermons: The Christian talk shows of Southern Baptist minister Pat Robertson, who attempted a presidential nomination for the Republican ticket in 1988.

Although Trump's candidacy was preceded by such TV phenomena as Ronald Reagan or, more recently, by conservative social movements like the Tea Party, both interpreted as examples of populism (Troy 2005; Scokpol and Williamson 2012). Trump's ideological vagueness epitomizes Laclau's (2005) ideal of populism as an empty shell in which all societal dissatisfactions can be filled in. Trump sidelined during his campaign any of the classic conservative causes, and this might have been one of the reasons for his success. As Laclau (2005) points out, populism's symbolic simplicity is a condition for its efficacy, as the linkage of "heterogeneous social demands" (96) under a single banner may only be achieved through their maximum simplification around the least common denominator: the leader of the political experiment.

Given Trump's seeming populist pedigree, we decided to focus on his medium of choice, Twitter, to characterize his discourse in comparison to that of his Democratic rival and to ascertain which rhetorical features make their respective discourses popular in terms of their virality. Our aim was twofold: on one hand, we wanted to empirically define the rhetorical traits of populism, looking at which figures and tropes were more commonly used by Trump, a presumably more populist candidate than Clinton; on the other hand, we wanted to determine which rhetorical traits, populist or not, were associated with a higher likelihood of being shared by users.

Methods and Measures

This chapter compares the discourse of Trump and Clinton on Twitter during the 2016 presidential campaign through a content analysis of their official accounts, @realDonaldTrump and @HillaryClinton, looking for traces of populism.

A strategic sample of 188 tweets was selected by limiting the time frame to the dates comprised between the candidate's respective nominations (July 28, 2016, for Clinton and July 21, 2016, for Trump) and the Election Day (November 8, 2016) and by selecting the twenty most relevant and top tweets, according to Twitter, while looking for keywords related to the following six campaign topics: economy, terrorism, women, immigration, gun control, and healthcare.[1] For Twitter, the "Top results" are those that have had more retweets or likes, so they are a proxy for the more popular tweets dealing with the keywords entered in the search query.[2] Not all campaign topics yielded an equal number of tweets: In some cases, the number of tweets for a given topic was fewer than twenty, whereas in others, the number exceeded twenty.

To ascertain the populist features in each of the candidates, we devised a coding protocol that looked for what the literature defines as typical populist gimmicks. From Waisbord and Amado (2016), we took the following populist constants: "antagonistic discourse" (5), such as attacks or threats to a rival, "self-promotion discourse" (5), such as tweets about campaign activity or past accomplishments, and "fixation with the press" (5), such as tweets that mention media outlets or individual journalists. From Engesser et al. (2016), we borrowed the variables "advocating for the people" (1109), verifiable in tweets in which the candidate presents her/himself as a champion for the regular folk; "attacking the elite" (1109), as seen in the criticism to economic or political powerholders; and "restoring sovereignty," whenever a suggestion to take back national and popular control of the country from other political or economic forces is voiced. Finally, from Hawkins (2010), we inferred two further populist features: (i) the preference of perceived legitimacy over the established legal order—if a law is considered not legitimate, the leader usually calls for its breach; and (ii) the overhaul of the current system as the only possible solution to societal problems—according to this logic, widespread corruption would render the extant political institutions unsustainable.

Despite populism is conventionally defined as mostly a rhetorical rather than an ideological phenomenon, few studies have tried to codify the recurrent rhetorical figures associated with populist discourses. Therefore, we resorted to classic handbooks on public speaking and rhetoric (Spang 2009; Leith 2012; Sánchez García 2012) to build a dictionary of rhetorical strategies, dividing them into *tropes* (e.g. metaphor, hyperbole, irony), *schemes* (e.g. alliteration, antithesis, apostrophe), and *fallacies* (e.g. *ad populum, ad hominem, ad logicam*).[3]

For each tweet, our unit of analysis, we considered its type: original tweets, retweets, replies, or mentions; its virality: number of likes, retweets, and replies; the presence of multimedia features: insertion of external links, images, or videos; and the use of paralinguistic resources, such as writing using all capitals, or including exclamation and interrogation marks. The candidates' mentions to other Twitter users and the hashtags included in their tweets were also recorded, as these reveal their patterns of interaction with other public figures or organizations (e.g. rival candidates, media companies) and their preferred way of conceptualizing key problems in the form of mottos of tags (e.g. #BigLeagueTruth, #ObamacareFail).

Results and Analysis

Our data support the widely held belief among academia and the press that Donald Trump is a populist leader. When analyzing his campaign tweets, he clearly surpasses Hillary Clinton in all the discursive traits associated with populism except the 'advocacy of the people,' where the Democrat is more outstanding, and 'antagonist discourse,' where both candidates are almost tied, as shown in Figure 1.1.

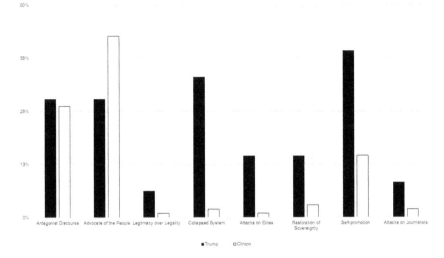

FIGURE 1.1 Percent recurrence of populist discursive traits in Trump and Clinton tweets.

The Democrat presents herself as a champion of street-level Americans in 43% of her tweets, as compared to 28% in the Republican. Clinton would often tweet quotations of her own speeches, using the first person plural pronouns to emphasize her identification with the common folk: ""Comprehensive immigration reform will grow our economy and keep families together, and it's the right thing to do." —Hillary" [*sic*] (Clinton September 29, 2016).

The harsh tone of the campaign is reflected in the similar proportion of tweets that include disqualifications of the rival: The "antagonist discourse" dimension is present in 27% of Trump's tweets and 26% of Clinton's. Perhaps this is a battlefield to which the Democrat was drawn by the Republican candidate, who would be successful in coining Clinton as "Crooked [...]" (Trump July 27, 2016). Qualitatively, however, Clinton's disqualifications of Trump are found to be milder and gentler than those of the media and real estate tycoon. For instance, while Clinton would say her rival is "[...] wrong [...]" and "[...] disrespectful [...]" (Clinton September 6, 2016), Trump would insinuate that his contenders engage in immoral behavior, when he pointed readers to a video showing "[...] Joe Biden's Long History Of Grabbing, Kissing and Groping Women Who Are Cringing: [...]" [*sic*] (Trump October 17, 2016).

Taking aside the two exceptions referred above, Trump reigns high in his recurrence to typical populist discursive strategies. Particularly frequent are his calls to overhaul the current political system ("Collapsed System" category, present in one-third, or 33% of his tweets as compared to 2% in Clinton). For Trump, the healthcare reform initiated by Barack Obama is "[...] a total disaster [...]", hence the need to "[...] REPEAL AND REPLACE!" (November 3,

2016). The Republican candidate sees the press as complicit in a defamation campaign against him. The "[…] dishonest media […]" do not report the facts (August 12, 2016) and are "[…] rigging […]" the election by publishing allegedly false sexual scandal stories (October 16, 2016). Trump is also quick to denounce his rival's husband, nicknamed as "Wild Bill" in clear reference to his own sexual scandals while in the White House, for receiving birthday gifts from countries tied to the Islamic State of Iraq and Syria (ISIS) terrorist group: "A country that Crooked Hillary says has funded ISIS also gave Wild Bill $1 million for his birthday? SO CORRUPT!" (October 16, 2016). Trump presents himself as the best option to clean up the system, making recurring calls to "[…] #DrainTheSwamp!" (October 20, 2016).

The "Self-promotion" category, another mark of populist leaders, is far more common in Trump's discourse (39% vs. 14% in Clinton). Trump will constantly refer to the large crowds he managed to gather at his political rallies and to their plural composition: "@Patrici: Crowd at Trump Rally in Akron, Ohio is a Sea of Women, Minorities, Independents, Dems […] via @gatewaypundit" (August 29, 2016). As a means of countering the constant accusations of misogyny, Trump would reply by pointing to a link in which the reader would access his long "[…] History Of Empowering Women […]" (October 9, 2016).

Our sample registers "Attacks on Elites" and calls to the "Restoration of Sovereignty" in one out of every ten tweets from Trump, but these traits are hardly present in Clinton. Trump says he was "[…] never a fan of Colin Powell […]", calling his decisions on Iraq a "[…] disaster […]" (September 14, 2016). His opinion about former Defense Secretary Robert Gates is very similar: "[…] a total disaster!" (September 17, 2016).

The instances in which legitimacy is prioritized over the rule of law ('Legitimacy over Legality') or the press is attacked ('Attacks on Journalists') are not very frequent in our sample: they are present in less than 10% of the tweets of any of the two candidates. However, Trump is three times more likely than Clinton to use these characteristic populist strategies, as when he said he would "[…] tear it up […]" if he does not get a good renegotiation of NAFTA (October 19, 2016), or when he decried "The phony story in the failing @nytimes is a TOTAL FABRICATION. […]" (October 13, 2016).

Once that it has been shown that Trump is, as compared to Clinton, a candidate who showcases several of the discursive and ideological constants associated with populist leaders, the next step is to ascertain which are the rhetorical figures most commonly employed by the two rivals. If Trump is shown to master a set of rhetorical devices, we would be closer to discovering the formula of populist oratory.

If such a formula exists, one of its principal components would be the rhetorical figures of the apostrophe. In 53% of Trump's tweets (as compared to just in 7% of Clinton's tweets), the orator is addressing a person who is not present (see Figure 1.2). Rather than, as in classic oratory, invoking the Gods or the

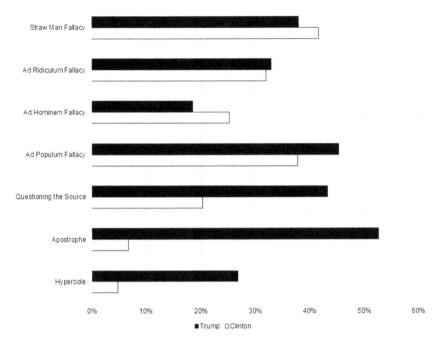

FIGURE 1.2   Percent recurrence of rhetorical tropes, figures, and fallacies in Trump and Clinton tweets.

country's forebears, Trump constantly pokes rivals and thanks friends in front of his audience of Twitter readers. To wit: "Paul Ryan, a man who doesn't know how to win (including failed run four years ago), must start focusing on the budget, military, vets etc." (Trump October 16, 2016), ".@dbongino You were fantastic in defending both the Second Amendment and me last night on @CNN. Don Lemon is a lightweight - dumb as a rock" (August 10, 2016).

A key ingredient of Trump's rhetorical formula is the disqualification of the source of given information in 43% of the Republican's tweets versus 20% of Clinton's. The so-called liberal media, *The New York Times* and CNN, among others, were some of his most frequent targets. Populist leaders claim to be representing the real truth, and Trump is no exception: One of his most frequent hashtags in our sample calls his readers to join the #BigLeagueTruth.

Alliteration, the repetition of words with similar sounds, is a scheme that facilitates memorization. Trump if five times more likely than Clinton to resort to this figure (20% of Trump's tweets vs. 5% of Clinton's): "[...] our economy will be STRONG & our people will be SAFE." (October 22, 2016); "[...] More Taxes. More Spending. [...]" (October 19, 2016); "REPEAL AND REPLACE OBAMACARE!" (October 26, 2016).

Trump is usually mocked by TV comedians for hyperbolic language. For the Republican leader, everything is "[...] massive [...]" (September 6, 2016) or "[...] Huge [...]" (May 17, 2016). Our evidence supports that impression. Trump is five times more likely than Clinton to use exaggerations (27% Trump and 5% Clinton): "Crooked Hillary Clinton wants to flood our country with Syrian immigrants that we know little or nothing about. The danger is massive. NO!" (July 27, 2016); "Obama's disastrous judgment gave us ISIS, rise of Iran, and the worst economic numbers since the Great Depression!" (August 4, 2016).

With other rhetorical figures, the proportion of their use is far more balanced: Trump slightly surpasses Clinton in the *ad populum* fallacy (e.g. "everybody knows that..."), with a recurrence in 45% and 38% of their respective Twitter accounts. The *ad ridiculum* fallacy (33% Trump and 32% Clinton) and the straw man fallacy (38% Trump and 42% Clinton), both aimed at ridiculing the opponent, register a similar presence in both candidates. Trump says Clinton's decisions "[...] have led to the deaths of many [...]" (Trump August 1, 2016) and have encouraged "[...] policies that spread ISIS [...]" (September 30, 2016), whereas Clinton calls Trump "[...] a bully. [...]" (Clinton October 19, 2016), a "[...] tax evader." (September 26, 2016) and as one of "[...] the greatest risks to the world economy. [...]" (October 19, 2016).

The only rhetorical device where Clinton is clearly superior is irony (11% Clinton and 5% Trump). Irony is a sophisticated figure that demands intelligence from both the messenger and the receiver, who are complicit in their understanding of a claim that aims at implying the contrary of what it asserts. On this ground, Clinton is the true master: "Wonder if Trump has shown Pence his "secret plan" to defeat ISIS. We're still waiting. #VPDebate" [*sic*] (October 4, 2016); "Now that's pretty rich coming from a guy who paid $0 in taxes for 18 years: [...]" (October 2, 2016).

Some oral traits of human speech, such as voice inflections to shout or enquire the audience, must be typographically represented with exclamation points and interrogation marks. If Clinton wonders or asks in her tweets in a similar proportion as Trump (in approximately 5% of the occasions), Trump clearly introduces more exclamatory marks than Clinton: if the Democrat barely uses this device, Trump includes exclamations in one-third (33%) of his tweets (see Figure 1.3).

Another way of shouting typographically is by writing texts with all capital letters (ALL CAPS), and Trump is well known for this: up to 53% of his tweets include texts that break the Internet etiquette of civilized language, a feature that is particularly non-existent in Clinton's tweets. Therefore, in what refers to paralinguistic devices, Trump confirms his liking for histrionic and hyperbolic performances: "[...] SO CORRUPT!" (Trump October 16, 2016), "I will stop RADICAL ISLAMIC TERRORISM in this country!" (October 20, 2016), "[...] VOTE so we can replace Obamacare [...]" (November 4, 2016), "I will be making a major speech on ILLEGAL IMMIGRATION on Wednesday in the GREAT State of Arizona. [...]" (August 28, 2016).

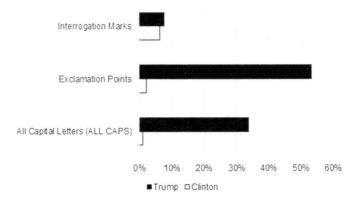

FIGURE 1.3 Percent recurrence of paralinguistic marks in Trump and Clinton tweets.

Twitter allows for the inclusion of hypertexts (external links) and multimedia features (images and videos). Clinton includes videos far more frequently than Trump (35% of the Democrat's tweets vs. 5% of the Republican's), whereas Trump beats Clinton in the proportion of tweets with images (21% Trump and 15% Clinton) and with external links (25% Trump and 17% Clinton).

One aspect of interest is the virality of tweets and its potential relationship with the constants of populist discourse, the rhetorical figures, and the proportion of multimedia and paralinguistic features. To test the hypothesis that these categories are predictive of more virality on Twitter, we ran an ordinary least regression (OLS) model in which virality is a dependent variable of all the other variables studied, aggregated in indices as follows[4]:

Discourse: Antagonistic Discourse; Advocate of the People; Legitimacy over Legality; Collapsed System; Attacks on Elites; Restoration of Sovereignty; Self-promotion; Attacks on Journalists.

Rhetoric: rhetorical tropes, figures, and fallacies.
Paralinguistic Marks: tweets containing Interrogation Marks, Exclamation Points, and All Capital Letters (ALL CAPS).
Media: tweets containing external links, videos, and images.

Our sampling procedure was strategic and not random, that is, we purposefully searched for the top twenty tweets in each of the six categories of interest (economy, healthcare, the right to bear arms, terrorism, immigration, and women). Because those twenty tweets are determined by Twitter itself by paying attention mostly to their virality, our sample is likely to have less variance than a randomly selected one. Therefore, there is a problem of endogeneity that we are aware of, and that is one of the main limitations of the study, along with the limited number of cases ($n = 188$) under analysis (see Table 1.1).

TABLE 1.1 OLS regression predicting virality of Trump and Clinton tweets

Variables	Multivariate OLS		
	Aggregated	Trump	Clinton
Media (inclusion of multimedia features)	−0.177** (0.088)	−0.297*** (0.079)	0.003 (0.160)
Paralinguistic (use of paralinguistic marks)	0.267*** (0.069)	0.117** (0.054)	0.095 (0.180)
Discursive (traditional populist traits)	0.081 (0.058)	0.028 (0.044)	−0.013 (0.153)
Rhetoric (rhetorical figures, tropes, and fallacies)	0.127*** (0.032)	0.053** (0.026)	0.160** (0.063)
Constant	9.65*** (0.161)	10.4*** (0.119)	9.38 (0.281)
R-squared	0.24	0.27	0.07
Observations	189	92	97
The dependent variable has been logged			

Robust standard errors are in parenthesis.
***$p < 0.01$, **$p < 0.5$, *$p < 0.1$.

Results at aggregated level confirm our expectations showing that media, paralinguistic, and rhetoric categories are key determinants for a tweet to get viral. Surprisingly, the use of multimedia resources seems to prevent Trump's tweets from becoming more popular. This counter-intuitive result might be related to the fact that, for the tweets chosen, the number of posts with a multimedia features was extremely low (less than 10%), which might influence the direction of the relationship.

Surprisingly, the "populist discursive traits" figure (see Figure 1.1), which includes the constants of populist discourse according to the literature, from attacks on elites to self-promotion, by way of attacks to the press or other political rivals, has no significant predictive power when explaining virality.

In sum, rhetorical devices and paralinguistic marks like exclamation points are more relevant than the populist thin ideological traits to explain the likelihood that a tweet would go viral. With all due caveats, given our small sample and our acknowledged selection bias, we prioritized campaign topics over randomness. It seems that on Twitter, form and style are more popular than ideological substance, however slim that substance might be in the case of populism.

Conclusion: Form Matters More than Content

The discourse of Donald Trump shows a higher recurrence of populist ideological features as compared to Hillary Clinton, especially when considering the traits of self-promotion and attacks to the political system. As the Republican candidate, Trump took advantage of his rival in all the discursive features except when advocating for the people, where the Democratic candidate surpassed Trump by a high margin. In any case, Trump's populist discourse makes an extensive use of rhetorical devices: the apostrophe, the disqualification of sources, and the *ad populum* fallacy. On the other hand, while Clinton's display of rhetorical tropes, figures, and fallacies is not as impressive, she does make a recurrent use of *ad populum*, *ad hominem*, and *ad logicam* fallacies, addressing most of her attacks to Trump.

The differences between the two candidates become sharper when considering the typographic representation of their Twitter language. Trump writes expressions in all capital letters in more than half of his tweets, and exclamation marks are included in one-third of them. It seems the Republican candidate was desperate for making himself heard, as in net-etiquette terms the use of ALL CAPS is equivalent to shouting at the audience. On the contrary, Clinton, with a more restrained use of paralinguistic features, symbolizes a more linear and considered language pattern. As for the multimedia affordances of Twitter, such as external links, images, and videos, Clinton stands out for her recurrent insertion of videos, a strategy whose success is yet to be determined, but that our research indicates that it would not be effective in terms of engaging the audience.

Trump clearly exceeds Clinton in all metrics of audience response: likes, retweets, and replies. In our sample, Trump's tweets were twice as likely to be retweeted as Clinton's. Surprisingly, Trump's success in engaging the audience has no clear bearance on the classic traits of populist discourse: advocacy for the regular folk; attacks to the economic, political, or media elites. Rather, it seems that rhetorical prowess, in terms of the variety of rhetorical figures used, and the presence of paralinguistic marks of exclamation are what makes the audience "like" or retweet. In other words, form is found to be more relevant than content when it comes to explaining the virality of populist discourse.

Trump was among the least popular candidates to ever face a presidential election, and his disapproval rate was as high as 70% when he was sworn in as president in January 2017. But his aggressive, hyperbolic, and polarizing tone might have pressed the right emotional keys to allow populism to reach the highest office in the United States.

Notes

1 These were the precise search terms for each of the six campaign categories: (i) economy: "economy," "debt," "income," "taxes," "budget"; (ii) terrorism: "terrorism," "Daesh," "ISIS," "terror," "jihadists"; (iii) women: "women," "glass ceiling"; (iv) immigration: "immigration," "immigrants"; (v) gun control: "weapons," "pistols," "guns," "bullets," "Amendment," "defense"; (vi) healthcare: "healthcare," "ObamaCare," "public health," "universal healthcare."
2 Twitter's own explanation of how the "top tweets" are selected is available here: https://help.twitter.com/es/using-twitter/top-search-results-faqs

3 This is the full list of rhetorical figures considered in the coding protocol: (i) tropes: metaphor, metonymy, hyperbole, irony, rhetorical question, hyperbaton; (ii) schemes: alliteration, antithesis, apostrophe, asyndeton; (iii) logical fallacies: questioning the source, *ad populum, ad hominem, ad ridiculum*, straw-man, victimhood.
4 The indices were the result of the sum of items that a tweet accounts for each category. Therefore, the *Rhetoric* category will get a maximum of 15 and *Media* 3, and so on.

Bibliography

Allison, Bill, Mira Rojanasakul, Brittany Harris, and Cedric Sam. "Tracking the 2016 presidential money race." *Bloomberg Politics*, December 9, 2016, accessed November 10, 2017, www.bloomberg.com/politics/graphics/2016-presidential-campaign-fundraising/

Baynes, Chris. "Donald Trump says he would not be President without Twitter." *The Independent*, October 22, 2017, accessed November 10, 2017, www.independent.co.uk/news/world/americas/us-politics/donald-trump-tweets-twitter-social-media-facebook-instagram-fox-business-network-would-not-be-a8013491.html

Berlet, Chip and Matthew N. Lyons. *Right-Wing Populism in America: Too Close for Comfort*. New York: Guilford Press, 2000.

Boorstin, Daniel J. *The Image: A Guide to Pseudo-Events in America*. New York: Vintage Books, 2012 (Original ed. 1962).

Clement, Scott. "Negative views of Donald Trump just hit a new campaign high: 7 in 10 Americans." *Washington Post*, June 15, 2016, accessed October 10, 2017, www.washingtonpost.com/news/the-fix/wp/2016/06/15/negative-views-of-donald-trump-just-hit-a-new-high-7-in-10-americans/

Clinton, Hillary. Twitter Post. October 2, 2016, 11:50 A.M. https://twitter.com/HillaryClinton/status/782653906513981444

Clinton, Hillary. Twitter Post. October 4, 2016, 6:53 P.M. https://twitter.com/hillaryclinton/status/783485209807298560

Clinton, Hillary. Twitter Post. October 19, 2016, 6:43 P.M. https://twitter.com/hillaryclinton/status/788918452669014017

Clinton, Hillary. Twitter Post. October 19, 2016, 6:57 P.M. https://twitter.com/HillaryClinton/status/788921932590768129

Clinton, Hillary. Twitter Post. September 6, 2016, 11:58 A.M. https://twitter.com/HillaryClinton/status/773233995207303168

Clinton, Hillary. Twitter Post. September 26, 2016, 6:39 P.M. https://twitter.com/hillaryclinton/status/780582541019475968

Collanyi, Bence, Philip Howard, and Samuel C. Woolley. "Bots and Automation over Twitter during the U.S. Election." Computational Propaganda Project Data Memo. Oxford Internet Institute, Oxford, November 17, 2016.

Cowls, Josh. "From Trump Tower to the White House, in 140 Characters: The Hyper-Mediated Election of a Paranoid Populist President." M.Sc. Thesis, Massachusetts Institute of Technology, Cambridge, 2017.

Darwish, Kareem, Walid Magdy, and Tahar Zanouda. "Trump vs. Hillary: What went Viral during the 2016 US Presidential Election." *Social Informatics* 10539 (2017): 143–61.

Decker, Cathleen. "Donald Trump Undoes His Third and Best Debate Performance in Just a Few Words." *Los Angeles Times*, October 22, 2016, accessed October 10, 2017, www.latimes.com/politics/la-na-pol-third-debate-analysis-20161020-snap-story.html

Engesser, Sven, Nicole Ernst, Frank Esser, and Florin Büchel. "Populism and Social Media: How Politicians Spread a Fragmented Ideology." *Information, Communication & Society* 20 (July 2016): 1109–26.

Enli, Gunn. "Twitter as Arena for the Authentic Outsider: Exploring the Social Media Campaigns of Trump and Clinton in the 2016 US Presidential Election." *European Journal of Communication* 32 (February 2017): 50–61.

Farber, Madeline. "Donald Trump's Approval Ratings Have Hit a Historic Low Before He Takes Office." *Time*, January 17, 2017, accessed November 10, 2017, http://time.com/4636142/donald-trump-inauguration-polls-approval-ratings/

Hawkins, Kirk A. *Venezuela's Chavismo and Populism in Comparative Perspective*. Cambridge and New York: Cambridge University Press, 2010.

Heer, Jeet. "America's First Postmodern President." *The New Republic*, July 8, 2017, accessed October 10, 2017, https://newrepublic.com/article/143730/americas-first-postmodern-president

Higgins, Tim. "The Post-TV Candidate." *Bloomberg Businessweek* (June 6, 2016): 28–29.

Hodges, Adam. "Trump's Formulaic Twitter Insults." *Anthropology News* 58 (18 January 2017): 206–10.

Jagers, Jan and Stefaan Walgrave. "Populism as Political Communication Style: An Empirical Study of Political Parties' Discourse in Belgium." *European Journal of Political Research* 46 (May 2007): 319–45.

Jamieson, Kathleen Hall and Doron Taussig. "Disruption, Demonization, Deliverance, and Norm Destruction: The Rhetorical Signature of Donald J. Trump." *Political Science Quarterly* 132 (Winter 2017–18): 618–49.

Kentish, Ben. "Donald Trump Has Lost Popular Vote by Greater Margin Than Any US President." *The Independent*, December 12, 2016, accessed November 10, 2017, www.independent.co.uk/news/world/americas/us-elections/donald-trump-lost-popular-vote-hillary-clinton-us-election-president-history-a7470116.html

Korostelina, Karina V. *Trump Effect*. New York: Routledge, 2017.

Kreis, Ramona. "The 'Tweet Politics' of President Trump." *Journal of Language and Politics* 16 (June 2017): 607–18. doi:10.1075/jlp.17032.kre.

Laclau, Ernesto. *On Populist Reason*. London and New York: Verso, 2005.

Lakoff, George. "Trump's Twitter Distraction." George Lakoff's Blog, March 7, 2017, accessed October 10, 2017, https://georgelakoff.com/2017/03/07/trumps-twitter-distraction/

Lee, Jasmine C. and Kevin Quealy. "All the People, Places and Things Donald Trump has Insulted on Twitter since Declaring His Candidacy for President." *The New York Times* (October 24, 2016): A10, updated list available at www.nytimes.com/interactive/2016/01/28/upshot/donald-trump-twitter-insults.html

Leith, Sam. *You Talkin' to Me? Rhetoric from Aristotle to Obama*. London: Profile Books, 2012.

Lui, Kevin. "Poll: Two-Thirds of Americans Want Donald Trump to Delete His Twitter Account." *Fortune*, January 11, 2017, accessed November 10, 2017, http://fortune.com/2017/01/11/real-donald-trump-twitter-delete-account/

Micklethwait, John and Adrian Wooldrige. *The Right Nation: Conservative Power in America*. New York: Penguin, 2004.

Monnat, Shannon M. and David L. Brown. "More than a Rural Revolt: Landscapes of Despair and the 2016 Presidential Election." *Journal of Rural Studies* 55 (September 2017): 227–36.

Mudde, Cas. "Reflexiones Sobre un Concepto y Su Uso." *Letras Libres* 127 (April 2012), accessed October 10, 2017, www.letraslibres.com/espana-mexico/revista/reflexiones-sobre-un-concepto-y-su-uso

Owen, Diana. "Characteristics of US Elections in the Digital Media Age". In *Internet Election Campaigns in the United States, Japan, South Korea, and Taiwan*, edited by Shoko Kiyohara, Kazuhiro Maeshima and Diana Owen, 27–53. London: Palgrave Macmillan, 2018.

Pew Research Center. "Election 2016: Campaigns as a Direct Source of News." July 18, 2016, accessed October 10, 2017, www.journalism.org/2016/07/18/election-2016-campaigns-as-a-direct-source-of-news/

Sánchez García, Francisco José. *Retórica parlamentaria española*. Madrid: Síntesis, 2012.

Scokpol, Theda and Vanessa Williamson. *The Tea Party and the Remaking of Republican Conservatism*. Oxford and New York: Oxford University Press, 2012.

Shanahan, Marie K. *Journalism, Online Comments, and the Future of Public Discourse*. New York: Routledge, 2018.

Shane, Scott. "The Fake Americans Russia Created to Influence the Election." *The New York Times*, September 7, 2017, accessed October 10, 2017, www.nytimes.com/2017/09/07/us/politics/russia-facebook-twitter-election.html

Shorenstein Center. "Molly Ball: Election 2016 and the Media." Shorenstein Center of Media, Politics and Public Policy, September 13, 2016, accessed October 10, 2017, https://shorensteincenter.org/molly-ball/

Spang, Kurt. *Persuasión: Fundamentos de Retórica*. Pamplona: EUNSA, 2009.

Strauss, Barry. "Populares and Populists." *The New Criterion* 35 (October 2016): 4–11.

Tharoor, Ishaan. "Trump's Twitter Feed is a Gateway to Authoritarianism." *Washington Post*, March 6, 2017, accessed October 10, 2017, www.washingtonpost.com/news/worldviews/wp/2017/03/06/trumps-twitter-feed-is-a-gateway-to-authoritarianism/

Troy, Gil. *Morning in America: How Reagan Invented the 1980s*. Princeton, NJ: Princeton University Press, 2005.

Trump, Donald J. and Tony Schwartz. *Trump: The Art of the Deal*. New York: Ballantine Books, 2015 (Original Ed., 1987).

Trump, Donald. Twitter Post. May 3, 2016, 4:02 P.M. https://twitter.com/realDonaldTrump/status/727634574298255361

Trump, Donald. Twitter Post. May 17, 2016, 7:21 A.M. https://twitter.com/realDonaldTrump/status/732576889538260992

Trump, Donald. Twitter Post. May 17, 2016, 7:41 P.M. https://twitter.com/realdonaldtrump/status/732762977825349632

Trump, Donald. Twitter Post. July 13, 2015, 9:21 A.M. https://twitter.com/realDonaldTrump/status/620629175897096193

Trump, Donald. Twitter Post. July 23, 2015, 3:36 A.M. https://twitter.com/realDonaldTrump/status/624166285363015681

Trump, Donald. Twitter Post. July 25, 2016, 6:47 A.M. https://twitter.com/realDonaldTrump/status/757573051215147008

Trump, Donald. Twitter Post. July 27, 2016, 3:08 A.M. https://twitter.com/realDonaldTrump/status/758242674646323200

Trump, Donald. Twitter Post. August 1, 2016, 3:46 P.M. https://twitter.com/realdonaldtrump/status/760245342231158785

Trump, Donald. Twitter Post. August 4, 2016, 7:19 P.M. https://twitter.com/realDonaldTrump/status/761386025323225088

Trump, Donald. Twitter Post. August 10, 2016, 8:08 A.M. https://twitter.com/realDonaldTrump/status/763391459110313984

Trump, Donald. Twitter Post. August 12, 2016, 6:01 A.M. https://twitter.com/realDonaldTrump/status/764084294704697344

Trump, Donald. Twitter Post. August 28, 2016, 4:27 P.M. https://twitter.com/realDonaldTrump/status/770040258796855296

Trump, Donald. Twitter Post. August 29, 2016, 3:03 P.M. https://twitter.com/realDonaldTrump/status/770248186241900544

Trump, Donald. Twitter Post. September 6, 2016, 8:31 A.M. https://twitter.com/realDonaldTrump/status/773181751749402624

Trump, Donald. Twitter Post. September 14, 2016, 8:59 P.M. https://twitter.com/realDonaldTrump/status/776269061823074304

Trump, Donald. Twitter Post. September 17, 2016, 4:51 A.M. https://twitter.com/realdonaldtrump/status/777112789672341504

Trump, Donald. Twitter Post. September 30, 2016, 11:24 A.M. https://twitter.com/realDonaldTrump/status/781922648645185536

Trump, Donald. Twitter Post. October 9, 2016, 6:24 P.M. https://twitter.com/realdonaldtrump/status/785289945837629440

Trump, Donald. Twitter Post. October 13, 2016, 6:35 A.M. https://twitter.com/realdonaldtrump/status/786560925113266176

Trump, Donald. Twitter Post. October 15, 2015, 7:00 P.M. https://twitter.com/realDonaldTrump/status/654839227612549120

Trump, Donald. Twitter Post. October 16, 2016, 4:36 A.M. https://twitter.com/realDonaldTrump/status/787618207444131840

Trump, Donald. Twitter Post. October 16, 2016, 6:15 A.M. https://twitter.com/realDonaldTrump/status/787643017234636800

Trump, Donald. Twitter Post. October 16, 2016, 1:54 P.M. https://twitter.com/realDonaldTrump/status/787758668565581824

Trump, Donald. Twitter Post. October 17, 2016, 5:19 A.M. https://twitter.com/realDonaldTrump/status/787991439196229632

Trump, Donald. Twitter Post. October 19, 2016, 6:44 P.M. https://twitter.com/realdonaldtrump/status/788918810040344576

Trump, Donald. Twitter Post. October 19, 2016, 6:45 P.M. https://twitter.com/realdonaldtrump/status/788919099275390976

Trump, Donald. Twitter Post. October 20, 2016, 8:52 A.M. https://twitter.com/realdonaldtrump/status/789132223479947264

Trump, Donald. Twitter Post. October 22, 2016, 11:40 A.M. https://twitter.com/realDonaldTrump/status/789899250834534400

Trump, Donald. Twitter Post. October 26, 2016, 4:02 A.M. https://twitter.com/realDonaldTrump/status/791233632593739776

Trump, Donald. Twitter Post. November 3, 2016, 5:34 A.M. https://twitter.com/realDonaldTrump/status/794155725152980992

Trump, Donald. Twitter Post. November 4, 2016, 4:14 P.M. https://twitter.com/realDonaldTrump/status/794679364289986560

Uscinski, Joseph E. "How 2016 Has Become the 'Conspiracy Theory' Election." The LSE US Centre Blog, May 5, 2016, accessed October 10, 2017, http://blogs.lse.ac.uk/usappblog/2016/05/05/how-2016-has-become-the-conspiracy-theory-election/

Waisbord, Silvio and Adriana Amado. "Populist Communication by Digital Means: Presidential Twitter in Latin America." *Information, Communication & Society* 20 (November 2016): 1330–46.

Washington Post Staff. "Transcript: Read Michelle Obama's Full Speech from the 2016 DNC." *Washington Post*, July 26, 2016, accessed October 10, 2017, www. washingtonpost.com/news/post-politics/wp/2016/07/26/transcript-read-michelle-obamas-full-speech-from-the-2016-dnc/

Williams, Christine B. (2017). "Introduction: Social Media, Political Marketing and the 2016 U.S. Election." *Journal of Political Marketing* 16 (June 2017): 207–11.

Wilson, Jason. "Hiding in Plain Sight: How the 'alt-right' is Weaponizing Irony to Spread Fascism." *The Guardian*, May 23, 2017, accessed October 10, 2017, www.theguardian. com/technology/2017/may/23/alt-right-online-humor-as-a-weapon-facism

Winberg, Oscar. "Insult Politics: Donald Trump, Right-Wing Populism, and Incendiary Language." *European Journal of American Studies* 12 (Summer 2017): 1–16.

2

OF TWIT-STORMS AND DEMAGOGUES

Trump, Illusory Truths of Patriotism, and the Language of the Twittersphere

Dawn F. Colley

It is a truism that Trump's use of Twitter is highly successful. He connects easily with his target audience, urges impulsive reactions, and effectively reframes debates to promote the acceptance of his own worldview. As Amanda Hess contends, the secret to Trump's success is that "He's cemented his reputation as a modern social media master by relying on age-old dick moves" (2016, para. 3). However, the factors that lead to Trump's effectiveness are actually more complicated and much more cunning. His tweets are ambiguous, deceptive, and divisive, and still, they garner instantaneous and vehement support. Such staunch and immediate endorsement of his ideas would be curious were it not for the fact that Trump's use of language and his promotion of team spirit suggest that he speaks for the people—and thus understands them—in a way that no other politician does. This pretense, coupled with the psychological phenomenon known as the illusory truth effect, creates the illusion of an outlier, a renegade who will shake up politics and #makeamericagreatagain. Yet, what he attempts to accomplish through his tweets has nothing to do with making America great; it has to do with urging the acceptance of what Trump believes to be his own greatness. By examining his language, his use of the Twittersphere, and the twit-storms he creates, we see Trump as a leader who is more interested in garnering power through provoking the emotions and prejudices of his audience; in short, we see a demagogue. Although Trump repeatedly encourages a team spirit, with us or against us mentality, the fact is that his machinations don't impact one side or the other; they influence everyone. The issue is no longer—and can no longer be—whether Republicans are right and Democrats are wrong, whether Conservatives are ignorant and Liberals are smug. The illusory truth effect and the language of the Twittersphere prime users to accept or to reject information that they read on Twitter passively. Trump exploits this situation to his benefit, and unless we understand the various factors that have led to Trump's twitter successes, not only will we be powerless to stop them, we might well fall prey to them.

New Media and the Twittersphere

The benefit of new media is that it offers a space for interactivity and collaboration while providing new platforms for users to contribute their voices to ongoing conversations. As Henriksen explains, "Where traditional mass media may be subjected to censorship and other less obvious restrictions, new media has made it possible for 'everyone' to participate in the exchange of information and views" (2011, 63). The potential for readers to be exposed to a more comprehensive understanding of whatever story is being reported on is one of the advantages to new media: Reports of an event often happen in real time, and the fact that any user can publish their opinions about that event suggests that the collective representation of the story is unbiased because it isn't filtered through a particular journalistic lens. As opposed to mass media, new media encourages "citizen producers" or "citizen journalists," as Anthea Irwin calls them, to post opinions and like, share, or comment on the ideas that others have offered (2011, 69). On one hand, such collaboration suggests that new media, and social media in particular, offers a space where everyone's involvement is welcomed and valued as a necessary contribution: We can better understand a situation when all perspectives are represented. On the other hand, user-generated content is fraught with issues: It's not required to prove any perspective that it offers, the platform shapes the messages in specific ways that users tend not to recognize, and it doesn't foster dialectic.[1] In the case of Twitter, these limitations are amplified.

Although the limitations of new media as a valid information source are becoming more apparent, the role that new media play as a news source continues to increase. Following a report published by the Pew Research Center, "more than half (55%) of Americans ages 50 or older report getting news on social media sites," which is a 10% increase from 2016, and 78% of those under fifty years get their news via social media (Shearer and Gottfried 2017, para. 2). The problem with this buy-in is twofold: collective representation of user-generated content simply doesn't happen because people tend to follow stories that offer one perspective and each story, each opinion offered by citizen journalists contains bias, even if unintentionally. As Irwin explains, "Whenever language is used, representational choices are made. There is always an angle of telling" (2011, 70). Brian L. Ott pushes this point further by suggesting that Irwin's "angle of telling" may well be intentionally deceptive. The problem, according to Ott, is that the news content found on social media consistently promotes "misleading stories from sources devoid of editorial standards. Moreover, it is specifically targeted to users based on their political proclivities (i.e. what items they 'like,' which sites they visit, and whom they're 'friends' with)" (2016, 65). And while Alfred

Hermida suggests that "social media services such as Twitter provide platforms for collaborative verification, based on a system of media that privileges distributed over centralized expertise, and collective over individual intelligence" (2012, 659–60), the actual intent to verify requires a desire to find the Truth, even at the expense of the desire to believe the truth of one's own perspective.

Another fallacy of social media is that there is a direct link between its interactivity and the co-creation of a body of knowledge through participation in those new media platforms. It is interactional, to be sure, but those exchanges do little to inspire real conversation—and without a dialog, we cannot hope to confront the issues that we face as a society or as a global community. On Facebook and Twitter, for example, users interact by simply posting their opinions, experiences, or responses; "friends" or "followers" then like, comment, share, or retweet what they read. Blogs afford individuals more opportunity to post extended explanations about their ideas, and viewers are typically invited to respond; the problem here is that the responses are asynchronous and therefore not conducive to a Socratic dialog. Throughout new media, there are few, if any, opportunities for rational debates that aim to educate participants and to solve problems. As Mark Thompson argues, "We are increasingly reluctant even to try to find a common language with which to engage with peoples and cultures whose values differ substantially from our own" (2016, 17). Worse yet, new media offers no standard for news reporting—users can simply post their version of the facts. What social media offers, then, in addition to user-generated knowledge is the potential for bad data: Misleading stories, erroneous claims, and self-serving statements of fact intend to communicate truths and to delude others into accepting them. When it comes to the restrictive and cacophonic space of the Twittersphere, the potential for misguiding and being misguided is heightened due to the limitations of Twitter's form.

Twitter's initial 140-character restriction led to a specific language of the Twittersphere, a style of communicating that remains unchanged by Twitter's decision to increase the character limit to 280.[2] This language is characterized by generic conventions, or standards of tweeting, that users collectively created to maximize their ability to communicate within that character limit. Incorporating hashtags, acronyms, links, images, and emojis permits users to include more information than long-form writing would allow, a practice which, in theory, is advantageous. Yet in practice, this structural shrinkage actually causes problems in comprehension and the ability to connect with people in meaningful ways. When every keystroke counts, the focus of the message becomes brevity, not elucidation, and tweeters therefore favor language that is blunt and reductive. As Ott explains, "When clever and even smart ideas are expressed on Twitter, the form demands that they are greatly simplified" (2016, 61). Worse yet is the suggestion that the very strategies that allow users to interact via Twitter both inhibit the potential to contribute anything thought-provoking to the Twittersphere and distract away from the ability to process a message critically. Ott continues, "the repeated production and consumption of simple messages, which endlessly redirect our attention elsewhere via hyperlinks, reshapes human cognition in ways that nurture simplemindedness and promote short attention-spans" (2016, 61). The fact that the way that readers engage with tweets is similarly unceremonious underscores Ott's point: respondents could compose a 140-character reply, "like" the tweet, or simply retweet it. There is no space for Socratic discussion; instead, it is read, "like," retweet, repeat.

This rapid and uncritical process was amplified by the Twittersphere's maximum character allowance, as this limitation denied the potential for users to explain their ideas fully and thus inhibits—sometimes significantly—the capability of readers to understand what they read fully. In the absence of a tweeter's explanation, the reader is then tasked with filling in the gaps that could not be bridged in the initial 140-character restriction. A recent Trump post, which proclaims wide acceptance of his Tax Cut and Reform Bill, demonstrates this point: "Democrats don't want massive tax cuts – how does that win elections? Great reviews for Tax Cut and Reform Bill" (Trump September 28, 2017). Although over 26,000 users commented on this tweet, over 17,000 retweeted it, and over 77,000 "liked" it as of March 12, 2018, the post is ambiguous at best and nonsensical at worst. The proclamation that "Democrats don't want massive tax cuts" is overly simplistic and denies not only the complexity of the proposed bill but also the Democrats' concerns about its consequences. In the subsequent question, "how does that win elections?" the antecedent of "that" is unclear. If it refers to Democrats not wanting massive tax cuts, and the implication is that this is a general Democratic stance, then the question suggests that the 'wanting,' not the 'doing,' wins elections. The final statement, "Great reviews for Tax Cut and Reform Bill," reads as a *non sequitur* and relies on the reader to find the connection to the declarative-interrogatory that precedes it; it also expects that the audience is not interested in knowing who reviewed the bill and determined that it was "great." The only qualifier is the plural "reviews," whether that indicates many or two is left to the reader to figure out. If a mark of effective composition is when a reader understands the intended message, without guesswork or analysis, then tweets such as this are either thoughtlessly posted or intentionally written poorly. On the surface, this tweet offers a rather simple perspective: Democrats want to tax you massively, they will never win elections because of this Trump-proclaimed fact, and the proposed bill is widely acknowledge to be #great. And this is the problem with Trump's use of Twitter and the twit-storms that he starts: His tweets rely on the reader to determine what he means, which suggests that the reader's perspective has just as much to do with the interpretation as the words that Trump uses.

Twitter does have utility in the public sphere, of course: It allows users to share information on a largely uncensored platform, which, in addition to the creation of community knowledge, has inspired the organization of peaceful protests. Additionally, first-person accounts posted in real time have the potential for more comprehensive reporting. As Alfred Hermida points out, this capacity has been "tapped by news organizations for gathering eyewitness reports as events unfold in real-time. Real-time messages from the public are seen as filling the news vacuum that tends to characterize the immediate aftermath of a breaking news event" (2012, 663). The problem with this type of reporting is that the tweeter's bias isn't necessarily accounted for: The statement will be perspectival, which has the potential to limit understanding even when the intent is to increase it. Certainly, Twitter works really well for exchanges that don't require explanation or engagement in ideas, but as a platform for communicating about and working to resolve the issues that we face as a country and as a world, it is a disaster. Necessarily, stark compositions that are too brief to explain a thought adequately, combined with the desire to increase the length of a message through the use of acronyms and emojis, lead to more confusion than clarity, and the fact is that "liking," retweeting, or commenting on a post doesn't lead participants to a better understanding of the issue under discussion. That Trump is a vociferous tweeter using the complications of the platform to his benefit merits attention.

Plain Speech and Plainly Spoken Truths

The unsophisticated and brash demands of the Twitter genre make the platform ideal for a speaker like Trump, who has cultivated a persona that is similarly, if overtly, artless and foolhardy. From his declaration that Syrian refugees are potential terrorists to his allegation that Mexican immigrants are rapists to his self-promotion, "I know more about ISIS than the generals do. Believe me," Trump consistently proffers unfiltered access to his worldview, which centers on his own superiority (Trump 2015, 52:42).[3] In contrast to the standard political speech favored by lawyer-politicians who, deservedly or not, are largely discredited as liars and manipulators, Trump's plain speech comes as a welcome change. Scholars Keir Martin and Jakob Krause-Jensen explain: "His unpredictable TV appearances and his *faux pas* were experienced like a breath of fresh air in the spin-doctored, tele-prompted, and opinion-polled political establishment…The fact that he 'says what he thinks' came to represent a truthfulness, which to many, counted more than consistency and factual truth" (2017, 7–8). That the unfiltered pretense of his speech creates an illusion of truth that supersedes actual truth has not only to do with Trump's rejection of politicalese but also the fact that his stark statements seem guileless: They suggest that he's willing to tell the truth no matter the consequences, and it is this alacrity that permits Trump to maintain his credibility.

These factors also work to separate Trump from another group: the smug liberal elite. As Emmett Rensin argues, the smug style of American liberalism "is a way of conducting politics, predicated on the belief that American life is not divided by moral difference or policy divergence—not really—but by the failure of half the country to know what's good for them" (2016, para. 1).[4] And this is precisely the mindset from which Trump's language—and his use of Twitter—distinguishes him. Virginia Heffernan explains that "He embraces odd abbreviations, erratic capitalization and typos in his invariably reactive rants: 'illegal imm,' 'Presidential Primaries,' 'He is do [*sic*] totally biased.' @realDonaldTrump is the opposite of aloof, the opposite of polished" (2016, para. 3). This uncontrolled, hasty approach to communication also seems to be its strength: Trump is credible not because he understands and is capable of handling the issues that we face as a nation but because his words are, ostensibly, not clothed in the colors of rhetoric. As such, his target audience is invited to accept what he says at face value; his words are believable for the very fact they are not well considered. This plain style also suggests that he is of the people and for the people. As opposed to the smug liberal elite that speaks *for* the citizenry, Trump's use of language intimates that he speaks 'with' them, using 'their' language while reinforcing an *esprit de corps* with his supporters.

(Deceptively) Plain Style of Trump's Tweets, the National Football League, and the Issue of Patriotism

Trump utilizes the team spirit stratagem to great effect. On September 22, 2017, he exemplified this everyman linguistic style during a campaign rally in Huntsville, Alabama. Nearly, 38 minutes into a speech that was intended to drum up support for candidate Luther Strange, Trump employed the strategies of polarization and false dichotomy to capitalize on the extreme divisiveness of current American politics. He began, "Luther and I, and everyone in this arena tonight, are unified by the same great American values. We're proud of our country. We respect our flag" (Trump 2017, 43:22).[5] As he paused for cheers from the crowd, his focus shifted from what makes this assembly outstanding—pride for their country and respect for the flag—to the oppositional other that will underscore the ethos of his supporters: National Football League (NFL) players protesting during the national anthem. In an ostensible aside, Trump queried, "Wouldn't you love to see one of these NFL owners, when somebody disrespects our flag, to say, 'Get that son of a bitch off the field right now. Out. He's fired. He's fired!' You know, some owner is going to do that. He's going to say, 'That guy that disrespects our flag, he's fired'" (43:43). In this moment, Trump reframed the complicated and complex issues of racial inequality and police brutality into a far simpler issue: one of patriotism defined by standing at attention during the national anthem; those who kneel are "sons of bitches" that shouldn't have a job. The offensiveness of this language, coupled with the darker insinuation that anyone Trump deems unpatriotic should be castigated, is outmatched by Trump's solidification of the crowd's team spirit. Through the 'us vs. them,' 'we're right, they're wrong' dichotomy that Trump consistently employs, he successfully bandied his audience against a common adversary, a strategy that primes them to work not on behalf of the nation but on behalf of Trump.

Trump began calling upon his "team" the very next day. On September 23, 2017, Roger Goodell, the commissioner of the NFL, publically criticized Trump's remarks as ignorant: "Divisive comments like these demonstrate an unfortunate lack of respect for the NFL, our great game and all of our players, and a failure to understand the overwhelming force for good our clubs and players represent in our communities" (2017, para. 1). Trump's response? A twit-storm. From September 23 to October 23, 2017, Trump tweeted eighteen times about the NFL protests, tweets which intended to mobilize his supporters within the frame of national patriotism that he had defined and which, combined, provoked more than 821,000 comments, 527,530 retweets, and 2,275,736 "likes," as of March 12, 2018. Simply because Goodell condemned Trump's comments, Trump encouraged his followers—through a tweet—to condemn the NFL: "Roger Goodell of NFL just put out a statement trying to justify the total disrespect certain players show to our country. Tell them to stand!" (Trump September 23, 2017). By proclaiming that the impetus of Goodell's statement is to attempt to "justify the total disrespect certain players show to our country," Trump effectively dismissed the condemnation of his choice to define protesters as "sons of bitches" who, if we believe the tweet that he fired off 4 hours and 14 minutes prior to this one, refuse to recognize their privilege. That Goodell's statement does not so much as suggest a rationalization of any player disrespecting the United States is insignificant; what matters is Trump's imputation, which is accepted by the 152,604 people who "liked" the tweet, as of March 12, 2018. Furthermore, he not only encouraged the audience to stand in opposition to Goodell and thus the NFL but he also weakened Goodell's ethos through the phrase "tries to justify." Goodell is thus, at once, an anti-patriot and wholly ineffective: According to Trump's accusation, Goodell attempted a justification, and he failed because there is no justification. The fact that Trump invented this reproach doesn't matter; what does, to Trump, is that it worked.

Over the following sixteen tweets, Trump increasingly encouraged his supporters to put pressure on the NFL, while simultaneously exaggerating his followers' success in applying that pressure.

On September 24, 2017, at 3:44 A.M., Trump suggested that "If NFL fans refuse to go to games until players stop disrespecting our Flag & Country, you will see change take place fast. Fire or suspend!" (Trump). After 29 minutes, he proclaimed that NFL attendance and ratings had significantly decreased because patriotic citizens "stay away": "...NFL attendance and ratings are WAY DOWN. Boring games yes, but many stay away because they love our country. League should back U.S." (Trump September 24, 2017). As with the examples above, this tweet is ambiguous and suggests something *like* verity but doesn't provide the evidence to prove its point. Instead, it relies on the plain style to intimate truth while its truth value is, at best, partial. Although Trump contends that attendance and ratings are not just down, they are WAY DOWN, Manuela Tobias explains that "there's little evidence to suggest people are boycotting the NFL. Most of the professional sports franchises are dealing with declines in popularity" (2017b, para. 34). Yet, Trump gets his audience to believe that there is a direct correlation between the protest and a decrease in viewership: "…NFL attendance and ratings are WAY DOWN [...]" due to his claim that "[...] many stay away because they love our country. [...]" (Trump September 24, 2017). The first statement is an exaggeration, and the second, an equivocation. The third—"League should back U.S."—implies that the NFL has an obligation to support the country, and although this declaration seems to encourage patriotism, the broad strokes with which Trump paints this duty hint at an insidious undercurrent: such support should be unrestricted and uncritical. More troubling is the fact that Trump makes this statement at 4:13 A.M., slightly more than 4 hours before the first game was scheduled to start at 9:30 A.M. In other words, after 29 minutes, he encourages his fan base not to attend the games, he declares that his team's boycott has already worked.

Trump reinforced this team spirit mentality by declaring that the NFL receives an unmerited benefit which his own supporters are denied. In a tweet on October 10, 2017, Trump provokes further vilification of the NFL based on what he implies is a lack of fairness: "Why is the NFL getting massive tax breaks while at the same time disrespecting our Anthem, Flag and Country? Change tax law!" (Trump). Trump clearly expects that this question will work to motivate his supporters to oppose the NFL because the situation, as he framed it, is unjust: hardworking, patriotic Americans do not receive "massive" tax breaks, but the disrespectful NFL does. The problem, again, has to do with the dubiousness of his wording. It is unclear what tax breaks he's referring to or what tax law needs to be changed. As Manuela Tobias explains, "Since 2015, the NFL hasn't benefitted from a not-for-profit tax break enjoyed by many professional sports league offices. However, it does enjoy tax exemptions on municipal bonds used to build stadiums" (2017a, para. 22). A 2016 study published by Brookings reports that these tax exemptions resulted in a $1.11 billion loss over a fifteen-year period for the federal government (Gold et al. 2016). While the claim that the NFL benefits from this type of tax break is true, the declaration that these exemptions are "massive" is not. But in Trump's realm of alternative facts, data doesn't matter because the objective is not to promote a real conversation about serious issues; rather it is to provoke an emotional response within the Twittersphere—both from those who support him and those who don't.

On the surface, Trump's tweets read like brief, often impetuous communiqués from an individual who cares more about the act of communicating, of keeping his followers in the know, than about the rules that govern such communications, and through this style, he reaffirms for those supporters that he speaks their language and therefore understands their problems. In an article published in the *Personality and Social Psychology Bulletin,* Matthew L. Newman et al. argue that there is "an interrelationship between the content of a communication and the style of language used to tell it" (2003, 673). If this is true, if content and style are interrelated, then Trump's ostensibly plain, purportedly non-rhetorical style suggests plain, guileless content. The deceptive simplicity of Trump's language suggests that he isn't using rhetoric as a means to engage with and lead his audience to a particular conclusion; he's merely speaking truth, openly and directly. This linguistic style distinguishes him from the standard rhetoric of politicians whose cautious *savoir faire* tends to be interpreted as double-speak and deceptive. But there is a subtlety to Trump's tweets that belies the notion that his brash outspokenness is without agenda; he's using common words, but he's not speaking a common language. Instead, he's using the pretense of plain speech for his own gain.

Language Revelations and the Trump Persona

Trump's affinity for brash, boorish, and offensive speech earns him, at once, praise from supporters who appreciate his anti-politician persona and staunch disapproval from those who reject the content of such speech and fear its normalization. For these audiences, he is either a powerful and effective leader who will "make America great again" or a woefully unqualified, cocksure malefactor. Yet, both of these perspectives, and the many others that pervade public forums, are born from an analysis of the language that Trump uses. In his book, *Language and Identity: National, Ethnic, Religious,* John E. Joseph argues that the way people speak—"inseparably from what they say"—plays a significant part in our conception of who that person is (2004, 3). In moments when our contact with people is purely linguistic, as it is on Twitter, Joseph suggests that "Under these circumstances we seem to be able to size them up, to feel that we know *who they really are*—that 'deep' identity again—more satisfactorily than when we only see them and have no linguistic contact" (2004, 3, emphasis in original). Annabelle Mooney's point illustrates this claim. She writes, "Even in a single language like English, there are many ways of representing the world. These representations are often the result of particular habitual ways of thinking, or worldviews" (2011, 35). In other words, in seeking to understand who a person is, we look to the language that he or she uses to find repeated patterns which communicate a speaker's ideology or worldview.

In this way, Trump's decision to use Twitter to gain support for his slant on the NFL protests is telling. On September 24, 2017, in addition to the two tweets above, he issued a third that was published at 3:25 P.M., slightly over 2 hours after the start of the Stateside games. This tweet—"Sports fans should never condone players that do not stand proud for their National Anthem or their Country. NFL should change policy!"—is in direct response to the start of a league-wide protest, where the number of players taking a knee during the national anthem increased dramatically (Trump). At 4:39 the next morning, Trump replied with a tweet meant to preemptively frame his followers' response to this demonstration: "The issue of kneeling has nothing to do with race. It is about respect for our Country, Flag and National Anthem. NFL mustrespect this!" (Trump September 25, 2017). As George Lakoff explains, "the idea of preemptive framing is to frame an issue before other people get a chance to, to put the idea out there first…You have to understand what the framing is and what the framing is he's trying to avoid" (2017). In this tweet, then, Trump offers an interpretation that moves the impetus of the protest away from racial inequality and police brutality and reframes the action of kneeling as unpatriotic: "[…] It is about respect for our Country, Flag, and National Anthem. […]" (Trump September 25, 2017). The purpose of the final exclamation—"NFL must respect this!"—is to reinforce the viewpoint that Trump initiated in his first two tweets about the protests: The NFL is the adversary that Trump's team of supporters is meant to oppose.

The fact that Trump preemptively frames his followers' response hints at an alternate agenda to his insistence that the players stand for the anthem. According to Euan McKirdy, "Players from all 28 teams in the league that played Sunday participated in some form of protest" in an "unprecedented show of defiance against US President Donald Trump Sunday" (2017, para. 2 and para. 1). McKirdy's suggestion is apt: Players joined the protest en masse because of Trump's inflammatory remarks in Alabama and his subsequent derogatory tweets about the NFL. As Julius Thomas of the Miami Dolphins explained, "To have the president trying to intimidate people—I wanted to send a message that I don't condone that. I'm not O.K. with somebody trying to prevent someone from standing up for what they think is important"; LeSean McCoy of the Buffalo Bills also clarified his reason for participation, saying, "I can't stand and support something where our leader of this country is just acting like a jerk, you know, angry and upset about N.F.L. players protesting in a peaceful manner" (Hoffman et al. 2017). So, Trump was partially correct. The protests on September 24, 2017 were not about race, but they were also not about "our Country, Flag and National Anthem." They were about Trump, and they were intended to be a very public rejection of his supercilious, authoritarian, and repeated incitation that protesters be castigated. In short, NFL players, coaches, and owners in the Sunday games joined together to question the legitimacy of a seated president calling protesters "sons of bitches" who should be fired for engaging in an act that is protected under the First Amendment of the Constitution.

The preemptive framing, however, allows Trump to push the protesters' disrespect of him into contempt for the United States; if we accept his frame, the protesters aren't anti-Trump, they're anti-America. He then bolsters the conflation of himself with America through the repetition of keywords. In the eighteen tweets that Trump posted about the NFL protests, he mentions "country" fourteen times, "flag" seven times, "anthem" eleven times, "disrespect" five times, "disrespected" once, and "respect," "disrespecting," and "stand" seven times. The objective throughout these tweets is to push acquiescence, to force players and coaches to take a literal "stand" in support of Trump. The September 25, 2017 protest was an outward display of defiance, of a refusal to acknowledge his power; the remedy, for Trump, is a public display of obedience, which would signal to the world—and to himself—that the dissenters had submitted to his authority. Trump's incessant need, displayed through these tweets, to use incendiary tactics to promote his self-aggrandizing worldview signals a type of leadership that thrives off of reactionary tactics and divisive strategies. Throughout his tweets about the NFL protests, Trump repeatedly reinforces the team spirit mentality that he initially cultivated during the speech in Alabama: Followers of his Twitter account are encouraged to view, immediately and concretely, the irreparable divide between the protesters and the patriots who have accepted that the act of kneeling is an absolute disrespect for the country, the flag, and the national anthem.

The us versus them dynamic that Trump works to cultivate is problematic for the very reason that it denies the potential for dialog with anyone who is not in the 'us.' Them is the 'other,' the anti-American, in the case of supporters of the protests, or pro-loser, and in the case of Democrats who don't want the enormous tax cuts that Trump is offering. In the tweet above, Trump declared that "Democrats don't want massive tax cuts – how does that win elections? Great reviews for Tax Cut and Reform Bill." (Trump September 28, 2017). Although the rhetorical frame is slight, it illustrates Trump's desire to create division between his supporters, who he expects to agree with his statement immediately, and those who were working against this proposed legislation. He very easily could have flipped the order— "Great reviews for Tax Cut and Reform Bill. Democrats don't want massive tax cuts. This is why they lost"— which would have focused his audience's attention on the amazing reviews that the proposed bill had received. Instead, he frames the "Great reviews" through the lens of Democratic opposition. The Democrats "don't want massive tax cuts," which the bill would purportedly allow, and the bill's supporters, who are not mentioned, think the proposed legislation is "great." What this arrangement suggests, then, is that Trump is less concerned about garnering bipartisan support for this bill and is instead focused on solidifying ideological divides between his supporters and those who oppose him. This slant also allows him to frame the conversation. By moving focus away from the consequences of the "massive tax cuts," he effectively shifts his readers' attention to an easier target of conversation: the other, the objectors, the Democrats. And such a shift is necessary, considering CNBC journalist Jacob Pramuk's explanation that "the outline [offered by Republican supporters] lacked some key details, including how to pay for the tax cuts without significantly increasing the federal budget deficit" (2017, para. 7). Whether about tax cuts or NFL protests, a lack of support, for Trump, doesn't signal the need to assess the merits of opposing viewpoints in an effort to modify his original position, if necessary; instead, it evinces a need to malign and to silence dissidents by provoking a vocal, sustained, and emotional response from his followers.

The extent to which Trump's tweets are hyperemotional has led writers such as Virginia Heffernan to label him a "proud male hysteric," and this declaration of hysteria is not off-base (2016, para. 3). Zachary Crockett notes that 76% of Trump's tweets contain exclamation points, and Caitlin Dewey argues, "A personification of the Trump Twitter voice would not look like Trump himself, smug and besuited and relatively composed as he always seems. It would be someone on the verge of a hysterical breakdown or a profound religious awakening" (2016, image3; 2016, para. 4). Strikingly, the success of Trump's emotional provocations has to do with Twitter. In the Twittersphere, emotion is read, not heard, which invites the reader to participate in the emotion through creation, as he or she reads a tweet. Trump scoffs at Democrats' attempts to defeat his ideas about tax reform or sneers at NFL protesters who challenge his authority, and his audience likewise ridicules those purportedly unpatriotic positions because the linguistic cues of framing, CAPS, and exclamations require that the reader adopt the writer's voice to 'hear' the message correctly. Even readers who reject the team spirit emotions that Trump intends to provoke are subject to emotional reactions against such provocations. On either side, tweeters are meant to read and to respond to tweets quickly by "liking," "retweeting," or commenting, and they are meant to be emotional in their responses.

Trump's use of Twitter, in short, makes him a demagogue. He garners support through inflaming the passions of those who listen to him or read what he tweets while hindering deliberation and rational thought. His tweets consistently and unabashedly trigger emotional reactions from the vast majority who read his messages—both supporters and oppositionists alike. As Michael Barbaro notes, "In a pattern that has played out over and over, he makes a provocative remark…and hundreds of thousands of strangers defend him, spread his message and engage in emotional debates with his critics, all the while ensuring that he remains the subject of constant conversation" (2016). And in that central position, he controls the story, his supporters' understanding of and reactions to the issues that he tweets about, and his readers' ability to see those with whom they disagree as intelligent individuals who might have differing perspectives but who are nonetheless capable of rational, respectful dialog. To be sure, part of the issue has to do with Twitter as a social media platform: its initial 140-character cap was exceptionally limiting and did not allow even scrupulous writers to engage in meaningful dialectics. In Trump's hands, Twitter becomes a means to insult 'them,' to deceive 'us,' and to gain acceptance of his authority by exploiting prejudice and ignorance. He creates twit-storms to derail conversation, to concretize divides, and to prevent any type of progress that doesn't demonstrate his power.

The issue, at its core, is his language: Trump's use of language on Twitter intends to shape the response of his audience in a specific way, which is the goal of both rhetoricians and Sophists. Considering the "new regime of language in the White House," Adam Hodges argues that "Insults, by their very nature, accord with the schoolyard bully persona, but [Trump's] tweets also epitomize the rhetorical moves of the snake oil salesman—the language of advertising at its slimiest" (2017). While Hodges is correct—Trump is a bully—this designation alone doesn't offer a strategy of dealing with an aggressor, and it doesn't suggest a way of understanding why he has gotten so much support. Gleb Tsipursky, an Assistant Professor in the Decision Science Collaborative and History Department at Ohio State University, offers a different perspective. Where he defines the "Intentional System," as cognition based on intelligent, reflective reasoning and the "Autopilot System" as emotional, intuitive responses, Tsipursky argues that "Politicians skilled in the art of public speaking can take advantage of our cognitive biases to shape our opinions. They do so through making points based less on evidence, reason, and logic—the Intentional System's strengths—and instead playing to the much more powerful Autopilot System that guides our thinking" (2016, para. 3). A reader's cognitive bias, then, predisposes that individual to reject or to accept the message that Trump relays based on the extent to which that message is congruous with that reader's perspective, a fact that complicates our ability to respond intelligently to Trump's efforts. Another such complication is the illusory truth effect.

Repetition, the Illusory Truth Effect, and Audience Assent

In 1977, Lynn Hasher, David Goldstein, and Thomas Toppino discovered that the truth value of statements increases with repetition; that is, the more familiar an individual is with a statement, the more likely he or she will be to rate that statement as valid. What's more, "the increase in validity ratings with repetition was equivalent for true and false statements, despite the fact that subjects succeeded in discriminating between them" (Hasher et al. 1977, 112). This phenomenon has been termed the illusory truth effect. While perhaps startling, acceptance of information—even while that information is known to be flawed or flat-out incorrect—has to do with fluency, as Wei-Chun Wang et al. have proven. In their study, published in the *Journal of Cognitive Neuroscience*, they scanned participants with functional magnetic resonance imaging (fMRI) to gauge the activation of the perirhinal cortex (PRC) to determine whether illusory truths are "mediated by brain regions previously linked to fluency" (2016, 739). They found that "the neuroimaging analyses indicate that activity in PRC mediated illusory truth. Specifically, activity increased as a function of perceived truth of repeated (i.e., fluent) statements but decreased as a function of perceived truth of new statements" (Wang et al., 2016, 743). Fluency, it seems, is the key to acceptance, as Elizabeth J. Marsh et al. confirm: "More generally, the ease with which we process information (i.e., fluency) serves as an extraneous cue for many judgments, including truth; perceptions of truthfulness increase when information pops to mind or even when statements are easy to read" (2016, 109). This type of neural processing, where the brain associates ease of understanding with accuracy, is so strong that it can override previously accepted facts. In "Knowledge Does Not Protect Against Illusory Truth," Lisa K. Fazio et al. test the assumption that knowledge limits the illusory truth effect. Their study demonstrates that "repetition increased statements' perceived truth, regardless of whether stored knowledge could have been used to detect a contradiction"; they conclude, "people sometimes fail to bring their knowledge to bear and instead rely on fluency as a proximal cue" (2015, 996 and 999). In other words, that individuals don't necessarily rely on stored knowledge to assess the accuracy of new information is a function of the brain: repetition leads to efficient processing, which in turn signals truth.

Through social media platforms such as Twitter, the illusory truth effect works to great advantage of tweeters like Trump. In their article in *Cyberpsychology, Behavior, and Social Networking*, Hyegyu Lee and Hyun Jung Oh argue that this effect is heightened by a lack of standard nonverbal cues on social media and the hasty judgments that such spaces promote: "people find it difficult to process information with sufficient time and effort, due to the information overload in online environments; people rather rely on heuristic cues available on social media to judge information credibility" (2017, 164). Looking to "likes," retweets, and comments, users not only judge accuracy based on their fluency with the information but also on how their peer group has assessed it. When Trump tweeted that "The issue of kneeling has nothing to do with race. It is about respect for our Country, Flag, and National Anthem. NFL must respect this!" over 54,000 users commented, 54,519 retweeted the post, and 202,813 "liked" it, as of March 12, 2018 (Trump September 25, 2017).[6] Certainly, there are dissenting comments, and some non-supporters retweeted in order to call attention to his statement, but even oppositional comments and retweets lend credence to the information that the tweet offers because of the illusory truth effect: users are engaging with and repeating the statement even as they work to oppose it. For those that agree, there is a chorus 202,813 strong whose "likes" ballyhoo illusory truth. Yet, that chorus may not be as robust as this number suggests. Douglas Guilbeault and Samuel Wooley explain in *The Atlantic* that "The widespread use of political bots solidifies polarization among citizens," as bots are "developed to automatically do tasks online, as a means for gaming online polls and artificially inflating social-media traffic" (2016). Thus, the influence of bots should not be underestimated: bots can easily be programmed to "like" and retweet all posts by a particular user; these automatic gestures increase the perception that the content of the tweet is valid; and users more readily accept that validity.

Peripheral cues such as "likes," comments, and retweets work together to reinforce the illusory truth effect by virtue of the fact that "likes" suggest acceptance and comments and retweets reiterate, and consequently strengthen, the information. While it might be comforting to assume that only Trump supporters are subject to the illusory truth effect, that he can only influence his team of supporters through the repetitions that he offers on Twitter, the fact is that our hardwired neural processing system has the capacity to enthrall even his staunchest detractors. In Gordon Pennycook et al.'s study, they found that "the familiarity effect was evident regardless of whether the items were concordant or discordant with stated political ideology," which means that inaccurate headlines and stories are "positively affected by familiarity even when there was a strong political motivation to reject them" (2017, 11–12). What this means, then, is that the issue of Trump's demagoguery, the issue of having a seated president using an online platform to deepen political divides by exploiting a team spirit dynamic, and the issue of people accepting his perspective as the most valid is not a problem between those who accept and those who reject Trump. It isn't a problem between Republicans and Democrats. And it isn't a problem between us and them. Certainly, there are individuals who are predisposed to assent to or to reject his perspective, but the core issue is linguistic in nature: how language must be used in the Twittersphere based on the constraints of the platform; how Trump uses repetition to bulldoze his perspective; how Trump's use of ambiguity requires the reader to figure out his meaning; and how the brain processes language. Independent of political ideology, the Twittersphere promotes the illusory truth effect and limits our potential not only to engage in earnest discourse but also to understand rightly any information gained in that sphere.

Delusory Realm of the Twittersphere

It would be easy to conclude this chapter by stating that we need to stop passively accepting mediated information. Such information offered via social media is, after all, a story driven by the perspective of the teller and governed by that individual's ideology—wittingly or not. Looking to Trump's response to the NFL protests, his tweets are clearly intended to promote acceptance of his perspective: he decides what information to include, what details to leave out, and how to frame the issue to elicit the response he desires. But his is merely one perspective, one story, which is formulated through a rapacious desire to be seen as 'the' unquestioned authority. That his story has been widely and vociferously accepted by his followers has more to do with his use of plain speech, his divisive tactics on Twitter, and his emotional and biased provocations than with actual content, rational ideas to solve important issues, or an ability to inspire people to embrace diversity and to work toward a stronger America. In short, the acceptance that Trump has gained results from the illusory truth effect and his demagoguery.

Although he's using a new platform, the tactics are not new: philosophers from Plato forward have decried the strategems of rhetoricians and Sophists alike who demonstrate interest in winning at any cost. As Mark Thompson notes, "Ever since Plato, critics of rhetoric have worried about instrumentality— the risk that eloquent but unscrupulous speakers will seek to convince not through the merit of their argument but by pressing the audience's buttons, in other words by using ideas, phrases, and professional tricks that they've learned and perfected over time to elicit a desired reaction" (2016, 19–20). In Trump's case, his lack of eloquence is a guise: his tweets don't read as rhetorically con- structed because the language he uses is plain and, in many cases, grammati- cally incorrect. His style seems untutored, but it works. It provokes. It divides. And it is perfectly situated on Twitter, where the constraints of that platform deny conversation and hinder attempts to understand better what others value, believe, and think. Yet knowing how our brains intake information can pre- pare us to "be intentional about influencing our own thinking and feeling patterns. We can evaluate reality more clearly, make better decisions, and im- prove our ability to achieve goals" (Tsipursky 2014, para. 1). Being aware of the process can lessen the impact of the illusory truth effect, and in combination with an understanding of the language of the Twittersphere, individuals may be better prepared to extend compassion to others instead of mindlessly revil- ing differences. The power of language to shape our connection to the world around us cannot be overestimated. As Jason Del Gandio points out, "Those who control language control the mind, and those who create language create reality" (2008, 107). In Trump's hands, the language of the Twittersphere is a weapon of mass deception. It is up to us to determine whether that weapon has power and how much damage it will do.

#theresistence #resistence #resist

Notes

1 Wikipedia is a great example of user-generated content, in that users provide re- search and sources to support the claims that are made on the pages, and other readers can verify information and make corrections when necessary. This stands in stark contrast to citizen producers in platforms such as Twitter who tend not to substantiate their claims.

2 As of November 7, 2017, Twitter increased the character count to 280. The tweets quoted in this chapter occur before this date and were restricted to 140 characters.

3 There is no transcript available of this rally. The author listened to the speech and transcribed the quoted passage.

4 Both Rensin and Conor Friedersdorf ("What Critiques of 'Smug Liberals' Miss." *TheAtlantic.com*, last modified May 3, 2017. //www.theatlantic.com/politics/archive/ 2017/05/what-the-smug-liberals-critique-leaves-out/525189/) point out that all political movements include a self-righteous and superior faction within the larger group.

5 The speech starts at 5:40 of the video, which places the quotation at 43:22. While the transcript of the speech was originally published along with the video that publication has since been pulled from the website. The author listened to the rally and transcribed the quoted passages.

6 The use of bots to increase numbers of "likes" in social media platforms is a complicated issue, especially with respect to the fact that users rely on "likes" as heuristic cues in the determination of truth. Interested readers can turn to Douglas Guilbeault and S. Wooley's article, "How Twitter Bots are Shaping the Election," *TheAtlantic.com*, last modified Nov 1, 2016. //www.theatlantic.com/technology/archive/2016/11/election-bots/506072/.

Bibliography

Barbaro, Michael. "Pithy, Mean and Powerful: How Donald Trump Mastered Twitter for 2016." *NYTimes.com*, accessed October 2, 2017, www.nytimes.com/2015/10/06/us/politics/donald-trump-twitter-use-campaign-2016.html

Crockett, Zachary. "What I Learned Analyzing 7 Months of Donald Trump's Tweets." *Vox.com*, last modified May 16, 2016, www.vox.com/2016/5/16/11603854/donald-trump-twitter

Del Gandio, Jason. *Rhetoric for Radicals: A Handbook for 21st Century Activists*. Gabriola Island: New Society Publishers, 2008.

Dewey, Caitlin. "Donald Trump, Twitter, and the Art of the Exclamation Point." *WashingtonPost.com*, last modified July 22, 2016, www.washingtonpost.com/news/the-intersect/wp/2016/07/22/donald-trump-twitter-and-the-art-of-the-exclamation-point/?utm_term=.b1fd79feb118

Fazio, Lisa K., Nadia M. Brashier, B. Keith Payne, and Elizabeth J. Marsh. "Knowledge Does Not Protect Against Illusory Truth." *Journal of Experimental Psychology: General* 144, no. 5 (2015): 993–1002.

Gold, Alexander K., Austin J. Drukker, and Ted Gayer. "Why the Federal Government Should Stop Spending Billions on Private Sports Stadiums." *Brookings.edu*, last modified September 8, 2016, www.brookings.edu/research/why-the-federal-government-should-stop-spending-billions-on-private-sports-stadiums/

Goodell, Roger. "Statement from NFL Commissioner Roger Goodell." *nflcommunications.com*, accessed September 30, 2017, https://nflcommunications.com/Pages/Statement-From-NFL-Commissioner-Roger-Goodell.aspx

Guilbeault, Douglas and Samuel Wooley. "How Twitter Bots are Shaping the Election." *TheAtlantic.com*, last modified November 1, 2016, www.theatlantic.com/technology/archive/2016/11/election-bots/506072/

Hasher, Lynn, David Goldstein, and Thomas Toppino. "Frequency and the Conference of Referential Validity." *Journal of Verbal Learning and Verbal Behavior* 16 (1977): 107–12.

Heffernan, Virginia. "How the Twitter Candidate Trumped the Teleprompter President." *Politico.com*, last modified May/June 2016, www.politico.com/magazine/story/2016/04/2016-heffernan-twitter-media-donald-trump-barack-obama-teleprompter-president-213825

Henriksen, Berit Engøy. "Language and Politics." In *Language, Society, and Power: An Introduction*. 3rd ed. Eds. Annabelle Mooney, Jean Stilwell Peccei, Suzanne LaBelle, Berit Engay Hericksen, Eva Eppler, Anthea Irwin, Pia Pichler, Siân Preece, and Satori Soden. London: Routledge, 2011.

Hermida, Alfred. "Tweets and Truth: Journalism as a Discipline of Collaborative Verification." *Journalism Practice* 6, no. 5–6 (2012): 659–68. www.tandfonline.com/10.1080/17512786.2012.667269

Hess, Amanda. "How Trump Wins Twitter." *Slate.com*, accessed September 29, 2017, www.slate.com/articles/technology/future_tense/2016/02/donald_trump_is_the_best_at_twitter_here_s_why.html

Hodges, Adam. "Trump's Formulaic Twitter Insults." *Anthropology News* 58, no. 1 (January 18, 2017): e206–210. https://doi.org/10.1111/an.308

Hoffman, Benjamin, Victor Mather, and Jacey Fortin. "After Trump Blasts N.F.L., Players Kneel and Lock Arms in Solidarity." *NewYorkTimes.com*, last modified September 24, 2017, www.nytimes.com/2017/09/24/sports/nfl-trump-anthem-protests.html

Irwin, Anthea. "Language and the Media." In *Language, Society, and Power: An Introduction*. 3rd ed. Eds. Annabelle Mooney, Jean Stilwell Peccei, Suzanne LaBelle, Berit Engay Hericksen, Eva Eppler, Anthea Irwin, Pia Pichler, Siân Preece, and Satori Soden. London: Routledge, 2011.

Joseph, John E. *Language and Identity: National, Ethnic, Religious*. New York: Palgrave MacMillan, 2004.

Lakoff, George and Brooke Gladstone. "A Taxonomy of Trump's Tweets." Produced by WNYC Studios. *On the Media*, January 12, 2017, Podcast, www.wnyc.org/story/taxonomy-trump-tweets/

Lee, Hyegyu and Hyun Jung Oh. "Normative Mechanism of Rumor Dissemination on Twitter." *Cyberpsychology, Behavior, and Social Networking* 20, no. 3 (2017): 164–71.

Marsh, Elizabeth J., Allison D. Cantor, and Nadia M. Brashier. "Believing that Humans Swallow Spiders in their Sleep: False Beliefs as Side Effects of the Processes that Support Accurate Knowledge." *Psychology of Learning and Motivation* 64 (2016): 93–132.

Martin, Keir and Jakob Krause-Jensen. "Trump: Transacting Trickster." *Anthropology Today* 33, no. 3 (June 2017): 5–8.

McKirdy, Euan. "NFL Players, Owners Come Together to Denounce Trump's Anti-Protest Rant." *CNN.com*, last modified September 25, 2017, www.cnn.com/2017/09/25/politics/nfl-protests-weekend/index.html

Mooney, Annabelle. "Language Thought and Representation." In *Language, Society, and Power: An Introduction*. 3rd ed. Eds. Annabelle Mooney, Jean Stilwell Peccei, Suzanne LaBelle, Berit Engay Hericksen, Eva Eppler, Anthea Irwin, Pia Pichler, Siân Preece, and Satori Soden. London: Routledge, 2011.

Newman, Matthew L., James W. Pennebaker, Diane S. Berry, and Jane M. Richards. "Lying Words: Predicting Deception from Linguistic Styles." *PSPB* 29, no. 5 (May 2003): 665–75.

Ott, Brian L. "The Age of Twitter: Donald J. Trump and the Politics of Debasement." *Critical Studies in Mass Communication* 34, no. 1 (December 23, 2016): 59–68. https://doi.org/10.1080/15295036.2016.1266686

Pramuk, Jacob. "Senate Budget Proposal Calls for Bill Before Nov. 13, Allows for $1.5 Trillion in Tax Cuts." *CNBC.com*, last modified September 29, 2017, www.cnbc.com/2017/09/29/senate-budget-proposal-calls-for-tax-reform-bill-before-nov-13.html

Rensin, Emmett. "The Smug Style in American Liberalism." *Vox.com*, last modified April 21, 2016, www.vox.com/2016/4/21/11451378/smug-american-liberalism

Shearer, Eliza and Jeffrey Gottfried. "News Use across Social Media Platforms 2017." *Pew Research Center*, last modified September 7, 2017, www.journalism.org/2017/09/07/news-use-across-social-media-platforms-2017/

Thompson, Mark. *Enough Said: What's Gone Wrong with the Language of Politics?* New York: St. Martin's Press, 2016.

Tobias, Manuela. "Is the NFL Getting 'massive tax breaks,' as Donald Trump Said?" *Politifact.com*, last modified October 12, 2017a, www.politifact.com/truth-o-meter/statements/2017/oct/12/donald-trump/nfl-getting-massive-tax-breaks-donald-trump-said/

Tobias, Manuela. "Trump's Mostly False Claim that NFL Ratings Are 'Way Down.'" *Politifact.com*, last modified September 24, 2017b, www.politifact.com/truth-o-meter/statements/2017/sep/24/donald-trump/trumps-mostly-false-claim-nfl-ratings-are-way-down/Trump, Donald. Campaign Rally. Fort Dodge, IA, November 12, 2015. *FNN*, www.youtube.com/watch?v=kG6FrgMXcSs.

Trump, Donald. *Campaign Rally for Luther Strange.* Huntsville, AL, September 22, 2017, www.realclearpolitics.com/video/2017/09/23/full_video_president_trump_holds_campaign_rally_for_luther_strange_slams_nfl.html

Trump, Donald. Twitter Post, October 10, 2017, 3:13 A.M. https://twitter.com/realdonaldtrump/status/917694644481413120

Trump, Donald. Twitter Post. September 23, 2017, 3:25 P.M. https://twitter.com/realdonaldtrump/status/911718138747727872

Trump, Donald. Twitter Post. September 24, 2017, 4:13 A.M. https://twitter.com/realdonaldtrump/status/911911385176723457

Trump, Donald. Twitter Post. September 24, 2017, 3:44 A.M. https://twitter.com/realdonaldtrump/status/911904261553950720

Trump, Donald. Twitter Post. September 24, 2017, 3:25 P.M. https://twitter.com/realdonaldtrump/status/912080538755846144

Trump, Donald. Twitter Post. September 25, 2017, 4:39 A.M. https://twitter.com/realdonaldtrump/status/912280282224525312

Trump, Donald. Twitter Post. September 28, 2017, 4:55 A.M. https://twitter.com/realdonaldtrump/status/913371663789625344

Tsipursky, Glib. "Autopilot vs. Intentional System: The Rider and the Elephant." *Intentional Insights*, last modified November 14, 2014, https://intentionalinsights.org/autopilot-vs-intentional-system-the-rider-and-the-elephant-2/

Tsipursky, Glib. "How Our Biases Cause Us to Misinterpret Politics." *Psychology-Today.com*, last modified October 25, 2016, www.psychologytoday.com/blog/intentional-insights/201610/how-our-biases-cause-us-misinterpret-politics

Wang, Wei-Chun, Nadia M. Brashier, Erik A Wing, Elizabeth J. Marsh, and Roberto Cabeza. "On Known Unknowns: Fluency and the Neural Mechanisms of Illusory Truth." *Journal of Cognitive Neuroscience* 28, no. 5 (May 2016): 739–46.

3

THE DARK ALCHEMY OF DONALD TRUMP

Re-inventing Presidential Rhetorics through Christian and "New Age" Discourses

Lance Cummings

In an interview with Michael Gove and Kai Diekmann published on January 16, 2017, just before his inauguration, Donald Trump explained his reasoning for maintaining his @realDonaldTrump Twitter account, which at that time had 46 million followers (Trump 2017).[1] Trump would much rather "just let that build up," because "it's working." He can easily respond to the "dishonesty" of the press—"bing bing bing and I just keep going and they put it on and as soon as I tweet it out [it's breaking news]" (para. 64). It seems much like magic, right?

Undoubtedly, Donald Trump's use of Twitter falls in line with business principles that he has outlined in his books. For example, in his first book *The Art of the Deal*, Trump (1987) famously describes his media strategy. Instead of hiring public relations professionals, Trump relies on free press:

> One thing I've learned about the press is that they're always hungry for a good story, and the more sensational the better. It's in the nature of the job, and I understand that. The point is that if you are a little different, or a little outrageous, or if you do things that are bold or controversial, the press is going to write about you. I've always done things a little differently, I don't mind controversy, and my deals tend to be somewhat ambitious. Also, I achieved a lot when I was very young, and I chose to live a certain style. The result is that the press has always wanted to write about me.
>
> *(39)*

It doesn't really matter to Trump if the press is positive or negative—"the benefits of being written about have far outweighed the drawbacks" (39). The primary key for this approach is "truthful hyperbole" or an "innocent form of exaggeration" that "plays to people's fantasies" (40). This is perhaps the showmanship aspect of Trump's persona that has made him so successful in reality

TV and branding, but there are far deeper influences on how Trump engages the public through spaces like Twitter.

Many of Trump's strategies also reflect ways of thinking found in American business culture, much of which is proliferated through motivational books focused on delivering laws, principles, and formulas for success. In fact, Trump's own books reflect this genre. For example, in his introduction to *How to Get Rich*, Trump (2004) begins with three business rules:

1   "If you don't tell people about your success, they probably won't know about it."
2   "Keep it short, fast, and direct."
3   "Begin working at a young age. I did." (xiii–xiv)[2]

He uses the first to describe both the style and substance of his book. Judging by the cover alone, one might think the purpose of this book is to give advice on how to acquire wealth, but this purpose is only secondary to the primary purpose of letting his audience know of his success in a "straightforward and succinct" way (xiv). He implies that beneath this brevity is a "profundity" and "wisdom" that will lead his readers to riches (xiv). Clearly, these rules lend themselves well to the affordances of Twitter, which is very public and allows for only "short, fast, and direct" messages (xiv).

Easier to miss, though, is Trump's reliance on what might be called self-help and motivational rhetorics—many of which arise out of various religious rhetorics in "New Age" and Christian thought and meld with many twentieth-century business discourses.

Trump's connection with the positive thinking guru, Norman Vincent Peale, is common knowledge although rarely considered in recent analyses of Trump's discourse and his approach to Twitter. Trump's family regularly attended Peale's Marble Collegiate Church, where Peale focused his preaching on developing self-confidence through Christian principles derived from specific verses that could be used as a kind of hypnotic suggestion (Blair 2015, para. 3). Controlling the mind becomes a way to manifest success by overcoming negative thoughts such as guilt and fear. Presumably, Peale's goal was to help those weakened by lack of confidence to find their way in the world. Other authors have pointed out how Trump dislodges Peale's philosophy from its Christian context by creating his own cult of personality (Schmitz 2016, para. 11). "Losers" are those who are unable or unwilling to tap into this power, while "winners" build successful personalities for themselves. Trump has so vanquished weakness, guilt, and fear in his own mind that he is unable to sympathize with these struggles in others. This is what one might call the "dark side" of positive thinking. In Trump's definition, as presented in *How to Get Rich*, a "loser" is someone trapped in the "low altitude" of negative thinking (2004b, 71). Practicing positive thinking is a way to give the "Higher Self" a boost (75). Diminishing this "Higher Self" means a diminished life force. Although too much ego can lead to a "dictatorial personality," the greatest danger for Trump seems to be too little ego (75). Because Twitter blurs the boundaries between the private and the public, this online venue has become a perfect place for Trump to give this ego or Higher Self a boost while also persuading some audiences of his political perspectives.

Recent scholarship on Twitter has noted both a collapse of context and publicized privacy that enhances what some call the "enthymematic nature" of tweets (Cisneros and Nakayama 2015, 118). In other words, there is a latent logic behind many tweets that require the audience to participate in the 144-character (now 280 characters) argument by building on implicit assumptions. For example, racist tweets often use stereotypes of race and cultural logics of "whiteness" that followers must bring to the tweet to understand. Kevin Brock (2014) calls these rhetorical algorithms that intensify arguments and build identification by encouraging audiences to participate in the realities required for each tweet to make sense (2). But because Twitter tends to collapse context and flatten audiences, followers respond to these algorithms in different ways, explaining why many feel a strong identification with Trump, while others a strong aversion. More importantly, Twitter tends to blur the boundaries between the private and the public, creating a kind of "publicized privacy" (Sloop and Gunn 2010, 301). In other words, users tend to use Twitter as a form of social validation and self-promotion, as well as a form of expression and self-disclosure (Cisneros and Nakayama 2015, 117). In this context, twitter can be seen as a direct conduit for the mind—not only to promote ways of thinking through repetitive algorithms but also as a way to extend the self into the public sphere. These aspects of Twitter make it the perfect venue for building a "successful" persona and applying self-help strategies to audiences—not just to one's own mind.

Business motivational and self-help books are very common and have been for quite some time. Peale's philosophy can easily be folded in with authors like Brian Tracey, Stephen Covey, and Tony Robbins. But the rhetoric that undergirds these philosophies has a long history in the U.S., starting with the Puritans. Trumps use of language on Twitter is one logical end of these motivational and self-help rhetorics that seek to change reality through the power of language and positive thinking. Like alchemy, language's ability to recontextualize reality through the manipulation of definitions and ideas can transform anyone's reality into a successful one. Policy and rational approaches to national problems are irrelevant at best because positive thinking and its powerful linguistic alchemy can "make America great again" (MAGA) simply by changing America's attitude ("Donald J. Trump for President"). Twitter becomes a mechanism for deliberately altering reality through discourse. If I can change my personal reality through the power of positive thinking, then I can also change the public reality with the appropriate conduit, in this case, Twitter.

Amalgamating Christian and New Age Rhetorics into Business Literature

For the purposes of this chapter, it will be argued that motivational and self-help literature is a discursive category that lies at the margins of New Age thought. The term "New Age" has always been a vague term, referring to seemingly random combinations of spiritual ideas and practices. Thomas Luckman (1996), an early scholar on the New Age movement attributes its popularity to the slow disintegration of Christianity's hegemony, highlighting the individual's ability to collect "abundant psychological, therapeutic, magic, marginally scientific, and older esoteric material," repackaging them for specific applications. With the current rise of "spiritual, but not religious" approaches to religion, the term "New Age" is perhaps outmoded for the twenty-first century. Spiritual practices in the U.S. have increasingly become syncretic in nature, defying efforts to label and categorize. Even so, these ways of thinking have been deeply influenced by previous religious discourses and ideologies. For example, some scholars in religious studies have attached the term New Age to a particular set of practices and beliefs that criticize dualistic and reductionist ways of viewing life found in Western modernity while providing counter-narratives mostly derived from Eastern, spiritualist, and/or esoteric worldviews that emphasize the individual and her power to change a personal reality (AskeHave 2004, 8). Aupers and Houtman (2006) argue that this apparently random combination really revolves around a "doctrine of self-spirituality" that contests organized efforts to control spiritual practice and identity (206). By nature, New Age rhetorics are anti-establishment and focus primarily on the individual or self—two key traits of the Trump movement.

Even so, many New Age rhetorics, especially those associated with business and self-help, draw on Protestant ways of thinking. For example, business-oriented self-help books can easily be traced back to early American Puritans, who wrote guides to achieve material success through moral conduct (Weiss 1969, 4). Starting most prominently with Ralph Waldo Emerson, this advice shifted away from strictly Christian ideologies to what Richard Weiss (1969) calls the "mind-power" movement:

> God, in the mentalistic self-help tradition, is defined in Emersonian terms, as a Universal Intelligence or Over-Soul. The individual is held to be a partial incarnation of the cosmic force. The locus of divinity in man is his mind which relates to him, in a manner of speaking, to the Universal Mind and gives him access to its power. Translated into popular idiom, this provides the ideological basis for the conviction that all men can 'think' their way to success.
>
> *(14)*

In the nineteenth century, as business rhetorics developed, the professional *ethos* became shaped by "muscular Christianity," a religious movement meant to rescue men's masculinity from the "feminizing" forces of civilization and the church (Cummings 2017, 10). As the cultural image of success became associated with "business men," like Andrew Carnegie, John D. Rockefeller, and Henry Ford, many of these mind-power rhetorics became integral in imbricating success with personal power. For example, Dale Carnegie ([1936] 2010) was one of the first authors to identify passion and desire as keys to motivate people toward success in his book, *How to Win Friends and Influence People*. Napoleon Hill ([1937] 2011) spent years interviewing America's richest men to identify their key attributes in his book *Think and Grow Rich*, which was easily adapted by Norman Vincent Peale ([1952] 2003) in *The Power of Positive Thinking*, one of Donald Trump's most powerful influences.

Although many religious rhetorics inform this literature, writers tend to choose what best fits their situation or audience. For example, Norman Vincent Peale ([1952] 2003, 10) calls his approach to positive thinking "applied Christianity", a term first used by Peale's less religious predecessor, Napoleon Hill (2017, 12). Both of these authors were more likely to discuss "vibrations" and "energy" than God, relying heavily on battery and magnet metaphors when discussing a connection with the Divine like in Peale's book: "Personally, I believe that prayer is a sending out of vibrations from one person to another and to God. All the universe is in vibration. There are vibrations in molecules of a table. The air is filled with vibrations" (56). Tending to this connection is how we channel power for "constructive living" (57). For Peale, this meant cultivating Christian spirituality through Biblical principles that can be tested and utilized scientifically, much like a battery or magnet (38). One must shape the mind through positive thoughts to take advantage of these powers and energy. If you are unsuccessful, or a "loser," you and your negative thinking is to blame. Although Hill and Peale do not make this explicit claim, one can easily argue that wealth is a sign of God's approval, or at least, one's deep connection with God's positive energies.

Despite Donald Trump's apparent turn toward evangelicalism, his ingrained attitudes toward religion and God reflect this mind-power theology. Although he has been a self-professed Presbyterian for most of his adult life, Trump's primary religious experience occurred at Marble Collegiate Church in New York, while Peale was pastor and focused his preaching mostly on overcoming guilt and fear through positive thinking (Schmitz 2016, para. 7). In this context, Trump's assertion that he does not ask forgiveness makes complete sense because guilt simply gets in the way of positive thinking: "I'm not sure I have [asked for forgiveness]. I just go on and try to do a better job from there. ... I think if I do something wrong, I think, I justly [*sic*] and make it right. I don't bring God into that picture. I don't" (quoted in Scott 2015). More recently, Trump has partnered with Paula White (2008), a tele-evangelist who is now one of the President's religious advisors. Although associated by many with Pentecostalism and the prosperity Gospel, her core mission emerges from mind-power theology: "That's the principle I teach … Find your passion in life and figure out a way to make money" (1:27). The idea of finding one's "vocation," or God's calling, is nothing new and has been most famously hashed out by Max Weber ([1905] 2002) in his book *The Protestant Ethic and the "Spirit" of Capitalism*, where he argues that Protestant ethics, particularly Calvinist, inform the cultures of capitalism. But as the idea of the "business man" developed more fully later in the twentieth century, mind-power rhetorics began to inform the construction of the professional *ethos*; a successful business man is able to control his thoughts and stoke his deepest desires into reality.

For Napoleon Hill ([1937] 2011), the secret to developing this successful reality has to do with "feeding" the "subconscious mind" with the right desires, instead of allowing negative thoughts to reach the mind because "thoughts are truly things, for the reason that every material thing begins in the form of thought-energy" (343, 346). In fact, he sees prayer as a "science" that will eventually be taught in schools: "The subconscious mind is the intermediary, which translates one's prayers into terms which Infinite Intelligence can recognize, presents the message, and brings back the answer in the form of a definite plan or idea for procuring the object of the prayer" (352). Peale also focuses on "dynamic laws" and "spiritual formulas," outlining specific practices and procedures that lead to success (1, 6). Instead of desire, Peale encourages the "cultivation of peace of mind […] as a power center out of which comes driving energy for constructive personal and social living" (1). He promises that this peace of mind cannot be "defeated by anything" and leads to "improved health, and a never-ceasing flow of energy" (7). For Peale, there is no such thing as defeat, as long as you have peace of mind and the will power not to be defeated (7). Like authors before him, Trump (2004) also uses this metaphor of "frequency" and "wave length" to describe the power of positive thinking (even recommending Peale's book):

> I'm a tough-minded optimist. I learned a long time ago that my productivity was increased by a large percentage simply by learning to let go of negativity in all forms as quickly as I could. My commitment to excellence is thorough — so thorough that it negates the wavelength of negativity immediately. I used to have to zap negativity mentally. By now, it just bounces off me within a moment of getting near me.
>
> *(70–71)*

In other words, once a successful business man determines his deepest desire and cultivates the appropriate attitude, nothing can stand in his way. With the invention of social media, spaces like Twitter become a place where business men can cultivate these attitudes and desires through discursive strategies such as repetition and reassociation. Historically, Trump has used Twitter as a space to promote these ideas and techniques to his fan base.

Religion of Positivity on Twitter

A quick search for the term "God" at *Trump Twitter Archive* shows few substantive statements that go beyond platitudes. Trump often quotes well-known evangelists, such as Billy Graham and Billy Sunday, but more notably, he quotes his mother seven times between 2013 and 2015—a quote that also appears on the dedication page of his first book: "Trust in God and be true to yourself." Although the two statements in this quote may seem unrelated at first, in business success literature, finding one's passion and stoking your desire is the path to fulfillment. Trusting in God means trusting the potential God gives you (Cummings 2017). For example, Dale Carnegie associated the successful business man with desire and masculinity: "If your desire is pale and flabby, your achievements will also take on that hue and consistency. But if you go after this subject with persistence, and with the energy of a bull dog after a cat, nothing underneath the Milky Way will defeat you" (15). In *Think and Grow Rich*, Napoleon Hill focuses even more on the power of desire to make things happen:

> Will-power and desire, when properly combined, make an irresistible pair. Men who accumulate great fortunes are generally known as cold-blooded, and sometimes ruthless. Often they are misunderstood. What they have is will-power, which they mix with persistence, and place at the back of their desires to insure the attainment of their objectives.
>
> *(260)*

Peale associates desire with positive thinking: "Unless you really want something sufficiently to create an atmosphere of positive factors by your dynamic desire, it is likely to elude you" (99). In other words, one can create one's own conditions for success, as long as you persistently pursue your true desires. From this perspective, Twitter can be used to create the conditions for success.

When looking for evidence of Trump's beliefs in the *Trump Twitter Archive*, there are far more references to positive thinking. For example, Trump has quoted himself often: "Entrepreneurs: Be cautiously optimistic. Call it positive thinking with a lot of reality checks." (Trump April 2, 2014). He also gives his audience other kinds of advice along the same lines: "Entrepreneurs: View any conflict as an opportunity. Being positive could lead you into a fortunate situation." (Trump December 11, 2014). A good business person is in touch with their desire for success and fuel that desire with a positive spirit: "If you can't see it, you can't make it happen. Entrepreneurs, chase your dreams with resolute focus & determination. Be positive!" (October 17, 2014). Trump believes that by focusing on the positive that focus can be achieved: "Practice positive thinking--this will keep you focused while weeding out anything that is unnecessary, negative or detrimental." (June 27, 2014). Trump's election to the presidency is proof that positive thinking works; he wanted to be President, and his positive thinking turned that into reality. In the summer of his first year in office, Trump attributes the strength of the stock market to positive thinking: "Stock market hits another high with spirit and enthusiasm so positive. Jobs outlook looking very good! #MAGA" (July 12, 2017). "Spirit" and "enthusiasm" are all it takes to drive the economy and "MAGA." Some of Trump's followers identify with this positivity and use positivity as a *topos* for their tweets: ""@PaulaDuvall2: We're all enjoying you, as well, Mr. T.! You've inspired Hope and a Positive Spirit throughout America! God Bless you!" Nice" [*sic*] (August 13, 2016). Trump's twitter followers consistently see Trump as force for positivity: ""@Knight276: @realDonaldTrump @amstaffbru I have confidence trump can turn a negative into a positive. Trump can make America great again!" [*sic*] (June 29, 2015).[3] So Trump's slogan, "Make America Great Again," signifies a kind of alchemy. Policy will not necessarily transform America into greatness—only our positive thoughts.

Such a focus on positivity may seem contradictory to readers who only see the negative statements directed at specific people or groups of people, often using nicknames or slurs, like Pocahontas (Elizabeth Warren), Crooked Hillary, and Sloppy Steve [Bannon] (Trump November 3, 2017; January 4, 2018). Certainly, such strategies do not appear in books like *The Power of Positive Thinking*. But in Trump's world, people like Hillary Clinton have only themselves to blame because they have not cultivated a positive attitude. For Trump, they are losers, who have not yet tapped into this secret of success. According to Trump, Hillary lost her focus and is unable to see things in a positive light: "Crooked Hillary Clinton blames everybody (and every thing) but herself for her election loss. She lost the debates and lost her direction!" [*sic*] (Trump September 13, 2017). And during his campaign, one follower mocked Hillary Clinton for claiming a positive attitude: ".@HillaryClinton just claimed she has a "positive, optimistic view" for America. #Debates" [*sic*] (Official Team Trump October 9, 2016). The press should be getting America into a more positive and enthusiastic mindset by focusing on all the good things that have happened since his election, like the rise of the DOW: "Stock market hits another high with spirit and enthusiasm so positive. Jobs outlook looking very good! #MAGA" (Trump July 12, 2017). The more positivity and enthusiasm that can be drummed up in the press and online, the better the economy will be. It is also easy to overlook the many times that Trump tweets at stakeholders to get them to change to a more positive attitude. For example, when attempting to get legislation done in his first year in office, he often tweeted at congress: "Republican Senators are working hard to get their failed ObamaCare replacement approved. I will be at my desk, pen in hand!" (July 14, 2017). Twitter becomes a way to cheer his team on: "The approval process for the biggest Tax Cut & Reform package in the history of our country will soon begin. Move fast Congress!" (September 13, 2017). People that oppose Trump are simply negative thoughts that need to be weeded out.

The influence of New Age rhetorics goes beyond simply the *topos* of positive thinking; many of the ideologies and rhetorical techniques show up in Trump's use of Twitter, particularly his use of language to glorify what he sees as his "Higher Self" and creative potential. The intention here is not to connect Trump politically or even religiously to the New Age movement, which spans far outside the realm of business self-help literature. In fact, many of the core tenets or practices of the New Age movement seem diametrically opposed to the politics and business persona of Donald Trump. At its core, though, the New Age movement seeks to erase the distinction between God and the human self (Hanegraaf 1996, 517). Although gradations of this erasure can vary, the possibility of making oneself God (or a god) arises as practitioners tap into the creative potential and Higher Self, drawing on any discourse, rhetorics, or practices that help achieve this purpose, whether Eastern religion or philosophy, esotericism, or even Christianity. For example, imagining God as an energy or vibration allows business self-help writers to blur the distinction between God. Ideologies behind these belief systems inform Trump's rhetoric, as well as the way he manipulates discourse on Twitter.

The belief system of New Age thinking is difficult to pin down because its cultural logic is syncretic by nature. In his article "If Language is a Game— These Are the Rules," Inger Askehave (2004) identifies several ideologies that can consistently be found in the New Age rhetorics that inform self-help literature: Holism; Spiritual Monism; Health and Healing; The Higher Self; Creative Potential/Self-Responsibility; Reincarnation; Karma Law (9–12). Although more esoteric worldviews that include reincarnation and healing can be tracked in business self-help literature, the core ideologies that influence how Donald Trump uses Twitter revolve primarily around "the Higher Self" and "creative potential/self-responsibility" (9–12). Both Hill ([1937] 2011, 312) and Peale ([1952] 2003, 31) introduce alternative practices such as meditation and visualization into the business world. The distinction between the Higher Self and God is minimal because tapping into these energies releases the potential to create our own realities, like God. If you are unhappy, then you simply have not tapped into this potential, according to thinkers like Hill and Peale.

In many ways, this Higher Self is the opposite of rationality, which gets in the way of intuition and spiritual development. Emotions such as guilt and fear arise from over-rationalizing and must be combatted with positive thoughts. For example, Peale quotes Henri Bergson, an influential French philosopher who "says that the surest way into truth is by perception, by intuition, by reasoning to a certain point, then by taking a 'mortal leap,' and by intuition attaining the truth" (199). Peale does not expand on Bergson's philosophy because he is only interested in short, motivational sayings that will illustrate for his readers his main thought. Here is a philosopher who eschews rationality and realizes there is a deeper way of being. Hill also is looking for ways to connect to this "Infinite Intelligence" that is often hindered by over-rationalizing. Fear and doubt must be vanquished to connect to this higher, more intuitive self:

> If you fill you mind with FEAR, doubt and unbelief in your ability to connect with, and use forces of Infinite Intelligence, the law of auto-suggestion will take this spirit of unbelief and use it as a pattern by which your subconscious mind will translate it into its physical equivalent.
>
> *(Hill [1937] 2011, 92)*

This explains much of Trump's (1987) behavior that may be labeled as "irrational," for example his chaotic management style, which he describes in *The Art of the Deal*. Trump generally describes himself as someone who keeps things flexible and likes to improvise. He introduces his work day by pointing out the lack of structure: "Most people are surprised by the way I work. I play it loose. I don't carry a briefcase. I try not to schedule too many meetings. I leave my door open. You can't be imaginative and entrepreneurial if you've got too much structure. I prefer to come to work each day and just see what develops" (3). When discussing the "elements of the deal," he explains that he likes to keep his options open by having "a lot of balls in the air" (35). He also doesn't like to rely on "number-crunchers," trusting his "gut feeling" and reaching beyond the rational and into the Higher Self (35).

Trump discusses his gut instincts often in his speeches and on Twitter. For example, his advice to entrepreneurs is to "Entrepreneurs: Cover your Bases. Know everything you can about what you're doing. Then go with your gut. Your instincts r there for a reason" [*sic*] (Trump December 11, 2014). During the campaign, he highlighted John Podesta's email that critiqued Hillary's instincts as "suboptimal" by tweeting a specific quote along with the WikiLeaks page: "Her instincts are suboptimal" (Official Team Trump October 19, 2016). Trump's followers also see Trump's instincts as counter to the machinations of career politicians: ""@theAgeofLeo: Your instincts on foreign policy & terrorism have been better than all of these so called experienced politicians combined."" (Trump March 25, 2016). Beyond simply a *topos* for tweets, Twitter is the perfect venue for functioning from one's intuitive self. Twitter allows users to communicate spontaneously and often—simulating microcosm of the mind. As a result, we can see Trump using many motivational techniques throughout his use of Twitter.

This focus on intuition also plays out in his sense of audience, which relies heavily on the moment, particularly when considering public speaking and negotiation. Trump never actually uses the term rhetoric, but uses negotiation as his structuring metaphor for understanding persuasion and audience. His basic premise is that deals should be made through persuasion, not through brute force. True power is "the ability to convince people to accept your ideas" (Trump 2004, 115). Trump asserts that people will not believe you just because your style and delivery are polished, the kind of rhetoric he associates with Barack Obama, for example in the 2012 presidential debates: "Obama is looking rhetorical and weak. @MittRomney is looking strong and sharp." (Trump October 16, 2012). For Trump, good negotiators make it easy for people to understand their argument by using metaphors, analogies, and humor. This strategy includes some elements of *ethos*, letting your audience know that "you're all on the same level in some way" (Trump 2004, 116). Bulldozing is not an effective approach: "You want people to accept your ideas, not merely be resigned to them because they think they can't fight back or are just plain exhausted by you. Don't browbeat them into believing you. Let them think the decision is theirs. It will give them a feeling of control" (116). Many would likely argue that these statements run counter to what we have seen of Trump's rhetoric more recently, especially on Twitter, but Trump is speaking primarily about *ethos* and his relationship to his audience. Later, in *How to Get Rich*, he has a chapter called "Let Your Guard Down, But Only on Purpose," implying that many of his more outrageous statements are merely negotiation tactics:

> If you say something seemingly off the cuff, you may get a revealing response. I might make an outrageous comment in a meeting to see whether the other people play along or take a stand and disagree. It's a good way of assessing the mettle of the folks across the table. Do they want to be liked? Are they comfortable with unpredictability? Are they capable of candor?
>
> *(129)*

Trump is describing a kind of listening rhetoric that is inventional in nature—he uses outrageous statements to get a sense of his audience and where he can go with them. These tactics are clearly reflected in Trump's ability to manipulate audiences at rallies, but they also come into play on Twitter, especially in how he uses language to recontextualize definitions that shape political realities.

Re-inventing the Power of Definitions on Twitter

In his article, Askehave also identifies elements of New Age rhetorics that are integral to how self-help discourse persuades readers to follow their prescriptions, primarily recontextualized words, metaphors, personifications, and parables. Understanding the linguistic elements and rhetorical devices is even more important when considering mind-power rhetorics because most business self-help gurus see language as key to changing the realities around us. For example, Hill's (2017) central practice involves writing down a statement of purpose, memorizing it, and then repeating it every day as a "form of prayer or affirmation" (12). Additionally, one of Peale's primary techniques is that of "suggestive articulation" or repeating out loud peaceful words: "Words have profound suggestive power, and there is healing in the very saying of them. Utter a series of panicky words and your mind will immediately go into a mild state of nervousness. [...] If, on the contrary, you speak peaceful, quieting words, your mind will react in a peaceful manner" (27). Although couched in terms of prayer and submission to God, anyone "obsessed by insecurity and inadequacy" must expose themselves to a "more positive pattern of ideas" through "repetitive suggestion or confidence ideas" (16). For Peale, these words are mostly comprised by Bible verses:

> The words we speak have a direct and definite effect upon our thoughts. Thoughts create words, for words are the vehicles of ideas. But words also affect thoughts and help to condition if not to create attitudes. In fact, what often passes for thinking starts with talk. Therefore, if the average conversation is scrutinized and disciplined to be sure that it contains peaceful expressions, the result will be peaceful ideas and ultimately, therefore, a peaceful mind.
>
> *(31)*

On the other side of this equation, we can create the "very condition we fear" through the power of our thoughts (17). Trump's association with Peale's approach to positive thinking may seem counter-intuitive, given some of the more hostile tweets found in Trump's feed, like those calling out "[...] Crooked Hillary [...]" or "[...] Sloppy Steve!" (Trump November 3, 2017; January 4, 2018). But content aside, the mechanism that drives Trump's use of Twitter is quite similar. If Trump repeats an idea enough on Twitter, that idea will become reality, especially when using techniques such as recontextualization. Trump's attempts to recontextualize Russian collusion is another example common throughout early 2018: "This memo totally vindicates "Trump" in probe. But the Russian Witch Hunt goes on and on. Their was no Collusion and there was no Obstruction (the word now used because, after one year of looking endlessly and finding NOTHING, collusion is dead). This is an American disgrace!" [*sic*] (February 3, 2018). The more Trump tweets about the absence of collusion, the more this term becomes associated with witch hunts.

Recontextualized words can be seen as a kind of alchemy that redefines key terms. Once these new definitions are accepted by readers, the presuppositions entailed by those new definitions are at once accepted (Askehave 2004, 15). As David Zarefsky (2004) notes, a core feature of presidential rhetoric in the twenty-first century is the power of definition: "Because of his prominent political position and his access to the means of communication, the president, by defining a situation, might be able to shape the context in which events or proposals are viewed by the public" (611). In particular, presidents are able to alter definitions through "association" and "dissociation," which involves separating terms from their original meanings or contexts and/or associating those terms with new meaning or contexts:

> The definition of the situation affects what counts as data for or against a proposal, highlights certain elements of the situation for use in arguments and obscures others, influences whether people will notice the situation and how they will handle it, describes causes and identifies remedies, and invites moral judgements about circumstances or individuals.
>
> *(612)*

For example, September 11 was defined as a war by analogously attaching the event to metaphors and discourse about war (612). Or dissociating the term peace from absence of war, so it could be attached to the idea of arms control (612). Or in Trump's case, dissociating the term "collusion" from Russia, so it can be associated with witch hunts and the Federal Bureau of Investigation (FBI). Combining these techniques with the power of repetition and distribution levied by Twitter, and Donald Trump's power to shape reality becomes a kind of alchemy that goes beyond what previous presidents have achieved. Trump's adept ability to do this on Twitter can be understood, though, through a positive thinking lens, which dictates that any negative thought must instantly be transformed into something positive. For example, Peale recommends that readers should never think of oneself as failing and replace such a thought with a mental image of success. When anything negative appears, one must "voice a positive thought to cancel it out" (22). If we think of Twitter through the metaphor of the mind, then this strategy would require counter-tweets to negativity. Ultimately, Peale's goal is for readers to realize their full selves: "Nobody can be you as efficiently as YOU can" (22). When estimating one's ability, one should "raise it by 10 percent." Twitter is a venue for making this happen, allowing personalities to reinforce positive images of themselves online. Trump takes this a step further, though, by not just countering negativity, but deflecting it onto other people.

Several examples of this positive thinking method can be found immediately after the election, as well as the inauguration, where "negative thoughts" about Trump's success in the election were questioned in several ways. First, as Hillary Clinton expanded her popular vote margins, Trump posted several tweets that reframed his win: "Campaigning to win the Electoral College is much more difficult & sophisticated than the popular vote. Hillary focused on the wrong states!" (Trump December 21, 2016). The fact that Trump won without the popular vote shows how sophisticated of a politician he is. If he needed the popular vote, he "would campaign differently" (December 21, 2016). Second, when attendance was visibly low at the inauguration, Trump posted a positive tweet about ratings: "Wow, television ratings just out: 31 million people watched the Inauguration, 11 million more than the very good ratings from 4 years ago!" (January 22, 2017). Trump keeps things as positive as possible, by focusing on all the people watching at home on TV, and probably online—not the actual in-person attendance. The inauguration crowd may not have been the biggest, but many people were still watching the event. Additionally, Trump's habit of picking the polls and articles that put him in the best light is not biased or misleading from a positive thinking perspective—it is simply a way to cultivate the mind from a positive thinking point of view. In fact, for Peale, attitudes are far more important than actual facts (19). Such tweets are meant to cultivate a "winning attitude," not just for Trump himself, but for his followers.

Trump does not stop at countering negativity with positive tweets, but he often deflects negativity toward others, essentially reversing the principles of positive thinking. For example, repeating nicknames, like "Crooked Hillary," associates Hillary with a negativity that can be hard to shake. Repeat the name "Crooked Hillary" enough and Hillary will forever be associated with the email scandal and criminality: "Look at the way Crooked Hillary is handling the e-mail case and the total mess she is in. She is unfit to be president. Bad judgement!" (Trump November 1, 2016). He has transformed reality, but from the opposite direction. Trump often deflects negativity toward his rivals: "So General Flynn lies to the FBI and his life is destroyed, while Crooked Hillary Clinton, on that now famous FBI holiday "interrogation" with no swearing in and no recording, lies, many times…and nothing happens to her? Rigged system, or just a double standard?" (December 2, 2017). Trump is dissociating the negativity of a rigged system from himself and reassociating it with his rivals. In the end, "losers" are responsible for their own failures because they aren't able use positive thinking to mold their desire into reality: "Crooked Hillary Clinton is the worst (and biggest) loser of all time. She just can't stop, which is so good for the Republican Party. Hillary, get on with your life and give it another try in three years!" (November 18, 2017). Such use of association is not necessarily a recommendation of business gurus like Hill and Peale, but an adaptation of their rhetorical strategies.

A third example of dissociation is his use of the term "racist." Up until his actual election, Trump also shifted the definition of "racist" from those who exert power to exclude people based on race to those who bring visibility to the African-American experience, directing most of his accusations of racism toward people like President Obama, Tavis Smiley, and Bryant Gumbel: "Why does @ThisWeekABC w/ @GStephanopoulos allow a hater & racist like @tavissmiley to waste good airtime? @ABC can do much better than him!" (January 11, 2016). By disassociating the term from its original definition, Trump is able to use it against his enemies. For example, he redefines the term as someone who uses race to advance their career: "Goofy Elizabeth Warren, sometimes referred to as Pocahontas, pretended to be a Native American in order to advance her career. Very racist!" (June 11, 2016). Through the manipulation of discourse, Trump does not fit the definition of racist while those he attacks on Twitter do. Such a use of recontextualization is not necessarily sanctioned by positive thinking gurus, but might be described as the dark side of this rhetorical alchemy.

Conclusion

Is Donald Trump a model for positive thinking proponents? Perhaps for some, but there are many components to these mind-power ideologies that are often contradicted by Trump's behavior, even though he may be using rhetorical techniques from these cultures of thought. For example, Hill (2017) provides several principles for dealing with conflict and anger, most of which involve keeping your cool: "The habit of making an incident out of petty annoyances is one of the things that most of us indulge in very greatly almost every day of our lives, instead of just looking at them, or winking at them, or keeping silent" (33). Part of cultivating a positive attitude involves controlling this aspect of our mental attitudes, but many people "get mad at the drop of the hat, and if a fellow doesn't drop the hat, they knock it off his head and then get mad" (103). Peale has an entire chapter on how anger affects the body and what kind of embodied techniques will help you "cool off" that anger (159–60). Such discipline runs counter to the showmanship we find in Donald Trump's twitter feed that more accurately reflects reality TV shows. Tweeting about television ratings or responding to followers about their "stupidity" does not really show constraint although these strategies have worked well for Trump to gather followers who like his authenticity and honesty. For Hill and Peale, such negativity will only attract negative people—a dark side of this kind of rhetoric that perhaps can be seen at his more violent rallies and in events, such as protests over the Confederate statue in Charlottesville in 2017 (Mathis-Lilley 2016; Griggs 2017). Trump's relationship to these violent movements is unclear, but they are at the very least an unintentional consequence of his ability to amplify this negativity through his use of motivational and self-help rhetorics.

Another way to read Trump is through Hill's philosophy, who identifies our biggest weakness, a fear of criticism. There is a fine line between developing a positive attitude for personal success and using positive thinking to publicly mask insecurities and doubt. Although one might argue that Trump manages a confident persona, avoiding Hill's symptoms of fear of criticism such as self-consciousness, lack of poise, and personality, he shows other deeper symptoms that Hill associates with an inferiority complex, alongside extravagance and lack of initiative ([1937] 2011, 402). In other words, Trump is neither timid nor nervous when around strangers and projects "firmness of decision, personal charm, and ability to express opinions definitely" (401). But he has a habit of "expressing self-approval" publicly:

> INFERIORITY COMPLEX. The habit of expressing self-approval by word of mouth and by actions, as a means of covering up a feeling of inferiority. Using 'big words' to impress others, (often without knowing the real meaning of the words). Imitating others in dress, speech and

manners. Boasting of imaginary achievements. This sometimes gives a surface appearance of a feeling of superiority.

(402)

His "extravagance" shows a need to "keep up with the Joneses" and his evasive answers and "alternative facts" show a "lack of initiative" (402). Twitter has become a place for Donald Trump to addictively exert the power of his inferiority complex through the rhetorical alchemy so often found in business self-help books.

The publicized privacy of the Twitter sphere blurs the distinction between personal motivation and self-adulation because Twitter often serves as a direct conduit to one's mind. Critiques of people's spontaneity on Twitter abound. Users may tweet "without thinking" or tweet about the most trivial things. Trump is no different. In fact, one can argue that Trump is manipulating the Twitter sphere as if it were a microcosm of his own mind. By changing the discourse or thoughts within that sphere, reality can be changed. But his ability to manipulate discourse is what makes Twitter so powerful, and the media's constant attention to Trump's tweets only amplifies that power. Perhaps, though, applying mind-power techniques to the Twitter sphere is where Trump goes wrong, mainly because he has internalized the media and Twitter feeds that revolve around him. Neither Peale nor Hill would likely accept the premise that we should manipulate the media or Twitter like we manipulate our own minds when developing a "positive attitude." Is Trump accessing his Higher Self? Is he releasing the full potential of his creative self on Twitter? Does his ability to manipulate Twitter demonstrate a closer relationship to the "divine energies" of God? Or are we actually looking at the opposite? The dark side of positive thinking.

Notes

1 On January 16, 2017, Trump stated in the interview that he had 46 million followers. On November 17, 2017, Trump had 36.4 million followers and 48 million followers as of February 19, 2018, on the @realDonaldTrump account.
2 The third rule is a bit mysterious and out of place, especially since Trump does not discuss this rule in his introduction. It appears as a caption to an image of himself as a boy carrying a pair of shoes in a wheelbarrow. But perhaps this is a clue that his book is not really a book of advice, but a construction of his *ethos*.
3 When looking at the context of these twitter exchanges, it is actually not clear these are Trump followers. Two of the accounts have been suspended and the other is tweeting mostly Russian news (as of February 22, 2018).

Bibliography

AskeHave, Inger. "If Language is a Game: These are the Rules: A Search into the Rhetoric of the Spiritual Self-Help Book *If Life is a Game: These are Rules.*" *Discourse & Society* 5, no. 1 (2004): 5–31.

Aupers, Stef and Dick Houtman. "Beyond the Spiritual Supermarket: The Social and Public Significance of New Age Spirituality." *Journal of Contemporary Religion* 21, no. 2 (2006): 201–22.

Blair, Gwenda. "How Norman Vincent Peale Taught Donald Trump to Worship himself." Politico, 2015, last modified October 6, 2015, www.politico.com/magazine/story/2015/10/donald-trump-2016-norman-vincent-peale-213220

Brock, Kevin. "Enthymeme as Rhetorical Algorithm." *Present Tense* 4, no. 1 (2014): 1–7.

Carnegie, Dale. *How to Win Friends and Influence People.* Reprint. New York: Simon & Schuster. Kindle eBook, [1936] 2010.

Carnegie, Dale. *Public Speaking and Influencing Men in Business.* Reprint. New York: American Book-Stratford Press, Inc., [1926] 1937.

Cisneros, David J. and Thomas K. Nakayama. "New Media, Old Racisms: Twitter, Miss America, and Cultural Logics of Race." *Journal of International and Intercultural Communication* 8, no. 2 (2015): 108–27.

Cummings, Lance. "Religion and the Professional Ethos: The YMCA, Dale Carnegie, and the 'Business Man.'" *Rhetoric, Professional Communication, and Globalization* 9, no. 1 (2017): 6–27.

"Donald J. Trump for President." accessed February 19, 2017, www.donaldtrump.com; www.donaldjtrump.com/

Griggs, Brandon. "Protests over Confederate Statue Shake Charlottesville, Virginia." *CNN*, 2017, last modified May 15, 2017, www.cnn.com/2017/05/15/us/charlottesville-lee-monument-spencer-protests-trnd/index.html

Hill, Napoleon. *Napoleon Hill is on the Air!* Grand Haven, MI: Napoleon Hill Foundation Press, 2017.

Hill, Napoleon. *Think and Grow Rich.* Reprint. Amazon Digital Services, LLC. Kindle eBook, [1937] 2011.

Hanegraaf, J.W. *New Age Religion and Western Culture—Esotericism in the Mirror of Secular Thought.* Leiden: Brill, 1996.

Luckman, Thomas. "The Privatisation of Religion and Morality." In *Detraditionalisation: Critical Reflections on Authority and Identity.* Eds. Paul Hellas, Scott Las, and Paul. Oxford: Blackwell, 1996 Morris, 72–86.

Marwick, Alice E. and dana boyd. "I Tweet Honestly, I Tweet Passionately: Twitter Users, Context Collapse, and the Imagined Audience." *New Media & Society* 13, no. 1 (2011): 114–33.

Mathis-Lilley. "A Continually Growing List of Violent Incidents at Trump Events." *Slate*, 2016, last modified April 25, 2016, www.slate.com/blogs/the_slatest/2016/03/02/a_list_of_violent_incidents_at_donald_trump_rallies_and_events.html

Official Team Trump. (@TeamTrump). Twitter Post. October 9, 2016, 6:08 P.M. https://twitter.com/TeamTrump/status/785285836191531008

Official Team Trump. (@TeamTrump). Twitter Post. October 19, 2016, 7:22 P.M. https://twitter.com/TeamTrump/status/788928278795055105

Peale, Norman Vincent. *The Power of Positive Thinking.* Reprint. New York: Simon & Schuster. Kindle eBook, [1952] 2003.

Trump, Donald. *The Times.* Interview by Michael Gove and Kai Diekmann, 2017, last modified January 16, 2017, www.thetimes.co.uk/article/full-transcript-of-interview-with-donald-trump-5d39sr09d.

Trump, Donald. *Trump: How to Get Rich.* New York: Random House, 2004.

Trump, Donald. *Trump: The Art of the Deal.* New York: Random House, Inc., 1987.

Trump, Donald. *Trump Twitter Archive,* last accessed September 20, 2017, www.trumptwitterarchive.com/

Trump, Donald. Twitter Post. April 2, 2014, 10:36 A.M. https://twitter.com/realdonaldtrump/status/451412881146658816

Trump, Donald. Twitter Post. August 13, 2016, 1:06 P.M. https://twitter.com/realdonaldtrump/status/764553771879899137

Trump, Donald. Twitter Post. December 11, 2014, 7:09 A.M. https://twitter.com/realdonaldtrump/status/543059935056388097

Trump, Donald. Twitter Post. December 11, 2014, 7:15 A.M. https://twitter.com/realdonaldtrump/status/543061508323016706

Trump, Donald. Twitter Post. December 21, 2016, 5:15 A.M. https://twitter.com/realdonaldtrump/status/811560662853939200

Trump, Donald. Twitter Post. February 3, 2018, 6:40 A.M. https://twitter.com/realdonaldtrump/status/959798743842349056

Trump, Donald. Twitter Post. January 4, 2018, 7:52 P.M. https://twitter.com/realDonaldTrump/status/949126530839572481

Trump, Donald. Twitter Post. January 22, 2017, 4:51 A.M. https://twitter.com/realdonaldtrump/status/823151124815507460

Trump, Donald. Twitter Post. July 12, 2017, 4:06 P.M. https://twitter.com/realdonaldtrump/status/885274148012011520

Trump, Donald. Twitter Post. July 14, 2017, 12:57 A.M. https://twitter.com/realdonaldtrump/status/885770227514052608

Trump, Donald. Twitter Post. June 11, 2016, 4:28 P.M. https://twitter.com/realdonaldtrump/status/741774067368402945

Trump, Donald. Twitter Post. June 27, 2014, 8:18 A.M. https://twitter.com/realdonaldtrump/status/482543454850138112

Trump, Donald. Twitter Post. June 29, 2015, 5:21 P.M. https://twitter.com/realdonaldtrump/status/615676500411551745

Trump, Donald. Twitter Post. March 25, 2016, 7:47 P.M. https://twitter.com/realdonaldtrump/status/713558033129930752

Trump, Donald. Twitter Post. November 1, 2016, 3:31 A.M. https://twitter.com/realdonaldtrump/status/793400131525677056

Trump, Donald. Twitter Post. November 3, 2017, 4:55 A.M. https://twitter.com/realdonaldtrump/status/926417546038923264

Trump, Donald. Twitter Post. November 18, 2017, 5:31A.M. https://twitter.com/realdonaldtrump/status/931877599034388480

Trump, Donald. Twitter Post. October 16, 2012, 6:43 P.M. https://twitter.com/realdonaldtrump/status/258382694520586240

Trump, Donald. Twitter Post. October 17, 2014, 1:51 A.M. https://twitter.com/realdonaldtrump/status/523214787178946560

Trump, Donald J. Twitter Post. September 13, 2017, 4:28 A.M. https://twitter.com/realdonaldtrump/status/907928888587808768

Trump, Donald. Twitter Post. September 13, 2017, 7:47 P.M. https://twitter.com/realdonaldtrump/status/908160218995068928

Schmitz, Matthew. "Donald Trump, Man of Faith." *First Things*, 2016, last modified August 2016, www.firstthings.com/article/2016/08/donald-trump-man-of-faith

Scott, Eugene. "Trump Believes in God, but Hasn't Sought Forgiveness." *CNN Politics*, 2015, last modified July 18, 2015, www.cnn.com/2015/07/18/politics/trump-has-never-sought-forgiveness/index.html

Sloop, John and Joshua Gunn. "Status Control: An Admonition Concerning the Publicized Privacy of Social Networking." *The Communication Review* 13 (2010): 289–90.

Weber, Max. *The Protestant Ethic and the "Spirit" of Capitalism and Other Writings.* New York: Penguin Classics. Kindle eBook. Reprint, [1905] 2002.

Weiss, Richard. *The American Myth of Success.* New York: Basic Books, Inc., 1969.

White, Paula. "Paula White Today Trump." *Youtube*, uploaded by pwmmin, April 29, 2008, https://youtu.be/EqcZ5NcnGYk

Zarefsky, David. "Presidential Rhetoric and the Power of Definition." *Presidential Studies Quarterly* 34, no. 3 (2004): 607–19.

PART II

Power and Abuse Abroad and at Home

Foreign Policy via Twitterverse, "Bullshit," and "Nut Job"

4

PRESIDENT TRUMP'S TWEETS ON THE MIDDLE EAST, NORTH KOREA, AND RUSSIA

The Constructive and the Unconstructive

Anish Dave

Introduction

In 2008, during his presidential run, President Obama used social media effectively "to reach voters and other stakeholders" (Aharony 2012, 591; Parmelee and Bichard 2012, 8). Since then, social media has become a communication platform of choice for politicians worldwide (Parmelee and Bichard 2012, 8). As of February 4, 2018, President Donald Trump had 47.4 million followers on Twitter, approximately 24 million followers on Facebook, 8.4 million followers on Instagram, and more than 111,000 subscribers to his YouTube channel. He has often said that using social media allows him to connect to people directly, letting them know his thinking about various issues (Mann 2017).

Throughout his presidential campaign, Trump's Twitter use often got him into trouble (Liptak 2016). Even after he became president, his media critics and others have sometimes criticized his social media communication, especially his Twitter communication (Mann 2017). On August 1, 2017, in a tweet, he declared that social media allowed him to present the truth, which media distorted (Trump). This chapter analyzes President Trump's use of Twitter to communicate his thoughts about the U.S. foreign policy. The importance of these tweets increases when considering Trump's strong criticism of past U.S. foreign policy as well as his critics' fear of his own foreign policy (Sestanovich 2017).

This chapter covers Trump's tweets since his inauguration on January 20, 2017 through January 4, 2018, spanning, roughly, eleven and a half months of his first term. Tweets were selected that related to foreign policy surrounding the Middle East, North Korea, and Russia; these tweets totaled 213 (see Table 4.1).

The most significant areas in Trump's tweets appeared to be the Middle East, North Korea, and Russia. These areas were more significant than others for several reasons. During his presidential campaign, Trump frequently mentioned the Islamic State of Iraq and Syria (ISIS), a terrorist group based in the Middle East, as an urgent foreign policy challenge. Additionally, as president, he tweeted the most about the Middle East, a total of ninety-six times. North Korea dominated the U.S. foreign policy agenda for much of 2017. Trump tweeted seventy-six times about this area. Finally, throughout his presidential campaign, Trump expressed his desire to work cooperatively with Russia to tackle major world problems. Although he tweeted about Russia fewer times as compared to the first two areas, forty-one, he appears to be convinced that the U.S. and Russia need to have a good relationship to solve a variety of world problems.

On the Middle East, Trump's tweets focused on terrorism. Conversely, he tweeted an unfair overgeneralization, which potentially detracts from his efforts to rally the world behind the mission of eradicating terrorism. On North Korea, in his early tweets, he seemed to rely on North Korea's neighbors to seek a solution to the crisis involving North Korea's pursuit of nuclear weapons. In later tweets, however, Trump appeared more involved and showed more respect for other countries working with him on the crisis. In a few tweets, however, he threatened North Korea and denigrated its dictator, potentially making it harder to persuade North Korea to reverse its pursuit of nuclear weapons. Finally, on Russia, Trump sought to balance different stakeholders. On the other hand, in a few tweets, he sought to divide Republicans and Democrats even as he continues to try to improve U.S.-Russia relations. Overall, Trump's foreign policy tweets offer a peek into his foreign policy agenda and ways of working.

Methods

Content analysis to categorize the tweets (Aharony 2012, 592–94) and critical discourse analysis (Griffin 2013) to analyze the tweets are used within this chapter. Context helped in determining which category a tweet should be assigned to and what topics might be combined into a category. Categories were created based on the tweets' content and the most suitable or simplest encompassing term under which to classify the tweets. Multiple tweets related to Russia warranted a separate category, a rule which was also followed for tweets related to North Korea. The category of Middle East not only comprised tweets related to countries in this region, several of which are US allies, but also included tweets related to concerns about terrorism or ISIS, concerns that often have origins in or implications for the region. The categories and the number of tweets for each category are shown in Table 4.1.

Critical discourse analysis seems apt for analyzing tweets, communications limited to 140 characters for the most part excluding accompanying materials because the writer is forced to select his or her message carefully to meet the length requirement. Twitter doubled the length from November 2017 (Kastrenakes 2018); as a result, some of Trump's tweets seemed a bit longer.

TABLE 4.1 Trump's tweets: topic categories

Subject of tweets	Number of tweets (January 20, 2017–January 4, 2018)
Middle East	96
North Korea	76
Russia	41
Total	213

According to Griffin, critical discourse analysis assumes that language is not "neutral" (97). Politicians' social media use provides many examples of language invested in a perspective or an ideology (Barbera 2015, 76). This chapter analyzes selected tweets from each of the three categories presented in Table 4.1.

Middle East

Trump's tweets in this area focus on terrorism. The tweets show that he is clear and result oriented about the need to confront and eradicate terrorism. Conversely, Trump tweeted an unfair overgeneralization involving whole countries, which can promote stereotypes and potentially detract from his goal of uniting the world to fight terrorism.

Trump visited the Middle East in May 2017, his first foreign trip as president, and his itinerary included Saudi Arabia, Israel, and the West Bank (Benzaquen et al. 2017). He also spoke to leaders of other countries in the region, including the United Arab Emirates (UAE), Bahrain, Kuwait, Qatar, and Oman (2017). In Saudi Arabia, Trump gave a speech calling on countries in the region to root out terrorism (Vitali 2017a, para. 3). In fact, he raised the subject of terrorism only a few days into his presidency. On January 29, 2017, in a tweet reacting to Senators McCain and Graham's criticism of his executive order known as the "travel ban" (Schallhorn 2018),[1] Trump wrote, "…Senators should focus their energies on ISIS, illegal immigration and border security instead of always looking to start World War III" (Trump). By mentioning ISIS as the first item in a short list of foreign policy goals, Trump communicated clarity about his foreign policy agenda. The tweet suggests that he believed dealing with ISIS to be his topmost foreign policy or national security challenge.

Trump tweeted about ISIS again, on July 12, 2017, informing Americans that "ISIS is on the run & will soon be wiped out of Syria & Iraq […]" (Trump). The tweet reminds one of Trump's campaign promise to "utterly destroy ISIS" (Johnson and DelReal 2016). Moreover, the tweet shows a result-oriented president—a frequent quality in his foreign policy tweets, as we will see—who named the two countries that were and continue to be ISIS's now shrunken territorial base (Barnard and Coker 2017),[2] in addition to pointing out that the group was in the process of being evicted.

Additionally, Trump described terrorism as a global challenge, tweeting, "All civilized nations must join together to protect human life and the sacred right of our citizens to live in safety and in peace." (Trump May 23, 2017). Coming a day after a terrorist attack in Manchester, U.K., the tweet recalled these words from candidate Trump's speech on terrorism in August 2016: "As President, I will call for an international conference focused on this goal" (Politico staff 2016, para. 67). The tweet also suggests that Trump views terrorism as a threat to humanity, a bare-bones characterization devoid of details or nuances. This attitude raises this threat above sectarian or geopolitical lenses. It is no longer a matter of a conflict or a region but antithetical to human life.

It is clear from Trump's tweets on terrorism that he seeks results, whether asking Senators McCain and Graham to focus on ISIS or informing Americans that ISIS will soon be eradicated. This emphasis is further seen in his tweets after Saudi Arabia and other countries in the region challenged Qatar about funding terrorists (Keatinge 2017). On June 6, 2017, Trump tweeted, "During my recent trip to the Middle East I stated that there can no longer be funding of Radical Ideology. Leaders pointed to Qatar - look!" (Trump). Through his tweet, Trump hints to his varied audience about the role he, as the President of the United States, may have played in an ongoing diplomatic crisis in which Saudi Arabia, Bahrain, the UAE, and Egypt ended diplomatic ties with Qatar over its suspected extremist funding (Tharoor 2017). Trump's tweet also demonstrates his commitment to fight terrorism; specifically, the tweet shows that he acted on a promise he made during a campaign speech to seek "international cooperation" to eliminate terrorists' funding (Politico staff 2016, para. 70).

In what perhaps shows his result-oriented approach more directly, a further tweet reads in part, "So good to see the Saudi Arabia visit with the King and 50 countries already paying off. [...]" (Trump June 6, 2017). Trump is referring to the showdown of prominent gulf countries with Qatar (Carlson 2017). In a separate tweet, Trump added that "[...] all reference was pointing to Qatar. Perhaps this will be the beginning of the end to the horror of terrorism!" (Trump June 6, 2017). In the tweet, Trump expresses his hope that terrorism can be defeated because of concrete actions such as calling Qatar out over its suspected funding of extremism. By referring to his visit with Saudi Arabia and leaders of fifty other countries, he also emphasizes cooperation to fight and eliminate terrorism. Lastly, the expressions "paying off," "leaders pointed to Qatar - look!" and "perhaps this will be the beginning of the end to the horror of terrorism" show Trump's penchant for concrete results.

However, in contrast to his appeal to nations to unite against terrorism, on June 5, 2017, Trump tweeted an unfair overgeneralization about entire countries in the Middle East and Africa: "That's right, we need a TRAVEL BAN for certain DANGEROUS countries, not some politically correct term that won't help us protect our people!" (Trump). The tweet came after a recent terror attack in London and amid ongoing legal wrangles over and revisions to his travel ban (Dolan and Kaleem 2017). In the tweet, Trump summarily describes the countries included in his travel ban—"Iran, Sudan, Somalia, Yemen, Syria, and Libya" (2017)—as "dangerous." Even if there exist extremist elements in these countries, describing entire countries as "dangerous" is an unfair overgeneralization. Indeed, a few days after the tweet, a court blocked the travel ban and quoted this tweet in its judgment (Westcott 2017). The judges stated that "the [Executive] Order does not offer a sufficient justification to suspend the entry of more than 180 million people on the basis of national-ity" (51).[3] The judges also cited a brief passage from a dissenting opinion in a World War II case involving people of Japanese origin: "[T]he exclusion order necessarily must rely for its reasonableness upon the assumption that all per-sons of Japanese ancestry may have a dangerous tendency to commit sabotage and espionage and to aid our Japanese enemy in other ways. It is difficult to believe that reason, logic or experience could be marshalled in support of such an assumption."[4] The dissenting judge's opinion highlighted an instance of an unfair overgeneralization. Trump's tweet calling whole countries "dangerous" is similar, which is perhaps why the judges rejecting the travel ban quoted this extract from the dissenting opinion. Such an unfair overgeneralization detracts from Trump's credibility when he asks the world to unite against ter-rorism. Additionally, because the travel ban affected countries where the ma-jority population is Muslim, it was rejected by a court on grounds of "religious discrimination" (Liptak 2017). Thus, it is not inconceivable that the tweet may alienate many Muslims around the world, who may not be unaware of such remarks in today's information age. A study by the Pew Research Center found that approximately 74% of Muslim Americans call the president "unfriendly" ("U.S. Muslims" 2017). Arguably, support and sympathy of Muslims around the world, who also suffer from terror attacks, are important to eradicate the threat of terrorism. Next, this chapter analyzes Trump's tweets on North Korea, which sparked a foreign policy crisis in 2017 due to its aggressive testing of missiles and a nuclear device.

North Korea

Founded in 1948, North Korea—or the Democratic People's Republic of Korea (DPRK) (French 2014, 7)—remained a serious foreign policy challenge for the U.S. in 2017. Since May 2017, North Korea tested several interconti-nental and "intermediate-range" missiles (Hamblin 2017). In September 2017, it conducted a nuclear test (Hamblin 2017). The foreign policy challenge of North Korea has spanned a few U.S. administrations (French 2014; Osnos 2017). According to a report in *The New York Times*, President Obama told Trump that North Korea was probably going to be his toughest foreign policy chal-lenge (Sanger and Broad 2017). Trump's tweets on North Korea show that he worked with North Korea's neighbors, mainly China and South Korea, to resolve the crisis involving North Korean ballistic missiles and nuclear weapons programs. On the other hand, several of his tweets threatened North Korea and attacked its dictator, which may potentially have alienated North Korea.

Trump first mentioned North Korea in a tweet on March 17, 2017: "North Korea is behaving very badly. They have been "playing" the United States for years. China has done little to help!" [*sic*] (Trump). Trump was referring to a checkered history of U.S. interactions with North Korea over the years, including the six-party talks involving China and Russia (Bajoria and Xu 2013). Trump also hinted at the fact that, although China offers critical economic support to North Korea, China has failed to prevent North Korea from conducting nuclear and missile tests (Beech 2017). Over the next nine and a half months, Trump tweeted frequently about North Korea, seventy-six times. However, unlike his more direct approach to issues involving the Middle East, in case of North Korea, Trump seems to have initially preferred delegating the crisis to China (Lind 2017; Revere 2017), often focusing on "substance" or results over process (Caminiti 2017). We have seen Trump's result-oriented approach in the previous section. In a similar vein but with an important difference, given his businessman background, perhaps unsurprisingly Trump seems to have partially fallen back to a role of a CEO while approaching the North Korea crisis. He sought cooperation of stakeholders such as China, cajoling it to do more with offers of incentives and intensifying pressure on it when North Korea appeared to ratchet up its provocative behavior. However, this approach largely proved ineffective to deal with the crisis, in that North Korea continued its missile tests (Lind 2017). Later, however, Trump appears to have become more involved himself, as will be seen from a few tweets referring to his frequent consultations with North Korea's neighbors.

On April 11, 2017, Trump tweeted an incentive for China, "I explained to the President of China that a trade deal with the U.S. will be far better for them if they solve the North Korean problem!" (Trump). On the face of it, Trump's tweet sounds like a good offer to China. However, the dynamics of U.S.-China relations with respect to North and South Korea will likely not be altered with some trade incentives (Rosenblum 2017). Additionally, Trump seems to assume that China could get North Korea to reverse its course, a plausible assumption given that China is North Korea's largest trading partner (Bajoria and Xu 2013; Lind 2017). However, the assumption has not worked, as of January 2018. While China has in the past taken steps to ensure that North Korea does not pursue nuclear weapons, China also faces risks in going too far with an economically weak neighbor whose unraveling may create a regional crisis (Beech 2017). On the same day, Trump also appeared to apply some pressure on China when he tweeted, "North Korea is looking for trouble. If China decides to help, that would be great. If not, we will solve the problem without them! U.S.A." (Trump April 11, 2017). This tweet seems to contradict the earlier tweet offering an incentive to China. The second tweet suggests that the U.S. is willing to solve this problem without China's help if necessary. However, it is not clear what the U.S. might do. Writing about the leadership of CEOs, Farkas and Wetlaufer stated that "whatever the approach … the CEO's role is to act decisively and boldly" (1996). If Trump believed that he was being decisive and bold in his message in the second tweet, such an attitude or style may not help with situations of complex negotiations typical in international diplomacy (Malhotra and Powell 2016), something Trump's later tweets show he seems to have realized, as we will see.

In an interview with CNBC, Deepak Malhotra, a Harvard Business School professor, commented about Trump's negotiating style (Caminiti 2017). Describing Trump's style as having been developed "in the rough-and-tumble world of high-end real estate," Malhotra emphasized putting "process before substance" in negotiations (2017), stating that focusing on process questions allows one to avoid making "substance mistakes" or mistakes in expecting results (2017). The crisis related to North Korea seems to demand an approach focused on process rather than on substance or results (Lind 2017; Revere 2017). Trump's second tweet shows an emphasis on substance or results versus on the process. Another important negotiation quality Malhotra highlighted in his interview is empathy (Caminiti 2017). He defines it as "the ability to take the perspective of the other party" (2017). Trump's second tweet also appears to lack empathy because the tweet assumes that China is not currently helping or doing so fully. In an article published in *The Philadelphia Tribune* titled "Will Trump's Hardball Tactic Work on China and North Korea?", Jennifer Lind asks the U.S. "to imagine this scenario [a collapse of North Korea] from China's perspective" (2017, para. 11). North Korea is China's neighbor and a "historically" (Connor 2017). China has several reasons why it does not want the North Korean regime to fall, among them a potential refugee crisis, loss of a "buffer" between itself and U.S. forces in South Korea, and likely occupation of the country by U.S. and South Korean forces (Lind 2017).

However, the next day, on April 12, 2017, Trump informed his audience that he "Had a very good call last night with the President of China concerning the menace of North Korea." (Trump). Trump's tweet was likely intended to allay any concerns that may have arisen over his previous tweet in which he appeared to be hinting at putting China on notice and looking to solve the North Korea crisis without the help of its great neighbor. Taking a similar tone, on April 13, 2017, Trump tweeted, "I have great confidence that China will properly deal with North Korea. If they are unable to do so, the U.S., with its allies, will! U.S.A." (Trump). Trump's use of the phrase "great confidence" suggests some reaffirmation of trust in China, a result perhaps of his telephone call with the Chinese leader. Returning to an incentive-based approach again, on April 16, 2017, Trump tweeted, "Why would I call China a currency manipulator when they are working with us on the North Korean problem? We will see what happens!" (Trump). Despite his campaign speeches promising to hold China accountable for currency manipulation, Trump decided not to label China a currency manipulator, telling *The Wall Street Journal* that he did not "want to throw a wrench into U.S.-China talks on North Korea" (Beavers 2017, para. 1). In the tweet, he let his audience know about his reasoning.

One can see in Trump's tweets CEO tactics of offering incentives, such as better trade deals, no currency manipulator label; applying pressure, as in "we will solve the problem without them," "we will see what happens!"; and motivating, as seen in "I have great confidence." Trump seems to rely on China, a partner, to "solve the problem" of North Korea, a phrase and approach typical of CEOs. Farkas and Wetlaufer referred to these aspects of CEO behavior, such as giving incentives, applying pressure, motivating, and solving problems (1996).

As the North Korea crisis continued to unfold, however, Trump's tweets began to change in their tenor. A few tweets should suffice to show the difference in tone and content compared to the earlier tweets. In early November 2017, Trump visited several Asian countries, including Japan, South Korea, China, Vietnam, and Philippines (The White House 2017). During the visit, in an address to the South Korean National Assembly, Trump discussed the threat from North Korea's pursuit of nuclear weapons (para. 5). On November 6, 2017, Trump tweeted, "Getting ready to leave for South Korea and meetings with President Moon, a fine gentleman. We will figure it all out!" (Trump). The tweet communicates not only Trump's admiration for South Korea's president but also an element of trust on and respect for a peer on the world stage, as seen in the second sentence starting with the first-person plural pronoun.

On November 9, 2017, Trump tweeted conspicuous praise of President Xi of China: "My meetings with President Xi Jinping were very productive on both trade and the subject of North Korea. He is a highly respected and powerful representative of his people. It was great being with him and Madame Peng Liyuan!" (Trump). In the tweet, Trump mentions full names of the Chinese President and the First Lady, a sign of respect. Finally, Trump mentions that his meetings included the subject of North Korea, and that the meetings were useful.

Lastly, on November 30, 2017, Trump tweeted the following progress report on the North Korea crisis: "The Chinese Envoy, who just returned from North Korea, seems to have had no impact on Little Rocket Man. Hard to believe his people, and the military, put up with living in such horrible conditions. Russia and China condemned the launch" (Trump). In the tweet, Trump refers to China's sending a senior official to North Korea "for the first time in two years" (Maza 2017). China's move came after Trump's visit to Asia in early November 2017. Trump also taunts the North Korean dictator Kim Jong-un, an issue discussed in the next paragraph. However, importantly, in the tweet, Trump mentions that both Russia and China "condemned the launch" of an intercontinental ballistic missile by North Korea. Trump's explicit mention of this fact is noteworthy because it suggests a greater respect for his partners working with him to resolve the North Korea crisis. This attitude is in marked contrast to the tone of Trump's initial tweets on North Korea, in some of which he appeared to question the commitment of China to resolve the North Korea crisis. By praising his partners for their efforts, Trump also appears to have moved away from excessive reliance on these countries to resolve the North Korea crisis.

Trump claimed credit for the resumption of dialog between North and South Korea in the early days of 2018 (McKirdy and Lee 2018), a development initiated by North Korea (Sang-Hun 2018a). The president of South Korea also credited Trump for having made the talks possible (Sang-Hun 2018b). Speaking to South Korea's National Assembly in November 2017, Trump was clear and firm that the U.S. would not accept nuclear weapons with North Korea (Trump's Speech 2017, para. 52). He also outlined briefly a vision for a peaceful Korean peninsula (para. 73). It is worth mentioning that Kim Jong-un, the North Korean dictator, expressed his desire to "create a peaceful environment on the Korean peninsula" in his "New Year's Address" (North Korea Leadership Watch 2018, para. 73). However, even if one gives Trump some credit for the beginning of talks between South Korea and North Korea, several of his tweets, along with other statements, may have strongly alienated North Korea. Notably, North Korea insists on keeping its nuclear weapons program outside the scope of its talks with its southern counterpart (Jeong 2018) and claims that its weapons programs are aimed at the U.S. (Silva 2017; Jeong 2018).

Trump has frequently threatened North Korea in his tweets. Additionally, in his tweets, he often uses demeaning terms for Kim Jong-un, such as "rocket man" or "little rocket man." On September 24, 2017, Trump tweeted, "Just heard Foreign Minister of North Korea speak at U. N. If he echoes thoughts of Little Rocket Man, they won't be around much longer!" (Trump). Trump's threatening tweet was in reaction to a speech at the United Nations by North Korea's foreign minister in which he called President Trump "mentally deranged" (Cummings 2017, para. 3). Trump also tweeted a threat he previously made to North Korea in his first speech to the United Nations in September 2017 (Vitali 2017b, para. 4): "The [emoji of U.S. flag] has great strength & patience, but if it is forced to defend itself or its allies, we will have no choice but to totally destroy #NoKo" (Trump September 19, 2017). The threat to destroy North Korea, issued both on the floor of the UN and in a tweet, can justifiably be termed as bullying of North Korea. The enormous difference in power between the U.S. and North Korea leaves little doubt about this conclusion. Trump's threats and taunts directed at North Korea make it difficult, if not impossible, for the U.S. to negotiate some type of resolution to the crisis created by North Korea's weapons programs.

Lastly, this chapter examines a few of Trump's tweets surrounding Russia, a former superpower that figured prominently in Trump's presidential campaign. The analysis suggests that Trump approached the task of improving U.S.-Russia relationship by balancing conflicting interests and stakeholders.

However, he also appears to have attempted to divide lawmakers and supporters of both parties while pursuing the goal of improving the U.S.-Russia relationship.

Russia

Throughout his presidential campaign, Trump argued that the U.S. should have a better relationship with Russia to solve the world's problems (Burns 2016; Miller 2017). Trump spoke passionately about enlisting Russia's help to defeat ISIS (Burns 2016). However, following his victory, the outgoing administration announced details of Russia's attempted interference in the presidential election (Sanger 2016). After Trump fired the Federal Bureau of Investigation (FBI) director James Comey, the Justice Department appointed a special counsel to investigate any Russian interference in the election, including possible links between the government of Russia and Trump's presidential campaign (Rod Rosenstein's Letter 2017). Given this context, Trump had to approach his relationship with Russia with discretion and wisdom. Within this chapter, the analysis of some of Trump's Russia tweets suggests that to some extent Trump succeeded in this difficult task, balancing stakeholders in the U.S.-Russia relationship. However, in a few tweets, Trump sought to divide Republicans and Democrats on Russia's role in the 2016 presidential elections. If Trump succeeds in drawing on his own party to pursue the goal of improving U.S.-Russia relations, in the short term he may have more flexibility in this foreign policy area; however, in the long run, building relations with a major world power based on partisan support along party lines may not be helpful.

On April 13, 2017, Trump tweeted his conviction that "Things will work out fine between the U.S.A. and Russia. At the right time everyone will come to their senses & there will be lasting peace!" (Trump). Trump's tweet came at a time of growing tensions with Russia (Miller 2017). The U.S. had recently launched an air strike against Syria over a suspected chemical weapons attack, and senior officials in Trump's administration had criticized Russia, Syria's ally (2017). Considering that Trump is known to regularly communicate via Twitter, it is not unreasonable to assume that world leaders, as well as U.S. politicians, probably read Trump's tweets. In fact, a Russian government spokesperson stated that Moscow considers Trump's tweets "as his official position," and that President Putin reads Trump's tweets (Reuters 2017). Trump's tweet therefore may have been directed at Russia, among others, a direct communication from him that he believed the two countries can improve their relations. In fact, a Trump adviser told the *Washington Post* that the president is "probably seeking to leave an opening for Putin to pursue better relations with the United States" (Miller 2017). If one also considers that the U.S.-Russia relationship suffered in recent times and that Trump pledged to improve the relations (Graham and Rojansky 2016; Miller 2017), one can see why Trump would express confidence in the future of the relationship. The tweet would likely seem agreeable to Russians if they read it, and it may not seem entirely inappropriate to members of Congress critical of Russia (Sullivan et al. 2017) but unwilling to return to Cold War days.

In a tweet that appeared to be aimed at members of Congress skeptical of Trump's overtures to Russia, Trump wrote on May 11, 2017, "Yesterday, on the same day- I had meetings with Russian Foreign Minister Sergei Lavrov and the FM of Ukraine, Pavlo Klimkin. #LetsMakePeace!" (Trump). The tweet came after Trump met with Russian diplomats, and Russia released pictures of the meeting (Strait Times 2017). Also, the tweet came shortly after Trump fired the FBI Director James Comey, who was investigating contacts between the Russian government and Trump's presidential campaign (Rod Rosenstein's Letter 2017; Strait Times 2017). In the tweet, Trump wants to reassure Congressional members that he can be trusted to be evenhanded in approaching the conflict between Russia and Ukraine. Moreover, using the hashtag #LetsMakePeace!, Trump signals to his audience that he is interested in resolving the dispute between Russia and Ukraine. However, some foreign policy specialists saw Trump's tweet as an unjustified equating of an aggressor, Russia, and a victim, Ukraine (Erickson 2017). Additionally, after Comey's firing, Trump may also have wanted to convey to members of Congress that he was not partisan toward Russia.

In both tweets above, we see a balancing on Trump's part, a desire for improved relations with Russia while acknowledging tacitly concerns of his audience about unlikelihood of such an outcome in the immediate future. As we also saw, in the second tweet, Trump seeks to quell any suspicions that he would favor Russia in Russia-Ukraine conflict.

Responding to a controversy regarding some intelligence he shared with Russian officials (Baker and Davis 2017), Trump tweeted on May 16, 2017, in part providing clues about why he is interested in improving relations with Russia: "[…] I want Russia to greatly step up their fight against ISIS & terrorism." (Trump). In both of his tweets, one related to his meeting with Russian and Ukrainian officials on the same day, and another related to his sharing of intelligence with Russian officials, Trump's result-oriented nature can be seen. He wants to make peace between Russia and Ukraine, and he wants Russia to "step up" its fight against ISIS. Although Trump has legal authority to share intelligence with anyone (Savage 2017), he tweeted reasons for his sharing some intelligence with Russian officials to defend himself from criticism by people who may consider this development troubling (Jackson 2017). His tweeting that he wants Russia to do more to fight ISIS may be seen by at least his supporters as a good reason to share intelligence with Russia (Williams 2017). This episode also hints at the importance Trump accords to US–Russia relationship; indeed, the *Washington Post* journalists Greg Miller and Greg Jaffe quoted a U.S.

intelligence operative as saying that the president shared more information than is usually shared by a president with U.S.'s allies (2017).

After his return from the G-20 summit in July 2017, where President Trump and President Putin met for the first time (Reilly 2017), Trump tweeted about a proposal Putin and he discussed. The proposal related to a joint cyber security initiative between the two countries. However, Trump found that Republicans in the Congress were opposed to the idea (Stewart and Volcovici 2017). In a face-saving tweet that nonetheless stressed the good that came out of his meeting with Russia's president, Trump tweeted on July 9, 2017, "The fact that President Putin and I discussed a Cyber Security unit doesn't mean I think it can happen. It can't-but a ceasefire can, & did!" [*sic*] (Trump). Trump referred to a ceasefire agreement reached with President Putin with respect to Syria. The tweet probably pacified members of Congress who were critical of the proposed initiative, as well as Russia, which may feel rebuffed at Trump's rejection of the idea he initially appears to have accepted (Stewart and Volcovici 2017). Additionally, by referring to the Syria ceasefire, a good outcome, the tweet also subtly pointed out to Russia that Trump values his relations with the country. In another tweet on the same day, Trump commented on the Syria ceasefire and offered his vision for the future of U.S.-Russia relations: "…We negotiated a ceasefire in parts of Syria which will save lives. Now it is time to move forward in working constructively with Russia!" (Trump July 9, 2017). Again, one sees Trump's result-oriented nature in the tweet: ceasefire, saving lives, "move forward in working constructively."

However, from a few of Trump's tweets, it appears that he would like to draw on support of members of his own party while adopting a combative stance with respect to Democrats as he pursues the goal of improving U.S.-Russia relations. Although in the short run this strategy, akin to a political wedge, may provide him with some backing from his own party, in the long run the strategy may be unhelpful to the U.S. foreign policy with Russia because Democrats may potentially become unenthusiastic about a Russia outreach. Following the first charges by the special counsel investigating contacts between Trump's campaign and the Russian government (Davis 2017), on October 29, 2017, Trump tweeted multiple messages complaining that there were no investigations into some issues involving Democrats, including the former Democratic presidential nominee Hillary Clinton while his campaign had been subjected to investigations. A brief analysis of two such tweets follows.

In the first tweet, a part-statement, Trump wrote, "…"collusion," which doesn't exist. The Dems are using this terrible (and bad for our country) Witch Hunt for evil politics, but the R's…" [*sic*] (Trump October 29, 2017). In the tweet, Trump denies any collusion between his presidential campaign and the Russian government. He describes the investigations into his campaign's contacts with Russia as a "witch hunt" and "evil politics." Although the "House Intelligence Committee Republicans" did not find any evidence of collusion between President Trump's campaign and Russia (Cheney 2018, para. 1), several investigations examining this matter are ongoing (2018). The second tweet referred to Republicans and read, "...are now fighting back like never before. There is so much GUILT by Democrats/Clinton, and now the facts are pouring out. DO SOMETHING!" (Trump October 29, 2017). In this tweet, Trump suggests that the Republicans have begun to address his concerns regarding problematic issues connected with Democrats. Indeed, a few days before these tweets, Republicans lawmakers in the House of Representatives had announced investigations into two such issues: a controversial uranium deal involving a Russian company and Secretary Clinton's emails (Lynch and Heavey 2017). Secretary Clinton's emails are also connected to the special counsel's Russia probe and specifically to the indictment of a former Trump campaign operative George Papadopoulos (Prokop 2017).

The two tweets suggest a possible strategy on Trump's part to divide Republicans and Democrats with respect to U.S.-Russia relations. If he can convince Republicans that the charge of collusion is baseless and politically motivated, as well as that there are problematic areas involving Democrats that have not been investigated, many Republicans may be more sympathetic to the president's view of needing to improve the U.S.-Russia relations, a foreign policy area that he frequently mentioned as a candidate and advocates for as president. Even if part of Trump's motivation in the tweets may be to rally his party in view of ongoing investigations into Russia and his presidential campaign, being able to take Republicans along as he pursues bettering U.S.-Russia ties offers him more flexibility. However, some Republicans would like to focus on Russia's role in the election interference, deeming it a serious foreign policy matter (Davis 2017).

Conclusion

This chapter analyzed President Trump's foreign policy tweets during the first eleven and a half months of his first term. This chapter focused on three areas in his tweets: the Middle East, North Korea, and Russia. On the Middle East, the analysis suggests that the emphasis in Trump's tweets was on the threat of terrorism. Urging the world to unite to eliminate terrorism, he closely communicated about and with the countries in the Middle East to advance this goal. Conversely, in a tweet, Trump made an unfair overgeneralization about entire countries, which detracts from his goal of uniting the world to eradicate terrorism.

Trump's tweets on North Korea show perhaps the widest range of his approaches to a foreign policy issue out of the three areas analyzed here. The analysis within this chapter suggests that at first President Trump seemed keen to delegate the crisis to North Korea's neighbors, in a CEO-like manner. In his later tweets, however, he appeared to show more involvement and more respect toward North Korea's neighbors. Conversely, his tweets attacking North Korea and its leader add to the animosity North Korea likely feels toward the U.S. This unnecessary animosity reduces a possibility of North Korea agreeing to negotiate with the U.S. or under U.S. leadership to reverse its course on nuclear weapons.

Perhaps North Korea is a crisis Trump did not want to have to deal with—although he was warned by President Obama (Sanger and Broad 2017)—which would explain why he seems to have relied so much on North Korea's powerful neighbor and benefactor, China. In a speech announcing changes in his administration's Cuba policy in Florida on June 16, 2017, Trump stated the following: "on my recent trip overseas... I also said countries should take greater responsibility for creating stability in their own regions" (The White House 2017, para. 27). The partial quote above provides some insight into why Trump seemingly relied on China to take the lead in solving the North Korean crisis.

Lastly, on Russia, Trump's tweets sought to balance different stakeholders, mainly Russia, on one hand, and Congress, on the other. However, in a few tweets, Trump sought to divide Republicans and Democrats even as he pursues his goal of improving U.S.-Russia relations. In resorting to this possible political wedge strategy, Trump may gain some short-term flexibility. However, he risks subjecting this important relationship to partisan party politics.

In all three areas, Trump's tweets communicate a result-oriented attitude, suggesting a president who believes in action. Indeed, referring to Trump's tweets on foreign policy, the secretary of state, Mr. Tillerson, said to CNN that "the President made the statements he did to try to 'motivate action'" (Watkins 2017). Thus, Trump's foreign policy tweets offer a part window into not only his foreign policy priorities but also into manner or approach of working. Trump himself mentioned the word "results" in a tweet on May 28, 2017, after his return from his first foreign trip as president (Savransky 2017): "Just returned from Europe. Trip was a great success for America. Hard work but big results!" (Trump). During the visit, Trump also spoke to world leaders about terrorism, among other issues.

Trump's tweeting about U.S. foreign policy is an unprecedented way of a U.S. president communicating with or about the world. World leaders have an important data point in his tweets. Finally, his foreign policy tweets provide updates to millions of his voters—and others—on how his foreign policy agenda is shaping up.

Notes

1 The order, dated January 27, 2017, sought to temporarily prevent immigrants from seven Muslim-majority countries, including Iran, Iraq, Syria, Libya, Somalia, Sudan, and Yemen, until the U.S. immigration authorities were satisfied with vetting procedures for these immigrants (The White House, January 27, 2017).
2 The ISIS had lost a substantial amount of its territory by November of 2017 (Barnard and Coker, November 3, 2017).
3 State of Hawaii; Ismail Elshikh v. Donald J. Trump, 17-15589 (DKW-KSC 2017) at 51, http://cdn.ca9.uscourts.gov/datastore/opinions/2017/06/12/17-15589.pdf.
4 Ibid.

Bibliography

Aharony, Noa. "Twitter Use by Three Political Leaders: An Exploratory Analysis." *Online Information Review* 36, no. 4 (2012): 587–603.

Bajoria, Jayshree and Beina Xu. "The Six Party Talks on North Korea's Nuclear Program." *Council on Foreign Relations*, September 30, 2013, www.cfr.org/backgrounder/six-party-talks-north-koreas-nuclear-program?utm_medium=social_share&utm_source=fb

Baker, Peter and Julie Hirschfeld Davis. "Trump Defends Sharing Information on ISIS Threat with Russia." *The New York Times*, May 16, 2017, www.nytimes.com/2017/05/16/us/politics/trump-intelligence-russia-classified.html?smid=fb-share

Barbera, Pablo. "Birds of the Same Feather Tweet Together: Bayesian Ideal Point Estimation Using Twitter Data." *Political Analysis* 23, no. 1 (2015): 76–91.

Barnard, Anne and Margaret Coker. "ISIS, Squeezed on Two Sides, Loses Syrian City and Border Crossing." *The New York Times*, November 3, 2017, www.nytimes.com/2017/11/03/world/middleeast/syria-isis-deir-al-zour.html

Beavers, Olivia. "Trump Won't Label China a Currency Manipulator." *The Hill*, April 12, 2017, http://thehill.com/business-a-lobbying/328541-trump-wont-call-china-a-currency-manipulator#.WhKF4RYZ3DU.facebook

Beech, Hannah. "China's North Korea Problem." *The New Yorker*, February 23, 2017, www.newyorker.com/news/news-desk/chinas-north-korea-problem

Benzaquen, Mercy, Russell Goldman, and Karen Yourish."President Trump's Schedule for His First Foreign Trip." *The New York Times*, May 24, 2017, www.nytimes.com/interactive/2017/05/19/world/middleeast/schedule-for-trump-first-trip-overseas.html

Burns, Alexander. "Donald Trump Reaffirms Support for Warmer Relations with Putin." *The New York Times*, August 1, 2016, www.nytimes.com/2016/08/02/us/politics/donald-trump-vladimir-putin-russia.html?smid=fb-share

Caminiti, Susan. "What Trump Doesn't Know about the Art of Negotiation." *CNBC*, June 7, 2017, www.cnbc.com/2017/06/07/what-trump-doesnt-know-about-the-art-of-negotiation.html

Carlson, Jeff. "Trump's Middle East Speech and the GCC's Rebuke of Qatar." *The Marketswork*, June 5, 2017, www.themarketswork.com/2017/06/05/trumps-middle-east-speech-the-gccs-rebuke-of-qatar/

Cheney, Kyle. "House Ends Russia Probe, Says No Trump-Kremlin Collusion." *Politico*, March 12, 2018, www.politico.com/story/2018/03/12/house-panel-russia-investigation-trump-457560

Connor, Neil. "Analysis: Why China Will Never Ditch Historic Ally North Korea for Donald Trump." *The Telegraph*, June 22, 2017, www.telegraph.co.uk/news/2017/06/22/china-will-never-ditch-historic-ally-north-korea-donald-trump/

Cummings, William. "Trump Threatens 'Little Rocket Man,' Says Kim 'May Not Be Around Much Longer.'" *USA Today*, September 24, 2017, www.usatoday.com/story/news/politics/onpolitics/2017/09/23/trump-threatens-little-rocket-man-says-kim-may-not-around-much-longer/697452001/

Davis, Julie Hirschfeld. "Trump Tries to Shift Focus as First Charges Reportedly Loom in Russia Case." *The New York Times*, October 29, 2017, www.nytimes.com/2017/10/29/us/politics/trump-clinton-mueller-russia.html

Dolan, Maura and Jaweed Kaleem. "U.S. Ninth Circuit Court of Appeals Refuses to Reinstate Trump's Travel Ban." *Los Angeles Times*, June 12, 2017, www.latimes.com/local/lanow/la-na-9thcircuit-travel-ban-20170530-story.html

Erickson, Amanda. "Trump's Tweet on Russia and Ukraine Wasn't Just Silly: It's Bad Diplomacy." *Washington Post*, May 12, 2017, www.washingtonpost.com/news/worldviews/wp/2017/05/12/trumps-tweet-on-russia-and-ukraine-wasnt-just-silly-its-bad-diplomacy/?utm_term=.f54c80c069d4

Farkas, Charles M. and Suzy Wetlaufer. "The Ways Chief Executive Officers Lead." *Harvard Business Review*, May June 1996, https://hbr.org/1996/05/the-ways-chief-executive-officers-lead

French, Paul. *North Korea: State of Paranoia*. Zed Books, 2014. ProQuest Ebook Central, https://ebookcentral.proquest.com/lib/gsw/detail.action?docID=1696467

Graham, Thomas and Matthew Rojansky. "America's Russia Policy Has Failed." *FP*, October 13, 2016, https://foreignpolicy.com/2016/10/13/americas-russia-policy-has-failed-clinton-trump-putin-ukraine-syria-how-to-fix/

Griffin, Gabrielle (Ed.). *Research Methods for English Studies*. Edinburgh, Scotland: Edinburgh University Press, 2013.

Hamblin, Abby. "North Korea: A Timeline of Jong Un's Aggression Since January." *The San Diego Union-Tribune*, September 15, 2017, www.sandiegouniontribune.com/opinion/the-conversation/sd-north-korea-nuclear-missile-timeline-20170915-htmlstory.html

Jackson, David. "Trump Defends Sharing 'Facts' with Russians; Reports Say Israel Gave Intel." *USA Today*, May 16, 2017, www.usatoday.com/story/news/politics/2017/05/16/donald-trump-russia-classified-the-washington-post/101740022/

Jeong, Andrew. "North Korea to Send Delegation to Winter Olympics, Refuses to Discuss Weapons." *The Wall Street Journal*, January 9, 2018, www.wsj.com/articles/koreas-near-olympics-deal-north-avoids-nuclear-talk-1515488910

Johnson, Jenna and Jose A. DelReal. "Trump Vows to 'Utterly Destroy ISIS' – But He Won't Say How." *Washington Post*, September 24, 2016, www.washingtonpost.com/politics/trump-vows-to-utterly-destroy-isis--but-he-wont-say-how/2016/09/24/911c6a74-7ffc-11e6-8d0c-fb6c00c90481_story.html?tid=ss_fb&utm_term=.002d6acb826c

Kastrenakes, Jacob. "Twitter Says People Are Tweeting More, But Not Longer, with 280-Character Limit." *The Verge*, February 8, 2018, www.theverge.com/2018/2/8/16990308/twitter-280-character-tweet-length

Keatinge, Tom. "Why Qatar Is the Focus of Terrorism Claims." *BBC News*, June 13, 2017, www.bbc.com/news/world-middle-east-40246734?SThisFB

Lind, Jennifer. "Will Trump's Hardball Tactic Work on China and North Korea?" *The Philadelphia Tribune*, August 12, 2017, www.phillytrib.com/commentary/will-trump-s-hardball-tactics-work-on-china-and-north/article_c43a9bc1-6e5b-578a-9a3b-0396565dd0cc.html?utm_medium=social&utm_source=facebook&utm_campaign=user-share

Liptak, Adam. "Trump Administration Asks Supreme Court to Revive Travel Ban." *The New York Times*, June 2, 2017, www.nytimes.com/2017/06/02/us/politics/trump-travel-ban-supreme-court.html

Liptak, Andrew. "In the Final Days of the Campaign, Trump's Aides Have Taken Away His Twitter Privileges." *The Verge*, November 6, 2016, www.theverge.com/2016/11/6/13545202/donald-trump-election-twitter

Lynch, Sarah N. and Susan Heavey. "House Republicans Launch Probes of Clinton Emails Decision, Uranium Deal." *Reuters*, October 24, 2017, www.reuters.com/article/us-usa-congress-clinton/house-republicans-launch-probes-of-clinton-emails-decision-uranium-deal-idUSKBN1CT29A

Malhotra, Deepak and Jonathan Powell. "What Donald Trump Doesn't Understand about Negotiation." *Harvard Business Review*, April 8, 2016, https://hbr.org/2016/04/what-donald-trump-doesnt-understand-about-negotiation

Mann, Windsor. "Stop Tweeting, Mr. President." *USA Today*, June 6, 2017. www.usatoday.com/story/opinion/2017/06/06/stop-tweeting-mr-president-windsor-mann-column/102551208/

Maza, Cristina. "Trump's Diplomacy Probably Pushed China to Start Talks with North Korea, Experts Say." *Newsweek*, November 15, 2017, www.newsweek.com/trump-china-north-korea-diplomat-visit-deal-712559

McKirdy, Euan and Taehoon Lee. "North Korea Accepts South's Offer to Meet for Talks." *CNN*, January 5, 2018, www.cnn.com/2018/01/04/asia/north-korea-south-korea-talks-intl/index.html

Miller, Greg. "On Russia, Trump and His Top National Security Aides Seem to be At Odds." *Washington Post,* April 18, 2017, www.washingtonpost.com/world/national-security/on-russia-trump-and-his-top-national-security-aides-seem-to-be-at-odds/2017/04/18/13fdc832-23bf-11e7-bb9d-8cd6118e1409_story.html?tid=ss_fb&utm_term=.9cc2bc3e4807

Miller, Greg and Greg Jaffe. "Trump Revealed Highly Classified Information to Russian Foreign Minister and Ambassador." *Washington Post*, May 15, 2017, www.washingtonpost.com/world/national-security/trump-revealed-highly-classified-information-to-russian-foreign-minister-and-ambassador/2017/05/15/530c172a-3960-11e7-9e48-c4f199710b69_story.html?utm_term=.cc50f8743ce1

North Korea Leadership Watch. "New Year's Address." 2018. www.nkleadershipwatch.org/2018/01/01/new-years-address/

Osnos, Evan. "The Risk of Nuclear War with North Korea." *The New Yorker*, September 18, 2017. www.newyorker.com/magazine/2017/09/18/the-risk-of-nuclear-war-with-north-korea

Parmelee, John H. and Shannon L. Bichard. *Politics and the Twitter Revolution: How Tweets Influence the Relationship between Political Leaders and the Public.* New York: Lexington Books, 2012.

Pew Research Center. "U.S. Muslims Concerned About Their Place in Society, but Continue to Believe in the American Dream." July 26, 2017. www.pewforum.org/2017/07/26/findings-from-pew-research-centers-2017-survey-of-us-muslims/

Politicostaff. "Full Text: Donald Trump's Speech on Fighting Terrorism." *Politico*, August 15, 2016, www.politico.com/story/2016/08/donald-trump-terrorism-speech-227025

Prokop, Andrew. "This Could Be the Most Important Revelation in All of Today's Trump-Russia News." *Vox*, October 30, 2017, www.vox.com/2017/10/30/16571462/george-papadopoulos-clinton-emails

Reilly, Katie. "President Trump Met Vladimir Putin for the First Time. Here's What a Body Language Expert Saw." *Time*, July 7, 2017, http://time.com/4849232/g20-summit-donald-trump-vladimir-putin-body-language/

Reuters. "Kremlin: We See Trump's Tweets as Official Statements." December 12, 2017, www.reuters.com/article/us-usa-trump-russia-twitter/kremlin-we-see-trumps-tweets-as-official-statements-idUSKBN1E6193?utm_source=Facebook&utm_medium=Social

Revere, Evans J. R. "The Trump Administration's North Korea Policy: Headed for Success or Failure." *Brookings*, July 10, 2017, www.brookings.edu/blog/order-from-chaos/2017/07/10/the-trump-administrations-north-korea-policy-headed-for-success-or-failure/

Rod Rosenstein's Letter Appointing Mueller Special Counsel. *The New York Times*, May 17, 2017, www.nytimes.com/interactive/2017/05/17/us/politics/document-Robert-Mueller-Special-Counsel-Russia.html

Rosenblum, Todd. "How to Persuade China to Abandon North Korea." *Politico*, July 18, 2017, www.politico.com/agenda/story/2017/07/18/china-north-korea-american-troops-removal-000476

Sang-Hun, Choe. "South Korea Proposes Border Talks with North Korea After Kim's Overture." *The New York Times*, January 2, 2018a, www.nytimes.com/2018/01/02/world/asia/south-north-korea-olympics-talks.html

Sang-Hun, Choe. "South Korea's Leader Credits Trump for North Korea Talks." *The New York Times*, January 10, 2018b, www.nytimes.com/2018/01/10/world/asia/moon-jae-in-trump-north-korea.html

Sanger, David E. "Obama Strikes Back at Russia for Election Hacking." *The New York Times*, December 29, 2016, www.nytimes.com/2016/12/29/us/politics/russia-election-hacking-sanctions.html?smid=fb-share

Sanger, David E. and William J. Broad. "Trump Inherits a Secret Cyberwar against North Korean Missiles." *The New York Times*, March 4, 2017. www.nytimes.com/2017/03/04/world/asia/north-korea-missile-program-sabotage.html?_r=0

Savage, Charlie. "How Government Secrets are Declassified and Disclosed." *The New York Times*, May 15, 2017, www.nytimes.com/2017/05/15/us/politics/trump-classified-secrets.html

Savransky, Rebecca. "Trump: 'Trip Was a Great Success for America.'" *The Hill*, May 28, 2017, http://thehill.com/homenews/administration/335451-trump-trip-was-a-great-success-for-america#.WhSk651z3n0.facebook

Schallhorn, Kaitlyn. "Trump Travel Ban: Timeline of a Legal Journey." *Fox News*, January 20, 2018, www.foxnews.com/politics/2018/01/20/trump-travel-ban-timeline-legal-journey.html

Sestanovich, Stephen. "The Brilliant Incoherence of Trump's Foreign Policy." *The Atlantic*, May 2017, www.theatlantic.com/magazine/archive/2017/05/the-brilliant-incoherence-of-trumps-foreign-policy/521430/?utm_source=fbb

Silva, Cristina. "North Korea Says Only U.S. Should Be Afraid of Its Nuclear Weapons." *Newsweek*, November 26, 2017, www.newsweek.com/north-korea-says-only-us-should-be-afraid-its-nuclear-weapons-other-nations-722698

Stewart, Phil and Valerie Volcovici. "Trump Backtracks on Cyber Unit with Russia After Harsh Criticism." *Reuters.* July 9, 2017, www.reuters.com/article/us-usa-trump-russia-cyber/trump-backtracks-on-cyber-unit-with-russia-after-harsh-criticism-idUSKBN19U0P4

Strait Times. "Donald Trump Urges Peace Between Russia and Ukraine in Tweet." May 12, 2017, www.straitstimes.com/world/united-states/donald-trump-urges-peace-between-russia-and-ukraine-in-tweet?&utm_source=facebook&utm_medium=social-media&utm_campaign=addtoany

Sullivan, Sean, Karoun Demirjian, and Paul Kane. "Senators from Both Parties Pledge to Deepen Probe of Russia and the 2016 Election." *Washington Post*, February 14, 2017. www.washingtonpost.com/powerpost/top-senate-republican-blunt-says-congress-should-probe-flynn-situation/2017/02/14/8abbcad4-f2d5-11e6-a9b0-ecee7ce475fc_story.html?tid=ss_fb&utm_term=.0250d9b0ff2a

Tharoor, Ishan. "The Persian Gulf Crisis over Qatar, Explained." *Washington Post*, June 6, 2017, www.washingtonpost.com/news/worldviews/wp/2017/06/06/the-persian-gulf-crisis-over-qatar-explained/?utm_term=.2d0178584546

The White House. "Executive Order Protecting the Nation from Foreign Terrorist Entry into the United States." January 27, 2017. www.whitehouse.gov/presidential-actions/executive-order-protecting-nation-foreign-terrorist-entry-united-states/

The White House. "Inside President Trump's Trip to Asia." November 15, 2017. www.whitehouse.gov/articles/president-trumps-trip-asia/

The White House. "Remarks by President Trump on the Policy of the United States Towards Cuba." June 16, 2017. www.whitehouse.gov/briefings-statements/remarks-president-trump-policy-united-states-towards-cuba/

Trump, Donald. Twitter Post. April 11, 2017, 4:59 A.M. https://twitter.com/realDonaldTrump/status/851766546825347076

Trump, Donald. Twitter Post. April 11, 2017, 5:03 A.M. https://twitter.com/realDonaldTrump/status/851767718248361986

Trump, Donald. Twitter Post. April 12, 2017, 5:22 A.M. https://twitter.com/realDonaldTrump/status/852134796436398086

Trump, Donald. Twitter Post. April 13, 2017, 6:08 A.M. https://twitter.com/realDonaldTrump/status/852508752142114816

Trump, Donald. Twitter Post. April 13, 2017, 6:16 A.M. https://twitter.com/realdonaldtrump/status/852510810287075329

Trump, Donald. Twitter Post. April 16, 2017, 5:18 A.M. https://twitter.com/realdonaldtrump/status/853583417916755968

Trump, Donald. Twitter Post. August 1, 2017, 6:55 A.M. https://twitter.com/realDonaldTrump/status/892383242535481344

Trump, Donald. Twitter Post. January 29, 2017, 1:49 PM. https://twitter.com/realDonaldTrump/status/825823217025691648

Trump, Donald. Twitter Post. June 5, 2017, 6:20 P.M. https://twitter.com/realdonaldtrump/status/871899511525961728

Trump, Donald. Twitter Post. June 6, 2017, 5:06 A.M. https://twitter.com/realDonaldTrump/status/872062159789985792

Trump, Donald. Twitter Post. June 6, 2017, 6:36 A.M. https://twitter.com/realDonaldTrump/status/872084870620520448

Trump, Donald. Twitter Post. June 6, 2017, 6:44 A.M. https://twitter.com/realDonaldTrump/status/872086906804240384

Trump, Donald. Twitter Post. July 9, 2017, 4:37 A.M. https://twitter.com/realdonaldtrump/status/884013689736769536

Trump, Donald. Twitter Post. July 9, 2017, 5:45 P.M. https://twitter.com/realdonaldtrump/status/884211874518192128

Trump, Donald. Twitter Post. July 12, 2017. 4:05 A.M. https://twitter.com/realDonaldTrump/status/885092844511387654

Trump, Donald. Twitter Post. March 17, 2017, 6:07 A.M. https://twitter.com/realDonaldTrump/status/842724011234791424

Trump, Donald. Twitter Post. May 11, 2017, 2:54 P.M. https://twitter.com/realdonaldtrump/status/862788002594127873

Trump, Donald. Twitter Post. May 16, 2017, 4:13 A.M. https://twitter.com/realdonaldtrump/status/864438529472049152

Trump, Donald. Twitter Post. May 23, 2017, 8:58 A.M. https://twitter.com/realDonaldTrump/status/867047119974170625

Trump, Donald. Twitter Post. May 28, 2017, 5:10 A.M. https://twitter.com/realdonaldtrump/status/868801710038372352

Trump, Donald. Twitter Post. November 6, 2017, 1:28 P.M. https://twitter.com/realdonaldtrump/status/927648870796070912

Trump, Donald. Twitter Post. November 9, 2017, 3:44 P.M. https://twitter.com/realdonaldtrump/status/928770248370728960

Trump, Donald. Twitter Post. November 30, 2017, 4:25 A.M. https://twitter.com/realdonaldtrump/status/936209447747190784

Trump, Donald. Twitter Post. October 29, 2017, 7:09 A.M. https://twitter.com/realdonaldtrump/status/924639422066384896

Trump, Donald. Twitter Post. October 29, 2017, 7:17 A.M. https://twitter.com/realdonaldtrump/status/924641278947622913

Trump, Donald. Twitter Post. September 19, 2017, 10:22 A.M. https://twitter.com/realdonaldtrump/status/910192375267561472

Trump, Donald. Twitter Post. September 23, 2017, 8:08 P.M. https://twitter.com/realdonaldtrump/status/911789314169823232

Trump's Speech to South Korea's National Assembly. *CNN*, November 7, 2017. www.cnn.com/2017/11/07/politics/south-korea-trump-speech-full/index.html

Vitali, Ali. "Trump Tells the Muslim Leaders: 'Drive Out' the Terrorists." *NBC News*, May 21, 2017a, www.nbcnews.com/storyline/trump-s-first-foreign-trip/trump-speech-muslims-we-are-not-here-lecture-n762631

Vitali, Ali. "Trump Threatens to 'Totally Destroy' North Korea in First U.N. Speech." *NBC News*, September 21, 2017b, www.nbcnews.com/politics/white-house/trump-un-north-korean-leader-suicide-mission-n802596

Watkins, Eli. "Tillerson on North Korea: Diplomacy Will Continue 'Until the First Bomb Drops.'" *CNN*, October 16, 2017, www.cnn.com/2017/10/15/politics/rex-tillerson-north-korea-cnntv/index.html

Westcott, Lucy. "How Donald Trump's Travel Ban Tweets Were Used Against Him." *Newsweek*, June 12, 2017, www.newsweek.com/trump-travel-ban-tweets-used-against-him-624575

Williams, Jason. "In Ohio's Trump Country, Voters Say Meh about 'Leak' Charges." *USA Today*, May 16, 2017, www.usatoday.com/story/news/politics/onpolitics/2017/05/16/ohio-trump-country-voters-say-meh-about-leak-charges/101764804/

5

THE PARADOX OF DISSENT

Bullshit and the Twitter Presidency

Christopher Carter

It is perhaps unsurprising that Harry Frankfurt, a moral philosopher who began analyzing the discursive structure of "bullshit" in the mid-1980s, would in 2016 choose to focus on the public persona of Donald Trump. As the real estate billionaire vows to unify the American populace and restore the greatness of his fallen country, Trump embodies the orator for whom style outstrips veracity. His attitude toward truth, Frankfurt suggests, ranges between negation and general disregard, and in the movement from one to the other, clarifies the difference between deceit and bullshit. "The distinction between lying and bullshitting is fairly clear," Frankfurt (2016) writes, "The liar asserts something which he himself believes to be false. He deliberately misrepresents what he takes to be the truth. The bullshitter, on the other hand, is not constrained by any consideration of what may or may not be true." In a short book on the subject, Frankfurt (2005) depicts indifference to truth as a greater threat to rational discourse than deliberate dishonesty, which at least takes accuracy into account.[1]

Unfortunately, such indifference does not preclude lying. Frankfurt (2016) finds calculated falsehood in the mogul's assertion that New Jersey crowds openly celebrated the World Trade Center attack, and his claim to know nothing of David Duke or the Ku Klux Klan. In the first instance, eyewitness testimony exposed the fabrication; in the second, recordings of his earlier statements contradicted the assertions of ignorance. After acknowledging this pattern of dishonesty, Frankfurt (2016) details the bullshit problem by citing Trump's campaign pledge to deport millions of immigrants despite uncertainty as to "whether he would have both the authority and the means to do so." Unruffled by questions of plausibility, he "most likely made that pronouncement merely in order to create certain expectations and impressions in the minds of his listeners" (Frankfurt 2016). Lesser instances of the problem include the president's evaluations of his own talents, including his debating prowess and possession of "the greatest memory in the world" (Frankfurt 2016). The point of Frankfurt's half-comical critique is not that Trump fails to substantiate his boasts, but that he feels no need to do so. The swagger validates itself.

Despite the contemporary relevance of Frankfurt's thesis, however, it has some limitations—chief among them the reification of an autonomous rhetor who positions himself in relation to unmediated facts. That view entails a certain irony, given that Frankfurt concludes *On Bullshit* by coding sincerity and self-knowledge as instances of his focal theme. Attentive to the contradiction, James Fredal endeavors in "Rhetoric and Bullshit" (2011) to redefine Frankfurt's concept as a problem of social relations rather than individual integrity. The phenomenon occurs when participants in a discourse group make questionable assertions to structurally subordinate subjects while providing little to no support for the claim. The tweet "How low has President Obama gone to tapp my phones during the very sacred election process. This is Nixon/Watergate. Bad (or sick) guy!" exemplifies the technique, raising alarm among supporters while offering nothing to persuade the rest (Shear and Schmidt 2017). As Fredal would have it, bullshit inheres less in the utterance than in the system that normalizes it. In a contribution to what Fredal playfully calls "taurascatics"—thus naming Frankfurt's scatology of the taurus—he condemns the disintegration of dialog more than any merely bogus proclamation (2011, 245, 256). In that way, he exhibits a Freirean sensitivity to "narration sickness" (2000, 71), a malady wherein authority figures force their stories on others while forbidding negotiation or cross-examination. Fredal so detests this arrangement that he declines to call it rhetoric, an idea that for him signals the aspiration toward democratic interchange, if not always its practice (2011, 257). In such a view, taurascatics concerns not the operation of communicative tactics but the outright abandonment of communication in favor of self-certifying decree.

The contrasting association of rhetoric with democratic discourse has appeal insofar as it affirms the social construction of knowledge, presuming a politics that is unfinished in more than one sense, both lacking polish and defying conclusion. Fredal's resistance to unilateralism presumes not a clean alternative but one characterized by movement and messiness. Yet, the same features that make his definition attractive also render it suspect. By casting rhetoric as a kind of heroic turbulence, pitting it against the non-rhetoric that emerges whenever any party flaunts its material advantage, Fredal lends the patina of honor to rhetorical theory while limiting its analytical scope. His definition precludes studying bullshit as communication that is, like all rhetoric, keyed to specific situations. More salient for the purposes of this chapter, it preempts investigation of how such communication accords with the situation of the U.S. electorate. Troubling as authoritarian rhetoric may be to people conversant with the history of totalizing governments, we must grapple with its present efficacy in a political regime that purports to share Fredal's dedication to democracy.

Rather than contrast taurascatics with the study of rhetoric, then, the following discussion codes those lines of inquiry as interdependent. Even as demagogic nonsense comes to us in the figures and forms of rhetoric, it is also and only through rhetoric that we can contest it. Staging the contest depends on recognizing the structure of what we confront. This chapter therefore describes that structure as commonly unfolding in three phases. First comes the gaffe: some revelation or other expression of Freudian parapraxis, whereby the administration discloses something shameful about its history or motives. Second comes the request for explanation, which the executive branch meets with high-handed replies: an assertion that the press misunderstands or overemphasizes the affair, for example, or an assurance that no gaffe occurred in the first place. Third, the resulting furor culminates in a paradox of dissent: protesting the abuse of power becomes the pretext for further abuses. The recurrent, almost rote performance of those phases supports Fredal's point that the suppression of dialog derives not from isolated statements but from naturalized discursive economies. And in studying the economies that compose our ways of knowing, or what James Berlin (1988) characterizes as the social episteme, we study rhetoric in action.

That episteme features the recent flourishing of what Hannah Arendt (1968) and, more recently, Pankaj Mishra (2017) call negative solidarity. Such solidarity develops as those who felt under-served by the previous administration, resenting its social programs, advocacy for marginalized demographics, as well as its catering to "rootless cosmopolitans" and "transnational elites," generate political force from identification with each other (Mishra 2017, 209). With those bonds in place, the practice of eliciting dismayed queries from the press and then badgering the questioners starts to look like a way to invigorate the president's considerable following. Whether the technique begins by accident or arises from deliberation, it clearly works, drawing strength from the tweet-stream that excoriates both the press and the social movements that have broadened their visibility since his victory. Given that rationality provides little purchase in countering such opportunism, we may wonder whether any finely tuned argument can avoid triggering the paradox. The question becomes not how to reason with the Twitter presidency, but how to mobilize the segment of society that did not choose it, and fashion a coalition that outmatches Trump's own constituency. Given the disrespect he shows longstanding international allies such as France, Germany, and the United Kingdom (Cook 2017), and the perils of what Naomi Klein dubs "ecocidal capitalism" (2017, 228), a better question might be how to rally a global multitude in opposition to incipient fascism. Trump's tweet that Germany pays "FAR LESS that it should on NATO and military" (Nianias 2017), his mockery of London Mayor Sadiq Khan for a purportedly inadequate response to terrorism (Baker 2017), his retweeting of racist videos by Jayda Fransen of the far-right group Britain First (Weaver et al. 2017), and his mantra that Mexico will pay for his border wall (Tillett 2017) have all recast the U.S. as a menace to long-time friends, thus endangering the "greatness" and international stature he promises his followers. His withdrawal from the Paris Climate Accords (Clark 2017) further compromises that stature, raising concerns about the ecological sustainability of rogue nationalism, and prompting social movements to drill more resolutely through clogs in contemporary civic discourse.

Parapraxis

> When the steep glide began, people rose, fell, collided, swam in their seats. Then the serious screaming and moaning began. Almost immediately a voice from the flight deck was heard on the intercom: "We're falling out of the sky! We're going down! We're a silver gleaming death machine!" This outburst struck the passengers as an all but total breakdown of authority, competence and command presence and it brought on a round of fresh and desperate wailing.
>
> Don DeLillo, White Noise (1985, 90)

The fascistic respect for displays of power involves a general refusal to admit wrong. Such tendencies create the impression of an especially adamant White House administration, as their front-page blunders occur with astounding frequency. From remarks about preferring soldiers who do not get captured to spats with the parents of fallen troops, from revelations about groping women to racist stereotyping of urban spaces, from promotions of Ivanka Trump's clothing line to defenses of Russian authorities despite the hacking of U.S. election procedures, the trouble comes with a fury. And those concerns fail to touch the drama of the Muslim travel ban, the firing of FBI director James Comey, or the president's claim that Neo-Nazi rallies involve some "very fine people" (Gray 2017).

Although Trump clearly means what he says about white supremacists, he often stumbles in ways that resemble the workings of what Freudians call parapraxis, a linguistic or physiological slip that exposes delicate or perhaps humiliating information about a speaker. According to Freud's theory, such purported errors signal the operation of the unconscious, bubbling up from a stream of perceptions and desires that escape explicit awareness. His references to the concept relate to the individual psyche rather than the circulation of ideology although appropriating the term for the study of cultural rhetoric helps us think about how high-stakes gaffes expose social structures. The slip is not always Trump's; it may as readily come from members of his family, from White House counselor Kellyanne Conway, or others from his administration; more profoundly, it may come from the material-discursive context in which the Trump brand makes meaning.[2]

When Conway uses her media platform to advertise Ivanka's fashion interests, she reveals in unflattering ways the overlap between commercialism and governance, which the administration generally has to suppress to maintain the semblance of ethical propriety. And one-time press secretary Sean Spicer expresses a dazzling lack of historical savvy when he contrasts Nazi Germany with modern Syria, contending that not even Hitler used chemical weapons against his own people (Smith et al. 2017). It is hard to pinpoint the more disturbing implication of that claim, which might mean that Spicer, in the heat of the press conference, forgot the gassing of the Jews, or that he neglected to learn what chemical weapons were before defending the decision to bomb Syria for using them. Either way, his gaffe constitutes a form of systemic parapraxis wherein the valuing of brute strength overrides, in deep-seated, almost primal ways, the need to be informed.

In combination with evidence of an underprepared, incomplete cabinet, such public relations work evokes the moment in DeLillo's *White Noise* when engines fail during a flight to (a mercifully fictional) Iron City. Rather than attempting to reassure the passengers, a pilot explains over the intercom that the plane is now a "silver gleaming death machine" (1985, 90). A second pilot follows in tones more professional and subdued: "This is American two-one-three to the cockpit voice recorder. Now we know what it's like. It's worse than we'd ever imagined. They didn't prepare us for this at the death simulator in Denver. Our fear is pure, so totally stripped of distractions and pressures as to be a form of transcendental meditation. In less than three minutes we will touch down, so to speak" (1985, 90). Thus emerges the airline pilot's unconscious dread, the buried sense that when the machine malfunctions, his helplessness will become all too clear. The rhetorical effect of the announcements is the "all but total breakdown of authority" (1985, 90). When that breakdown affects large groups at the same time, it becomes international news: the plane crashes, the high-speed train derails, the levees break. Revealing the uncertainty of what Robert Hariman and John Louis Lucaites term "modernity's gamble" in *No Caption Needed: Iconic Photographs, Public Culture, and Liberal Democracy* (2007, 243), those events bring our faith in technologically mediated authority into plain and terrible view. Similarly, when national leaders signal that the governing structure is unsound, portions of the population may understandably start to panic. As European confidence in U.S. stability wanes, bombs rain down on Syria, and North Korea engages in persistent nuclear testing, the comparison between the federal government and fallible, high-stakes machines appears uncomfortably apt.

If we consider the stumbles of the executive as the malfunctioning of a social machine, the phenomenon of parapraxis begins to loosen its Freudian moorings. It no longer signals the operation of individual consciousness but rather a rhetorical ecology in the sense outlined in "The Importance of Harmony: An Ecological Metaphor for Writing Research." Such an ecology "is less about individual elements—author, invention, error—and more a narrative of interactions intrinsic to a system" (Fleckenstein et al. 2008, 392). The system typically circumvents its fissures so as to stave off its own disintegration, but at times negative feedback holds such urgency that it refuses to be obscured. And when slips occur within a rhetorical ecology, it becomes difficult to locate the source of the problem. The need to contain indiscretions and eliminate uncertainty as to their origins helps explain the Trump administration's fixation during the early stages of his tenure: "The real story turns out to be SURVEILLANCE and LEAKING!" he tweets, "Find the leakers" (Borger 2017). The White House endeavors to identify culprits, and scapegoats undergo public sanction as a way to impose discipline, but the leaks continue at a disquieting pace.

Those leaks include highlights from Trump's private conversations with foreign heads of state, Michael Flynn's meeting with Russian ambassador Sergey Kislyak, documents about the National Guard assisting with the deportation of immigrants, and other papers about the revival of CIA "black site" prisons once used to torture suspected terrorists—to name just a few controversial disclosures (Farhi 2017; Landler and Pérez-Peña 2017; Mazzetti and Savage 2017). But for an especially prescient example of a structural leak, a rogue eruption within the rhetorical ecology, we might look to Trump's campaign days when backstage recordings of his visit to *Access Hollywood* dominated broadcast news and social media. In the clip we see the luxury bus approach from a distance, accompanied by the audio of his conversation with Billy Bush as they prepare to meet Arianne Zucker: "You know, I'm automatically attracted to beautiful—I just start kissing them. It's like a magnet. Just kiss. I don't even wait. And when you're a star, they let you do it. You can do anything. […] Grab 'em by the pussy. You can do anything" (Bullock 2016). Bush would later lose his job for encouraging such talk although the tape was not enough to derail Trump's presidential bid. Once he explains what he does to women like Zucker, who stands waiting in the studio lot to meet him, the men exit the bus and adopt public personae.

The video shows nothing like a conventional slip of the tongue: Trump conveys his attitudes toward women, receives encouragement, and elaborates without shame. What it does show, however, is the rhetorical ecology refusing to leave his indiscretions on the bus. Human actants undoubtedly play key roles in that ecology, preparing the recording equipment, archiving the results, and disseminating the footage at an inopportune time for the campaign. Yet, the lively environment also plays a decisive part, lending multimodal form to the ideologies that infuse Trump's consciousness and the rhetorics that constitute his subjectivity. *Access Hollywood*'s audiovisual apparatus did not function primarily for surveillance purposes; the idea was to obtain material for the show while documenting Trump's guest spot on "Days of Our Lives" (Taylor 2016). That the sound and image would weigh against him ten years later in a political campaign could not have been foreseen. After lying dormant for a decade, the digital object takes on the sort of vibrancy Laurie Gries (2015) attributes to seemingly inert things in *Still Life with Rhetoric: A New Materialist Approach for Visual Rhetorics*. As contexts change, communicative materials acquire unexpected purposes, converging and contending with human agency without being equivalent to it.

What we encounter, then, in the circulation of the *Access Hollywood* video, is systemic parapraxis, emanating not from the tongue alone but coalescing as visual, aural, and kinetic modes. Against the will of someone who has profited magnificently from its functioning, the digital-organic ecology brings his fitness for office into doubt. It does so by exposing his sexism, and more generally, by indicating his treatment of people as the Heideggerean "standing reserve," existing only to serve his pleasures and comply with his demands (1977, 24). Those attitudes help to explain his demonization of the media when they question his inconsistencies and impetuous behavior. They also help to explain his expectation of loyalty, and quickness to fire Preet Bharara and James Comey when they fail to pledge their commitment. For much of the American populace, those firings suggest a plane in steep descent, with the rhetorical ecology steadily insisting on the breakdown of authority. The terror, so pure as to resemble transcendental meditation, is not the pilots' but our own.

Executive Taurascatics

> We're an empire now, and when we act, we create our own reality. [...]
> And you, all of you, will be left to just study what we do.
>
> *Karl Rove, Senior Advisor to*
> *George W. Bush (Suskind 2004)*

After the passengers in *White Noise* have given themselves over to catastrophe, the flight to Iron City regains engine power and the plane levels off. Airline employees resume their business, proceeding as though nothing consequential has occurred. Although the question of leveling off remains unsettled for U.S. publics, already we recognize the pretense that all is secure: Tucker Carlson appears on the nightly news to assure us of the president's quirky wisdom, Trump ranks his administration among the most productive in history, and Sarah Huckabee Sanders praises her employer for foreign relations work while characterizing contrary views as dubious reporting (Katz 2017; Reuters 2017). So begins the second phase of the White House's rhetorical pattern. Trump's unwillingness to engage at length with critical questions, and his angry outbursts when the press insists on answers, exemplify bullshit in the sense Fredal gives,

> Bullshit happens [...] when one party in an encounter feels superior enough (in position, authority, or rhetorical skill, for example) to dispense with the rituals of cooperative interaction, leading the other to feel

treated without deference; when one participant in an exchange appears to have been undeservedly slighted; or when one side of a dialogue is unjustly disregarded [...] Bullshit is, in this sense, hubris.

(2011, 256)

We have seen such disregard in Trump's refusal to take questions from Jim Acosta of CNN, and in Spicer's condescension toward April Ryan, bureau chief of American Urban Radio Networks (Henderson 2017; Wemple 2017). Admittedly, tensions have long existed between press secretaries and reporters. Acosta recalls icy treatment from the Obama administration, for instance, after he questioned their resolve in locating Islamic State of Iraq and Syria (ISIS) operatives. Rarely, however, has the White House so consistently attacked the media en masse for unflattering reports. A typical tweet from Trump proclaims, "The Fake News Media has never been so wrong or so dirty. Purposely incorrect stories and phony sources to meet their agenda of hate. Sad!" (Oborne and Roberts 2017). With that perspective in mind, Sanders answers many journalists' queries in noncommittal and outright dismissive fashion (Reuters 2017).

Perhaps such evasions are to be expected given their prevalence during the campaign. When Trump angrily apologized on October 6, 2016 for the *Access Hollywood* incident, he also cast the discussion as "locker room talk" (Keneally 2017). When star athletes responded that such behavior does not characterize their locker rooms, he refused to engage with them (Blau 2016). Unconvincing though it was, Trump's apology was exceptional in that it occurred at all. His is an especially aggressive style of bullshit, less similar to the epistemological horseplay Frankfurt outlines in his book than to dogmatic solipsism, a preoccupation with crafting the world in his own image.

He is hardly the first high-level official to take such an approach. In 2004, George W. Bush's Senior Advisor Karl Rove expressed a similar perspective when speaking to *The New York Times* reporter Ron Suskind: "We're an empire now, and when we act, we create our own reality. And while you're studying that reality—judiciously, as you will—we'll act again, creating other new realities, which you can study too, and that's how things will sort out. We're history's actors... and you, all of you, will be left to just study what we do" (Suskind 2004). Rove's hubris suggests another variation on the theme of Freirean "narration sickness," and an implicit scoffing at anything like the "problem posing" outlined in *Pedagogy of the Oppressed*. Problem posing may occur, he seems to say, and it will likely be quite sophisticated, but it will make no difference. In *No Is Not Enough*, Klein rejects the sort of deterministic assessment that Rove offers but concurs with the claim that mega-wealth marshals its own reality. "According to the internal logic of [Trump's] brand," she writes, "lying with impunity is all part of being the big boss. Being tethered to fixed, boring facts is for losers" (2017, 56). When people express outrage at his profiting from the presidency, he claims that "the president can't have a conflict of interest"

(Arnsdorf 2016); when they challenge his numbers regarding inauguration crowds or airport detainees, he accuses them of lying (Hunt 2017); when they contest his insinuations about a rash of terror attacks in Sweden, he gestures vaguely toward Fox News as his source (McCauslund 2017). As of November 2017, Fox remained one of the few networks exempt from his disdain, however disputed its commentary on Sweden or disgraceful its history of workplace harassment. In none of the cases does he provide an especially detailed defense; to do so risks affirming his answerability to something other than markets.

As "history's actors" deflect unpleasant queries (Suskind 2004), they help fortify the structure of the political economy. Management-worker relations exhibit a strong tendency toward unilateral discourse, which corresponds nicely with the system's design. In the Marxian description, that system presumes that a small group of people controls the means of production, whereas the rest sell their labor to sustain themselves, at a rate that permits the owning class to grow its wealth. The history of capitalism depends on the suppression of that contradiction—so much so, that people who bring it to public awareness draw swift and often violent rebuke. U.S. instances include the Haymarket Massacre and Pullman Strike of the late nineteenth century, the Lawrence Textile Strike and Ludlow Massacre of the early twentieth century, the Matewan and the Harlan County Wars of the 1920s and 1930s, as well as the Delano Grape Strike and Memphis Sanitation Strike of the explosive 1960s (Brenner et al. 2009, 33–35, 55, 230–31). Although deadly confrontations declined over the course of the century, ideological violence remained prevalent in Ronald Reagan's response to the Aircraft Controllers' Strike of the 1980s; reasserted itself in the mid-1990s when the courts ruled against the 2,500 member journalists' union in Detroit; and surfaced yet again in the intimidation of workers and hiring of replacement employees during the 2015 United Steelworkers Oil Refineries Strike.[3] If we keep Fredal's work in mind, we recognize the chronicle of U.S. capitalism as a history of bullshit.

Trump claims to be worker-friendly and has managed to attract many Rust Belt voters by appealing to their plight as "people forced against their will into universal competition" (Mishra 2017, 334). But his history as CEO demonstrates recurrent conflict with organized labor.[4] He has engaged in protracted battles with union organizers at his Chicago hotel and denied the right to bargain to culinary workers at another hotel in Las Vegas.[5] He has favored the anti-union policies of Wisconsin governor Scott Walker and supported so-called right-to-work laws that weaken unions by abolishing the requirement for dues, permitting some workers to benefit from labor negotiations without funding their organizations (Meyerson 2016). If that history does not make Trump's workplace politics clear enough, he nearly appointed Andrew Puzder to the position of Secretary of the Department of Labor—a man who openly opposes unions and has "floated the idea of automating his restaurants to avoid worker costs" (Hesson 2016). Although the labor movement has long withstood attacks from owners, managers, police, and the military, contemporary activists rightly wonder whether Trump's election is "an extinction-level event for American labor" (Meyerson 2016). At the very least, it signals the overclass' declining patience with employee efforts to influence workplace conditions.

By word and deed alike, the executive assures workers that the question of consent is immaterial—that, in Rove's sense, history makers will go on making history despite any objections from the powerless. Fredal, however, maintains a distinction between the totalizing aspirations of such logic and its actual effects, which are far from certain. He sees countering autocracy as the work of rhetoric: "If bullshit is one-sided discourse and arises in encounters characterized by the perception of arrogance and insult, then rhetoric must be defined as discourse that affords due regard to all participants in an encounter and all perspectives in a dialogue or discourse, particularly the non-dominant positions most likely to go unheard" (2011, 256). He thus links rhetoric to an ideal situation where every position has a chance to influence the rest, and he encourages sensitivity to perspectives that have gone mostly unnoticed or have undergone deliberate suppression in the history of civic negotiations. In "Disgusting Bullshit," Jenny Rice concurs with Fredal's recommendations, describing the "delicate beauty" of rhetoric as its maintenance of open, risky flows between embodied stances: "In a moment of exposure before my interlocutor, my beliefs are likewise exposed to the possibility of transformation. I may feel the frightening possibility that my core belief is questionable, or that my longstanding commitment to a cause may not be completely defensible" (470). Bullshit forbids such openness, she argues, and amounts to a "blockage of rhetorical eardrums" (470).

Rhetoric scholars have a laudable history of specifying those blockages, developing a symbiotic relationship with people who study race, indigeneity, feminism, sexuality, gender, disability, climate change, labor, surveillance, and the prison-industrial complex—to provide only a brief list of topics. Charles E. Morris and Stephen Howard Browne's *Readings on the Rhetoric of Social Protest* provides a sampling of those concerns. While contributors to that collection detail how activist collectives communicate, they also examine how entrenched institutions attempt to stanch the flow of discourse, working to delegitimize movements with support from such material rhetorics as fire hoses, dogs, tear gas, truncheons, guns, helicopters, and tanks. Fredal would likely frame those attempts to immobilize activism as bullshit, and students of social movement rhetoric would no doubt agree. Those students would not, however, be as apt to code bullshit as the opposite of rhetoric. In movement literature, rhetoric serves a wide array of positions within the dynamic sphere of politics, even those that endeavor to shut the dialog down. Autocratic rhetors strive toward a goal that they rarely if ever reach, often doing as much to catalyze backlash as to jam the discursive assemblage.

Given these uneven effects, Fredal's shrewd thinking merits a gentle amendment: rather than conceiving of bullshit as the antithesis of rhetoric, we might address it instead as a species of rhetoric that demands a vigilant counter-rhetoric to sustain the flow of ideas. That formulation avoids the problem of overcorrection. The popular inflection of rhetoric as deception is lamentable, but we need not reply by designating rhetorical practice as entirely above reproach. Framing it as politically variable dissociates the concept from some perfected version of the public sphere, recognizing the resource inequalities that suffuse public deliberations and how often deliberation gives way to violence.

That violence extends beyond human subjects to the material network through which they address each other. Authoritarian politics proceeds not only through the policies of the White House, but through the ubiquity of Trump's image. His quick-tempered tweets, nepotistic favors to his son-in-law, sumptuous dining, and travel routines all become international news and fodder for late night comedy shows (Feldman 2017a,b; Izadi 2017; Nevins 2017). The digital apparatus absorbs these lexia and recirculates them in rhizomatic fashion, often as memes that have little connection to their initial meanings. Even tweets that include jabberwockian nonsense, such as the "covfefe" mishap of May 2017, deepen his hold on collective consciousness (Flegenheimer 2017). Human actants help generate the memes, but the network affords the raw materials and the means of circulation. As the design of the Internet works to support communication even when multiple distribution points become inoperative, blockage or congealed information is not always the problem. With the Twitter presidency, the problem becomes a flow that is so overwhelming as to absorb and redirect most countercurrents. Such redirection provides a modicum of support for Rove's position: attention to executive taurascatics, no matter how incisive, often makes too little impact, struggling to explain what has occurred while remaining speculative in its theories of intervention.

Negative Solidarity and Traumatic Recurrence

> What I'd really like us to do would be to come out and tell the whole world: "Now you boys never mind about the moral side of this. We have power, and power is its own excuse!"
>
> *General Edgeways in Sinclair Lewis's*
> *It Can't Happen Here (2014, 8)*

In the months after Trump's victory, shocked voters sought explanation in multiple directions, some of which converged with the history of dystopian fiction and the cinema of political intrigue. George Orwell's *1984*, for example, took on immediate relevance with its vision of totalitarian governance grounded in linguistic trickery. As leaks about Trump's connections with Russia started to multiply in early 2017, and as allegations of his attempts to quash the investigation intensified, Alan J. Pakula's movie *All the President's Men* became another key intertext. A lesser-known example, but one that sold in a rush following the election, is Sinclair Lewis's seriocomic novel *It Can't Happen Here* (1935). The book portrays the ascent of Berzelius "Buzz" Windrip to the presidency amid swirling currents of nationalism, economic distress, violent rallies, and populist resentment of news media. Despite long odds, Windrip takes the White House while garnering tumultuous applause from his base, many of whom see the election as providential. In a perverse victory lap, he demotes Congress to an advisory role in national government, affording himself nearly unlimited latitude in policy creation.

From the novel's opening pages, it telegraphs the coming authoritarianism of Windrip's new administration. It begins with a political rally in which General Herbert W. Edgeways produces a distinctive form of civic parapraxis, intimating to the audience what he would say were he not constrained by social propriety (Lewis 2014, 8). The apophasis promotes leadership without moral limits, needing no external justification since "power is its own excuse" (2014, 8). Although such proclamations would seem to have frightening implications for populist audiences, his listeners receive his choreographed slip with gratitude. Feeling that weak leaders have failed them, they want not governmental overthrow but a voice that speaks in unambiguous tones the value of robust authority. Democracy has sown confusion; they desire bold, single-minded direction instead.

Eighty years later, such sentiment broke the boundaries of fiction and carried Trump to victory, if not on raw vote count then at least according to the dictates of the Electoral College. By July 2017, national support for Trump held firm at approximately 36%, which marked a seventy-year low for presidents at that stage of their tenure but nevertheless represented a startlingly high acceptance of a confirmed autocrat (Kenny 2017). Although he has not yet imitated Windrip by transforming Congress into a powerless supporting cast, he has disparaged all opposition and dismissed legislative negotiation as inefficient. Such repudiation proves attractive because the base dislikes dialog among differences: the system has for too long allowed people who do not rightly qualify as American to influence public life.

Such anti-democratic affect coalesces as an Arendtian negative solidarity, a weak bond with nevertheless fearsome consequences. The urge to "make America great again" captures Windrip's identitarian unease, and does more to generate enthusiasm for border walls and travel bans than strategies for domestic comity or enhanced international relations. From negative solidarity comes negative policy, advancing a sweeping program of exclusion while failing to specify an interior content. The crisis became clear in the summer of 2017, when politicians who opposed the Affordable Care Act for seven years could not agree on an alternative despite controlling both the House and Senate (Mascaro 2017). As the empty core of negative solidarity reveals itself, collectives with more developed programs step in to offer material alternatives. Those alternatives include revisions to affordable care, but more broadly, efforts to protect people across the country from police brutality, ensure the well-being of those with varied sexualities and gender identities, support employee efforts to control labor conditions, and maintain the long tradition of welcoming immigrants. With such issues in mind, people take to the streets, town halls, courthouses, shopping districts, campuses, and the workplace, claiming voice for those whom Orwellian bullshit works to silence.

When such outrages occur on Windrip's watch, he corrals dissenters into internment camps. Discursive repression becomes terrifyingly physical; violence toward nonconformist views becomes widespread and systematic. As of early spring 2018, we have not yet reached that point in Trump's America, one might observe with some combination of relief and foreboding. Yet, he has already encouraged his supporters to "punch" protesters "in the face"; he has validated armed neo-Nazis; he has inspired bills that would subject activists to high fines and jail time, and "in some states, protect drivers from liability if they strike someone taking part in a protest" (Gabbatt 2017); and his administration has threatened to cut funding to sanctuary cities while governors endeavor to imprison city officials who fail to support federal deportation initiatives (Jarvie 2017; Yee 2017). The current climate suggests not just the foresight of literary art but also the late tendency of Western politics toward self-parody, leaving the satirists no room to maneuver. The desire to exclude or incarcerate the threatening other powered Trump's rise primarily by demonizing immigrants, but that rhetoric also extended to the opposition candidate. "Lock her up" went the chant, and with such little humor that many people were genuinely disappointed when Trump did not deliver on the slogan (Gomez 2016).

But to point out the negativity of such solidarity has thus far only confirmed its hold. The bond is in one sense weak insofar as its adherents want little to do with each other; the idea of the collective only proves useful in its capacity to serve the *homo economicus*, which Mishra defines as "the autonomous, reasoning, rights-bearing individual, the quintessential product of industrialism and modern political philosophy," who has "realized his fantastical plans to bring all of human existence into the mesh of production and consumption" (2017, 75). Yet, the paradoxical bond among purportedly self-sufficient strangers derives powerful influence from its geopolitical scope, producing the sense of righteous confidence that Lewis associates with the "Corpos," who bring Windrip to power and protect his government against defamation. It is here that the paradox of dissent takes its most aggressive form: executive authority flows through the social body such that agents who want to maintain democracy's dynamism appear to the Corpos as a sign of systemic infirmity. Reflecting the operation of neoliberalism, such a condition recalls Jean Baudrillard's diagnosis of economic ideology in *Symbolic Exchange and Death*, where he delineates a "code in which capital finds its purest discourses"—a system of "symbolic violence inscribed everywhere in signs, even in the signs of the revolution" (2007, 10). When the Corpos take critical questioning itself to be the malady in need of cure, any utterance unflattering to the executive presents an opportunity to reassert dominance.

In the final phase of his bullshit schema, then, Trump mocks rebellion on his Twitter account while mobilizing antagonism toward demonstrators. He tweets that the U.S. "just had a very open and successful presidential election. Now professional protesters, incited by the media, are protesting. Very unfair!" (Henderson 2016). In another tweet, Trump remarks that "Professional anarchists, thugs and paid protesters are proving the point of the millions of people who voted to MAKE AMERICA GREAT AGAIN!" (Chang 2017). With such tweets, Trump aggravates what Mishra describes as a "claustrophobic" reaction to cultural heterogeneity, a digitally mediated "capacity for envious and resentful comparison" among "individuals with very different pasts," along with a yearning to push against perceived encroachment, whether by purportedly subsidized activists or the paperless immigrants they support (2017, 13). The pattern of stoking protest and then using the resulting news coverage to energize the base has the affective texture of a traumatic cycle. When amplifying the rhetoric of protest further motivates the very constituencies that brought the disaster about, the paradox amounts to a social form of what thinkers like Cathy Caruth (1996) and Dominick LaCapra (2001) depict as a psychic loop.

Scholarship on such loops considers how the suffering subject endeavors to rupture the cycle through modified behavior. Such thinking constitutes a variation on the Freudian dialectic of melancholia and mourning, wherein the melancholic remains caught in a pattern of compulsive performance while the mourner manages gradually to interrupt the pattern. Despite the resemblance between melancholia and taurascatic inertia, however, the idea of mourning has limitations as a way to counter Trump-era bullshit. Loosening the situation's hold on the subject does nothing to alter that situation, as disengagement from social trauma only permits the trauma to continue. More troubling still, mourning requires privilege that many activists plainly cannot claim, as when the repeal of the Affordable Care Act may cost the activist her life, or when having brown skin means confronting steady suspicion, harassment, violence, or even death.

Given such life-or-death stakes, there exists no time to mourn the overthrow of democracy by rhetorics of unilateralism and unchecked avarice. We must instead address that apparent overthrow as rhetorical through and through, however bent on seeming otherwise. By remembering the rhetorical character of bullshit, we retain its status as a performance, a complex range of appeals that pretend to inevitability. The performance has proven viable throughout 2016 and 2017, but its future remains uncertain. As with Windrip's overthrow by members of his own cabinet, the propagation of unfettered self-interest creates few durable loyalties within the White House. And the weak bonds of negative solidarity, no matter how powerful in the aggregate, expose their tenuousness when faced with the complexities of positive social policy. Such work feels too much like democracy.

Trump's lack of patience with democratic standards becomes further apparent in his interventions in police-community relations, as demonstrated by his instructions to law enforcement officers in Brentwood, New York: "Please don't be too nice. Like when you guys put somebody in the car, and you're protecting their head [...] You can take the hand away, O.K.?" (Rosenthal 2017). Almost immediately condemned by police in New York, California, Louisiana, and Florida, the speech indicates once more his conviction that power is its own excuse. Given that U.S. police have fatally shot nearly 1,000 people in each year since 2014 (Police Shootings 2017; Sullivan et al. 2017; Whitcomb 2017), with an alarming portion of them being African American, his tone-deaf pronouncements reaffirm that the ethos of federal authority is in steep decline, with no assurance that the engines will reignite.

Even though public activism has thus far mainly emboldened the White House while feeding into cycles of trauma, there can be no turning from mass protest. With the new shamelessness comes the need for unprecedented social movement, held together not by the negative bonds of jingoistic self-interest but the articulation of positive social policy rooted in international dialog. Given the president's affirmations of war and torture, repudiation of the Paris climate accord, religious intolerance, and his vow to protect American wealth whatever the cost to other countries, the well-being of people around the globe depends on problem posing that crosses hemispheres. Because the Trump administration appears unlikely to reproduce Lewis's vision of an overthrow from within the White House, and such an event would, at any rate, only alter the surfaces of authoritarianism, coalitions dedicated to democracy must make themselves a constant presence in public, face-to-face encounters as well as on social and broadcast media. Michael Hardt and Sandro Mezzadra call not only for amplification of such coalitions in the U.S. context but also for their extension across borders. They note the rise of right populism in large portions of Europe and South America and describe an alternative populism whose democratic ethos might overwhelm through sheer numbers the fascist hegemony that is currently taking shape.

It Can't Happen Here offers a sometimes comic, mostly revolting look at how such hegemony creeps in, highlighting campaign promises and public address that prefigure Trump's tweets in uncanny ways. The point of such dystopian fiction, Klein explains, is to envision possible futures so that we might deliberately "swerve" (2017, 185). In late 2017, as the president makes common cause with white nationalists, the need to swerve could not be clearer. Trump consistently demonstrates a conviction that domination "is its own excuse," and embodies "the belief that money and power provide license to impose one's will on others, whether that entitlement is expressed by grabbing women or grabbing the finite resources from a planet on the cusp of catastrophic warming" (Klein 2017, 10). To return a final time to Fredal's ideas, such grabbing is bullshit—a structural relation in which influence runs only one way. Massive, direct-action response is necessary to denaturalize such rhetoric and prevent its further spread. The alt-right may draw energy from those demonstrations, but their negative solidarity cannot match the transnational coalescence of groups committed to racial and economic justice, social and ecological heterogeneity.

The urgency of transnational activism stems not only from the desire to preserve democracy in the U.S. but also to maintain the livability of the planet. In an age where the American president poses "an existential threat" to the labor movement (Klein 2017, 107), the cry for a living wage has expanded into a species-level concern for life itself. Klein attributes the international character of that concern to the magnitude of Trump's threat: "With powers so vast and policies so reckless, everyone on this planet is potentially in the blast zone, the fallout zone, and certainly in the warming zone" (2017, 11). Groups banding across borders aim to forestall those devastating effects, to swerve in ways counseled by Sinclair and Klein alike. But those groups also work in more affirmative fashion to enact the dialog that has come so violently under threat, and to clarify the necessary interdependence of the social sphere and the ecosphere. The Standing Rock Sioux has shown the way, as have antifascist movements, women's marches, trans rallies, and "the huge demonstrations that have been held in cities across the [European] continent—from Berlin to Helsinki—to insist that migrants are welcome" (Klein 2017, 205). With those coalitions have come brutal forms of repression, along with forms of corporate expansion and pollution whose effects will be felt beyond our lifetimes. To contain and perhaps reverse those effects, we must see their purported inevitability as a rhetorical ploy. Only then can we mobilize rhetoric for contrary purposes, demanding rather than assuming its affiliation with democracy.

Notes

1 Frankfurt 2005, 61. Reflecting on student responses to Frankfurt's work, Jenny Rice notes that the bullshitter cares little whether what she or he says is "correct, incorrect, or approximate [...] what matters is whether or not his or her goal is accomplished" ("Introductory" 2015, 468).

2 At times there is no slip at all, but mere recklessness in the delivery of information. Such information includes Trump's admission to Lester Holt that he fired James Comey because the FBI Director did not acknowledge collusion with Russia as a "made-up story," an obvious "excuse by the Democrats for having lost an election they should have won" (Griffiths 2017). Given that Comey was investigating collusion at the time of the firing, the president's comments have triggered widespread concern about obstruction of justice.

3 See Brenner et al. (2009) for a compilation of perspectives on U.S. labor strikes and the violence that accompanies them.

4 Klein also locates Trump's contempt for struggling workers in his television show, which mocks "have-nots" and turns "the act of firing people into mass entertainment" (2017, 47-8).

5 See Cadei 2016; United 2016. The Culinary Workers Union Local 226 eventually obtained bargaining rights at Trump's hotel, but this hardly signals his friendliness toward workers (Lee 2016). It instead gives evidence of the victories labor attains through struggle, after many hours outside their work schedules spent in planning and protest.

Bibliography

All the President's Men. 1976. Directed by Alan J. Pakula. Hollywood, CA: Warner Brothers, 1997. DVD.

Arendt, Hannah. *Men in Dark Times*. San Diego, CA: Harcourt Brace and Company, 1968.

Arnsdorf, Isaac. "Trump: 'The President Can't Have a Conflict of Interest.'" *Politico*, November 22, 2016, www.politico.com/story/2016/11/trump-the-president-cant-have-a-conflict-of-interest-231760

Baker, Peter. "Trump's Off-the-Cuff Tweets Strain Foreign Ties." *The New York Times*, June 4, 2017, www.nytimes.com/2017/06/04/us/politics/britain-attack-trump-twitter-storm.html

Baudrillard, Jean. *Symbolic Exchange and Death*. Translated by Iain Hamilton Grant. London: Sage, 2007. First published in English in 1993 by Sage (London).

Berlin, James. "Rhetoric and Ideology in the Writing Class." *College English* 50, no. 1 (September 1988): 477–94.

Blau, Max. "Not 'Locker Room' Talk: Athletes Push Back on Trump Remark." *CNN*, October 10, 2016, www.cnn.com/2016/10/10/politics/locker-room-talk-athletes-respond-trnd/index.html

Borger, Julian. "Ex-Obama Adviser Denies Leaking Names of Officials in Trump-Russia Reports." *Guardian*, April 3, 2017, www.theguardian.com/us-news/2017/apr/03/trump-russia-carter-page-energy-industry-files-spy

Brenner, Aaron, Benjamin Day, and Immanuel Ness (Ed.). *The Encyclopedia of Strikes in American History*. New York: Routledge, 2009.

Bullock, Penn. "Transcript: Donald Trump's Taped Transcripts about Women." *The New York Times*, October 8, 2016, www.nytimes.com/2016/10/08/us/donald-trump-tape-transcript.html

Cadei, Emily. "Trump's Labor Pains: The Ups and Downs of His Union Relations." *Newsweek*, June 3, 2016, www.newsweek.com/trump-labor-pains-466220

Caruth, Cathy. *Unclaimed Experience: Trauma, Narrative, and History*. Baltimore, MD: Johns Hopkins University Press, 1996.

Chang, Clio. "The Anti-Protest Backlash." *New Republic*, February 28, 2017, https://newrepublic.com/article/140926/anti-protest-backlash-republicans-criminalize-dissent

Clark, Nick. "COP23: Testing Times for Paris Climate Pact after Trump Withdrawal." *Aljazeera*, November 5, 2017, www.aljazeera.com/blogs/europe/2017/11/cop23-testing-times-paris-climate-pact-trump-withdrawal-171105053122123.html

Cook, Jesselyn. "Here's a List of Countries and Leaders Trump Has Insulted since His Election." *Huffington Post*, November 5, 2017, www.huffingtonpost.com/entry/trump-insult-foreign-countries-leaders_us_59dd2769e4b0b26332e76d57

DeLillo, Don. *White Noise*. New York: Viking, 1985.

Farhi, Paul. "The Trump Administration Has Sprung a Leak. Many of Them, In Fact." *Washington Post*, February 5, 2017, www.washingtonpost.com/lifestyle/style/the-trump-administration-has-sprung-a-leak-many-of-them-in-fact/2017/02/05/a13fad24-ebe2-11e6-b4ff-ac2cf509efe5_story.html?utm_term=.a8789536b520

Feldman, Kate. "SEE IT: Stephen Colbert Goes After Jared Kushner and the Bureau of Obvious Nepotism on 'Late Show.'" *New York Daily News*, March 28, 2017a, www.nydailynews.com/entertainment/tv/stephen-colbert-jared-kushner-late-show-article-1.3011019

Feldman, Kate. "SEE IT: Stephen Colbert Mocks President Trump's Chocolate Cake Sales Pitch after Bombing Syria." *New York Daily News*, April 17, 2017b, www.

nydailynews.com/entertainment/tv/stephen-colbert-mocks-president-trump-chocolate-cake-article-1.3067107

Fleckenstein, Kristie S., Clay Spinuzzi, Rebecca J. Rickly, and Carole Clark Papper. "The Importance of Harmony: An Ecological Metaphor for Writing Research." *College Composition and Communication* 60, no. 2 (December 2008): 388–419.

Flegenheimer, Matt. "What's a 'Covfefe'? Trump Tweet Unites a Bewildered Nation." *The New York Times*, May 31, 3017, www.nytimes.com/2017/05/31/us/politics/covfefe-trump-twitter.html

Frankfurt, Harry G. "Donald Trump is BS, Says Expert in BS." *Time*, May 12, 2016, http://time.com/4321036/donald-trump-bs/

Frankfurt, Harry G. *On Bullshit*. 2005. Princeton, NJ: Princeton University Press.

Fredal, James. 2011. "Rhetoric and Bullshit." *College English* 73, no. 3 (January): 243–59.

Freire, Paulo. *Pedagogy of the Oppressed*. New York: Continuum, 2000. First published in 1968 by Seabury Press (New York).

Freud, Sigmund. *The Psychopathology of Everyday Life*. Translated by Anthea Bell. Introduction by Paul Keegan. New York: Penguin, 2003. First published in English in 1914 by T. Fisher Unwin (London).

Gabbatt, Adam. "Anti-Protest Bills Would 'Attack the Right to Speak Out' under Donald Trump." *Guardian*, May 8, 2017, www.theguardian.com/world/2017/may/08/donald-trump-anti-protest-bills

Gomez, Luis. "Trump Won't Prosecute Clinton, Supporters Rip 'Broken Promise.'" *San Diego Union-Tribune*, November 22, 2016, www.sandiegouniontribune.com/opinion/the-conversation/sd-no-special-prosecutor-to-go-after-hillary-clinton-says-trump-campaign-spokeswoman-20161122-htmlstory.html

Gray, Rosie. "Trump Defends White-Nationalist Protesters: 'Some Very Fine People on Both Sides.'" *The Atlantic*, August 15, 2017, www.theatlantic.com/politics/archive/2017/08/trump-defends-white-nationalist-protesters-some-very-fine-people-on-both-sides/537012/

Gries, Laurie. 2015. *Still Life with Rhetoric: A New Materialist Approach for Visual Rhetorics*. Logan, UT: Utah State University Press.

Griffiths, James. "Trump Says He Was Considering This 'Russia Thing' When He Fired Comey." *CNN*, May 12, 2017, www.cnn.com/2017/05/12/politics/trump-comey-russia-thing/index.html

Hardt, Michael and Sandro Mezzadra. "The Power of the Movements Facing Trump." *Occupy.com*, November 21, 2016, www.occupy.com/article/power-movements-facing-trump#sthash.cqKfZdE8.okcao26E.dpbs

Hariman, Robert, and John Louis Lucaites. 2007. *No Caption Needed: Iconic Photographs, Public Culture, and Liberal Democracy*. Chicago, IL: University of Chicago Press.

Heidegger, Martin. 1977. *"The Question Concerning Technology" and Other Essays*. New York: Harper.

Henderson, Barney. "President-Elect Donald Trump Blames Media for Inciting 'Unfair' Protests: Friday U. S. Election Briefing." *Telegraph*, November 11, 2016, www.telegraph.co.uk/news/2016/11/11/president-elect-donald-trump-turns-his-attention-on-cabinet-appo/

Henderson, Nia-Malika. "April Ryan Asked the Most Important Question of the Trump Presidency." *CNN*, March 30, 2017, www.cnn.com/2017/03/29/politics/april-ryan-sean-spicer-trump-presidency/index.html

Hesson, Ted. "Trump Launches War on Unions." *Politico*, December 8, 2016, www.politico.com/story/2016/12/trump-unions-war-232382

Hirshfeld-Davis, Julie. "Trump's Cabinet, with a Prod, Extols the 'Blessing' of Serving Him." *The New York Times*, June 12, 2017, www.nytimes.com/2017/06/12/us/politics/trump-boasts-of-record-setting-pace-of-activity.html

Hunt, Emily. "Trump's Inauguration Crowd: Sean Spicer's Claims Versus the Evidence." *Guardian*, January 22, 2017, www.theguardian.com/us-news/2017/jan/22/trump-inauguration-crowd-sean-spicers-claims-versus-the-evidence

Izadi, Elahe. "'Mr. Trump, Are You Trolling Us?': Baldwin Returns to SNL with Parody of Trump's Holt Interview." *Washington Post*, May 14, 2017, www.washingtonpost.com/news/arts-and-entertainment/wp/2017/05/14/mr-trump-are-you-trolling-us-alec-baldwin-once-again-returns-to-snl-as-trump/?utm_term=.5ac0bd8e831f

Jarvie, Jenny. "Texas's Ban on 'Sanctuary Cities' Could Put Police in Jail if They Fail to Enforce Immigration Holds." *Los Angeles Times*, May 4, 2017, www.latimes.com/nation/la-na-texas-sanctuary-law-20170504-story.html

Katz, Celeste. "White House Claims Trump Keeps 'The World from Chaos.'" *Newsweek*, October 6, 2017, www.newsweek.com/donald-trump-chaos-sarah-huckabee-sanders-international-relations-679952

Keneally, Meghan. "What Trump Previously Said about the 2005 'Access Hollywood' Tape That He's Now Questioning." *ABC News*, November 27, 2017, http://abcnews.go.com/US/trump-previously-2005-access-hollywood-tape-now-questioning/story?id=51406745

Kenny, Caroline. "Poll: Trump's Approval Rating Drops to 36%." *CNN Politics*, July 17, 2017, www.cnn.com/2017/07/16/politics/trump-poll-abc-wapo-approval/index.html

Klein, Naomi. 2017. *No Is Not Enough: Resisting Trump's Shock Politics and Winning the World We Need*. Chicago, IL: Haymarket.

LaCapra, Dominick. 2001. *Writing History, Writing Trauma*. Baltimore, MD: Johns Hopkins University Press.

Landler, Mark, and Richard Pérez-Peña. "Flynn Was Brought Down by Illegal Leaks to News Media, Trump Says." *The New York Times*, February 15, 2017, www.nytimes.com/2017/02/15/us/politics/trump-condemns-leaks-to-news-media-in-a-twitter-flurry.html

Lee, Kurtis. "Trump Hotel Employees in Las Vegas Secure a Contract with Powerful Culinary Workers Union." *Los Angeles Times*, December 21, 2016, www.latimes.com/politics/la-na-pol-trump-hotel-culinary-union-20161221-story.html

Lewis, Sinclair. *It Can't Happen Here*. New York: Signet, 2014. First published in 1935 by Doubleday (New York).

Mascaro, Lisa. "McCain, Two Other GOP Senators Join Democrats to Reject Last-Ditch Effort to Repeal Obamacare." *Los Angeles Times*, July 27, 2017, www.latimes.com/politics/la-na-pol-obamacare-senate-vote-20170728-story.html

Mayer, Jane. "Documenting Trump's Abuse of Women." *New Yorker*, October 24, 2016, www.newyorker.com/magazine/2016/10/24/documenting-trumps-abuse-of-women.

Mazzetti, Mark and Charlie Savage. "Leaked Draft of Executive Order Could Revise C.I.A. Prisons." *The New York Times*, January 25, 2017, www.nytimes.com/2017/01/25/us/politics/executive-order-leaked-draft-national-security-trump-administration.html?_r=0

McCauslund, Phil. "Donald Trump Explains Sweden Terror Comment that Baffled a Nation." *NBC News*, February 20, 2017, www.nbcnews.com/news/us-news/donald-trump-explains-sweden-terror-comment-baffled-nation-n723006

Meyerson, Harold. "Donald Trump Can Kill the American Union." *Washington Post*, November 23, 2016, www.washingtonpost.com/posteverything/wp/2016/11/23/donald-trump-could-kill-the-american-union/?utm_term=.6e2a5117c6bd

Mishra, Pankaj. 2017. *The Age of Anger: A History of the Present*. New York: Farrar, Straus, and Giroux.

Morris, Charles E. III and Stephen Howard Browne (Eds.). 2013. *Readings on the Rhetoric of Social Protest*. 3rd ed. State College, PA: Strata.

Nevins, Jake. "Late-Night Hosts Blast Trump's 'Crazy and Cruel' Ban on Transgender Troops." *Guardian*, July 27, 2017, www.theguardian.com/culture/2017/jul/27/late-night-hosts-blast-trumps-crazy-and-cruel-ban-on-transgender-troops

Nianias, Helen. "Trump Responds to Merkel Criticism with Furious Tweet Saying Germany Does Not Pay Its Way." *The Telegraph*, May 30, 2017, www.telegraph.co.uk/news/2017/05/30/trump-responds-merkel-criticism-furious-tweet-saying-germany/

Oborne, Peter and Tom Roberts. "How Donald Trump Has Cheapened the Language of Politics through Twitter and Right-Wing Media Allies." *Independent*, June 29, 2017, www.independent.co.uk/news/long_reads/how-donald-trump-has-cheapened-the-language-of-politics-through-twitter-and-right-wing-media-allies-a7802626.html

Orwell, George. *1984*. London: Secker and Warburg, 1949.

Police Shootings 2017 Database. *Washington Post*, www.washingtonpost.com/graphics/national/police-shootings-2017/

Reuters. "Sarah Huckabee Sanders Scolds 'Fake News.'" June 27, 2017, www.reuters.com/video/2017/06/27/sarah-huckabee-sanders-scolds-fake-news?videoId=371976395

Rice, Jenny. 2015. "Disgusting Bullshit." *Rhetoric Society Quarterly* 45, no. 5 (November): 462–64.

Rice, Jenny. 2015. "Introductory Bullshit." *Rhetoric Society Quarterly* 45, no. 5 (November): 468–72.

Rosenthal, Brian M. "Police Criticize Trump for Urging Officers Not to Be 'Too Nice' with Suspects." *The New York Times*, July 29, 2017, www.nytimes.com/2017/07/29/nyregion/trump-police-too-nice.html

Shear, Michael D. and Michael S. Schmidt. "Trump, Offering No Evidence, Says Obama Tapped His Phones." *The New York Times*, March 4, 2017, www.nytimes.com/2017/03/04/us/politics/trump-obama-tap-phones.html

Smith, David, Ben Jacobs, and Tom McCarthy. "Sean Spicer Apologizes for 'Even Hitler Didn't Use Chemical Weapons' Gaffe." *Guardian*, April 12, 2017, www.theguardian.com/us-news/2017/apr/11/sean-spicer-hitler-chemical-weapons-holocaust-assad

Sullivan, John, Reis Thebault, Julie Tate, and Jennifer Jenkins. "Number of Fatal Shootings by Police is Nearly Identical to Last Year." *Washington Post*, July 31, 2017, www.washingtonpost.com/investigations/number-of-fatal-shootings-by-police-is-nearly-identical-to-last-year/2017/07/01/98726cc6-5b5f-11e7-9fc6-c7ef4bc58d13_story.html?utm_term=.14a39306d1d8

Suskind, Ron. "Faith, Certainty, and the Presidency of George W. Bush." *The New York Times*, October 17, 2004, www.nytimes.com/2004/10/17/magazine/faith-certainty-and-the-presidency-of-george-w-bush.html?_r=0

Taylor, Jessica. "'You Can Do Anything': In 2005 Tape, Trump Brags about Groping, Kissing Women." *NPR*, October 7, 2016, www.npr.org/2016/10/07/497087141/donald-trump-caught-on-tape-making-vulgar-remarks-about-women

Tillett, Emily. "Mexico Responds to Trump's Tweets on Border Wall, NAFTA." *CBSNews.com*, August 28, 2017, www.cbsnews.com/news/mexico-responds-to-trumps-tweets-on-border-wall-nafta/

United Auto Workers. "Trump's Words and Actions When It Comes to Workers: Workers Always Lose." June 10, 2016, http://uaw.org/trumps-words-and-actions-when-it-comes-to-workers-workers-always-lose/

Weaver, Matthew, Robert Booth, and Ben Jacobs. "Theresa May Condemns Trump's Retweets of UK Far-Right Leader's Anti-Muslim Videos." *Guardian*, November 29, 2017, www.theguardian.com/us-news/2017/nov/29/trump-account-retweets-anti-muslim-videos-of-british-far-right-leader

Wemple, Erik. "Sean Spicer Attempts to Trash CNN Correspondent Jim Acosta." *Washington Post*, January 31, 2017, www.washingtonpost.com/blogs/erik-wemple/wp/2017/01/ 31/sean-spicer-attempts-to-trash-cnn-correspondent-jim-acosta/?utm_term=.36d498f51915

Whitcomb, Dan. "U.S. Deaths by Police Gunfire on Track to Reach 1,000 by 2017." *Reuters*, July 1, 2017, www.reuters.com/article/us-usa-police-shooting-idUSKBN19M3ST

Yee, Vivian. "Judge Blocks Trump Effort to Withhold Money from Sanctuary Cities." *The New York Times*, April 25, 2017, www.nytimes.com/2017/04/25/us/judge-blocks-trump-sanctuary-cities.html

6

CRAZY, INSANE, NUT JOB, WACKO, BASKET CASE, AND PSYCHO

Donald Trump's Tweets Surrounding Mental Health Issues and Attacks on Media Personalities

Sarah Smith-Frigerio and J. Brian Houston

Stigma surrounding mental illness is one of the biggest concerns facing public mental health today (World Health Organization 2013). Stigmatizing beliefs about mental health issues can prevent those who are experiencing a mental health crisis from disclosing their concerns or symptoms to family and friends. It can also prevent individuals from seeking mental health treatment, which can result in worsening symptoms. Additionally, stigma can lead to individuals who are not experiencing a mental health concern to distance themselves from someone who is experiencing mental health symptomology and thus withhold assistance from that individual. This can extend to someone who is perceived to be exhibiting symptomology or has exhibited symptomology in the past (Weiner 1995). News and entertainment media depictions of mental health issues have been found to be particularly negative and stereotypical, and thus have potential to increase mental health stigma (Wahl 1992).

The most effective approach identified for combatting mental health stigma involves the development and implementation of anti-stigma communication campaigns and educational workshops. In fact, several national and governmental organizations, such as the U.S. Substance Abuse and Mental Health Service Administration (SAMHSA), have recommended the creation and implementation of communication campaigns aimed at decreasing "negative attitudes and discrimination toward people with mental illness and/or substance use disorders and their family members" (2014, 26). Despite these recommendations, communicators often find themselves fighting for funding, fighting against well-ingrained stereotypes, and fighting to get messages in front of as many individuals as possible while ensuring the messages are culturally appropriate and are understood by the audience.

In addition to these challenges, with the election of U.S. President Donald Trump, mental health communicators in the U.S. now face a national political leader who may propagate stigmatizing messages regarding mental illness. The National Alliance on Mental Illness (NAMI) describes stigmatizing discourse as "epithets, nicknames, jokes, advertisements, and slurs that refer to persons with serious mental illnesses" (2016, 2) and has condemned this type of language as "acts of stigma and discrimination directed against persons with mental illnesses, whether by intent, ignorance, or insensitivity" (2016, 2). News coverage of President Trump has suggested that his discourse concerning mental illness and individuals experiencing mental health issues is highly negative and stigmatizing (Nuzzi 2016), but is this truly the case? How prevalent is this type of language in President Trump's public discourse, particularly on Twitter, which Trump has described as his medium of choice (Keith 2016)? And what implications might this discourse have for anti-stigma campaigns and efforts in the U.S.? This study sought to explore these issues with the following research questions:

RQ1: What discursive practices have President Trump employed when referencing mental illness in campaign and presidential messaging and on Twitter during and after his presidential campaign?
RQ2: Are these discursive practices stigmatizing, and if so, how?

Before examining the discourse of President Trump on and off Twitter, it is necessary to briefly discuss the history of anti-stigma communication efforts as it relates to mental health, as well as the importance of discourse itself in defining, controlling, and mitigating mental illness.

Development of Anti-stigma Messaging Campaigns

Anti-stigma messaging campaigns aimed at mental health issues began during the 1970s and 1980s, when most large psychiatric hospitals were closing and mental healthcare was transitioning to smaller community-based service providers in the U.S. (NAMI n.d.). These first small campaigns were implemented in an inconsistent and haphazard approach. Some of the best known national anti-stigma campaigns addressed depressive disorders in the 1990s (Byrne 2000). Research focusing on attitudes toward mental health concerns identified shifts among public opinion to viewing mental illness and substance abuse disorders as medical problems requiring treatment, particularly for depression (Pescosolido et al. 2010). That shift may have been related to the fact that these anti-stigma campaigns were introduced at an optimal time, when advertising of pharmaceutical drugs was first allowed in both television and print ads. Prozac and Paxil, prescription medications originally developed to treat depression, were some of the most prominent pharmaceutical advertising campaigns introduced after the relaxation of regulations surrounding prescription drug advertising (Elliot 1997; Payton and Thoits 2011). While stigmatized beliefs and discriminatory behavioral intentions regarding depressive disorders have decreased since anti-stigma campaigns addressing depression began over twenty years ago, other major disorders—such as substance abuse disorders and schizophrenia—have likely increased in the amount of stigma and discriminatory behavioral intentions in recent years (Parcesepe and Cabassa 2013). Stigmatizing news and entertainment content about these major disorders abound, and there have been few efforts to develop anti-stigma campaigns beyond the scope of depressive and anxiety disorders (Stuart 2016).

In 2007, *The Lancet*, a global medical research journal, called for the development of regionally specific mental health communication and education campaigns, along with the national policies to support those campaigns (Horton 2007). Many national organizations across the U.S., the United Kingdom, and Canada have answered the charge, and so has the World Health Organization. Primarily, these campaigns have attempted to alter the discourse surrounding mental illness from one of personal responsibility and blame to one of medicalization and biologically based causation (i.e. external causes and diminished personal responsibility) (Clark 2014). Policies in the U.S. have been developed and millions of dollars have been dedicated to anti-stigma workshops and communication campaigns implemented by public health professionals (Stuart 2016). Nevertheless, in 2016, *The Lancet* followed up on progress and found the approach was not effective. *The Lancet's* recommendation was to dedicate more funding in the future, effectively doubling down on the approach, to overcome the pervasive consequences of stigmatizing messaging found around the world (Summergrad 2016).

Anti-stigma health communication campaigns are believed to provide an important function in breaking down what Corrigan (2000) constitutes as the stigma to prejudice to discrimination sequence. This sequence, based on the conceptualization of attribution theory developed by Weiner (1995), has been a common approach in researching responses to individuals suffering from a mental health crisis. One example of the sequence is when stigmatizing messages in local and national news media, including depictions of the dangerousness or criminality of an individual experiencing a mental health crisis, leads viewers to develop prejudicial beliefs that individuals with mental health concerns must be socially distanced from everyday society, and placed in hospitals or prisons. This, in turn, leads to the development of discriminatory behaviors and policy to keep mentally ill individuals removed from society. Discriminatory behaviors can include things like refusing to provide an individual with a history of mental illness jobs, housing, and other professional and social opportunities.

Many scholars have examined how to counter stigmatizing messages to prevent the development of prejudicial beliefs as well as discriminatory behaviors. Corrigan (1998) and Hinshaw (2007) suggest that there are three main areas in which stigmatizing messages can be resisted: through protest; educational workshops; and personal contact with individuals who have experienced mental health concerns. Corrigan (2012) and Hinshaw (2007) further break down the best goals for each approach (i.e. protests are effective for seeking awareness or recognition of an issue), as well as the likely effectiveness of each approach. The most effective approach overall appears to be personal contact with individuals who have experienced a mental health concern (Rüsch et al. 2005). Face-to-face contact with individuals who have recovered from a mental health concern and are willing to share their experiences is somewhat impractical to implement from a public communication perspective, despite prevalence rates of nearly one in five adult Americans dealing with a mental health concern in any given year (NIMH n.d.). As a result of this impracticality, significant attention has been given to incorporating the personal narratives of individuals who have experienced a mental health concern in mass media channels, such as news coverage and entertainment media. Some examples of these endeavors include the development of media guides for journalists who are reporting on issues involving mental health concerns that provide recommendations for how journalists can best represent individuals they are covering (Team Up 2012). Additionally, Hinshaw (2007) proposes that personal narratives should involve everyday individuals, instead of celebrities so that individuals who read or view such content are able to relate their lived experiences to the individuals providing their perspectives and accounts in the anti-stigma messages.

There is evidence that anti-stigma campaigns involving personal accounts from individuals who have experienced a mental health concerns are effective. For instance, Corrigan and colleagues (2015) demonstrate that higher levels of familiarity with mental illness is one of the best indicators of an individual's propensity to not engage in stigmatized thoughts, prejudicial beliefs, and discriminatory behaviors related to mental health issues. Familiarity levels can range from having no previous contact with someone with mental health issues, to watching a documentary on mental health, to knowing a coworker or friend with a mental health issue, to having a nuclear family member (or themselves) dealing with a mental illness. Anti-stigmatizing content can help develop and reinforce familiarity levels among audience members. Additionally, levels of familiarity can provide a buffer against stereotypical or stigmatizing content so that individuals with higher levels of familiarity will reject stigmatizing content.

Not engaging in the pathway from stigmatized ideas to prejudicial beliefs to acts of discrimination may have positive impacts for both those who experience a mental health concern and those around them. Familiarity could make individuals more likely to seek mental health treatment, if needed. It could also mitigate mental health concerns from developing into serious mental illnesses. Familiarity could provide an avenue for supporting continued research and funding at national and local levels. It could allow those who have experienced a mental health concern to enter recovery, continue on in their professional and social lives, and overall, lead successful lives. Anti-stigma campaign mental health campaigns can be effective. However, campaigns may be less effective when public or political leaders are concurrently providing stigmatizing discourse that is widely consumed and shared.

Role of Discourse in Conceptualizing and Controlling Mental Illness

According to Foucault (1988), discourse has always been involved in the construction of what we define as mental illness and how we seek to either control or mitigate mental illness in individuals. Put more simply, in order for one to study how mental illness has been defined, or how those who may experience a mental health concern are treated or controlled, it is necessary to understand the discourses of power surrounding and related to these constructs. For instance, Foucault points out that through the Renaissance era, mental illness was not discussed as abnormal or deviant. In fact, it was oftentimes seen as a supernatural or religious experience. It was only in the Age of Reason that those who exhibited these types of eccentric, abnormal, or deviant behaviors were considered to be problematic and in need of removal from society.

Foucault (1988) argues that in today's medical era of managing mental illness, the goal oftentimes is not to treat or cure an individual who is experiencing a mental health concern, but to manage and control both the individual and their disease. In other words, the ways in which we socially construct the definitions of mental illness, as well as the appropriate responses to individuals with mental illness, are identified in the ways we speak and write about mental illness and those individuals with mental health concerns. Goffman (1968) explored a similar proposition. He noted that once a society has labeled something as a mental illness, it then becomes the charge of society to craft a response, through communicative acts, like policies, that both regulates the behaviors of those affected individuals and alerts them to their social roles. These arguments place significant importance upon public stigmatizing messages about mental health, as well as anti-stigma mental health communication campaigns. The ways we communicate about mental health within our society determine our attitudes about what is acceptable or unacceptable regarding mental health. Additionally, any changes in how we view and approach mental health issues will be the result of changes in our discourse and discursive acts.

Methodology: Examining the Discourse of Donald Trump

To develop a better understanding of U.S. President Donald Trump's discursive depictions of mental illness, in campaign and presidential messaging and on Twitter, we conducted two different analyses. The first analysis involved discourse analysis of news coverage and quotes from Trump's campaign and presidential messaging, beginning with the Republican presidential election primaries in June 2015 and ending in August 2017. The second analysis examined discourse in President Trump's Twitter feed related to mental health or mental illness. These complementary analyses demonstrate that Trump uses stigmatizing language in both his campaign/presidential discourse and on Twitter. Additionally, the analyses demonstrate that Trump may view individuals who are experiencing mental health concerns in a negative light, that he may perceive them to be dangerous and adversarial, and that he may not fully understand the scope of mental health disorders. The implications for mental illness stigma and the consequences for anti-stigma mental health campaigns are then considered in the discussion section of this chapter.

Campaign and Presidential Discourse

We first began with an analysis of Trump's campaign and presidential messaging related to mental health issues. To access these campaign and presidential messages, we searched news media coverage relating to Trump during the timeframe of June 2015 through August 2017 using the search terms "Trump" and "mental illness" through Google Scholar, with the news story filter. This search engine was chosen as the simplest and most comprehensive means for identifying news coverage of Trump's messages during his campaign and the first part of his presidency. From this search, we were able to discern eight distinctive instances of news media coverage concerning Trump's stance and the discourse he engaged in surrounding issues of mental health, including two significant instances that occurred before the campaign began, but were covered during the Republican primaries.

Those two incidents that occurred before the announcement of Trump's presidential campaign first involved criticism about a contestant on the television show, *Celebrity Apprentice*, which Donald Trump hosted, and second, an ongoing feud with television celebrity Rosie O'Donnell. Following critical remarks made by O'Donnell on the television show, *The View*, in late 2006 and early 2007, Trump made derogatory remarks about O'Donnell, including comments about her disclosure of her depressive disorder, stating at one appearance: "If I looked like Rosie, I'd struggle with depression, too" (Kaczynski 2016). Later, at another speaking engagement, Trump stated that, "if (O'Donnell) stopped looking in the mirror, I think she'd stop being so depressed" (Nuzzi 2016). Not only did this discourse disparage O'Donnell based on her physical appearance but it also trivialized depression as something that could be cured by avoidance or caring less about one's appearance. In another instance that occurred during *Celebrity Apprentice*, Trump eliminated (as part of the show's contest) a contestant named Stacie for being described as "crazy" by two of her teammates. During the scene in which Stacie was eliminated from the televised contest, Trump stated, "the first thing they've agreed on is that you're crazy. Stacie, if you have a problem, I don't want you running one of my companies"

(Nuzzi 2016). He then went on to state that he "just can't have a loose cannon on my hands" (2016). Again, Trump's message to Stacie disparaged and discredited her mental health. This discourse implies the unpredictability of individuals perceived as having a mental health concern and illustrates a tendency to dismiss such individuals, in both a figurative sense and a literal sense of terminating employment. Additionally, it is important to point out that if this elimination were to occur outside the realm of reality television, it would likely result in the violation of federal discrimination laws, such as the Americans with Disabilities Act (U.S. Department of Labor 1990). It is not legal to fire someone on the basis of a perceived disorder or disability, with no regard for potential accommodations or the individual's ability to complete job-related tasks.

Three discursive instances addressing mental health issues occurred during the 2015 Republican presidential primary campaign. The first was Trump's repeated remarks about primary competitor Ted Cruz's wife, Heidi Cruz. These remarks were made on Twitter, during campaign rallies, and during interviews. Trump repeatedly threatened to "spill the beans" on a mental health concern Mrs. Cruz had sought treatment for and had recovered from several years before (Nuzzi 2016). These threats demonstrate Trump's use of mental health status to discredit or disparage another individual—in this instance, Ted Cruz, by casting suspicion on his wife's well-being and competency. This also occurred in a more recent incident involving former FBI Director James Comey. Trump allegedly referred to former FBI Director Comey as a "nutjob" with delegates representing the Russian government during a meeting in the oval office in May 2017. More specifically, it was reported that Trump stated, "I just fired the head of the F.B.I. He was crazy, a real nut job" (Apuzzo et al. 2017). This alleged exchange referenced the possibility the FBI may begin an investigation into claims that Trump's campaign team colluded with the Russian government to garner an unfair advantage in the 2016 presidential election (2017). Again, this appears to be a discursive act on the President's part to discredit a political opponent, and justify his actions to remove Comey from his sphere.

The other two occurrences of discourse involving mental illness during the primaries involve discussions about gun control. In one instance, Trump described gun-free zones, such as schools and government buildings, as "target practice for sickos and the mentally ill" (Nuzzi 2016). The other instance involved appearances on NBC's *Meet the Press* and ABC's *This Week*. In both of the television shows, Trump expresses his opinion that guns don't matter in acts of mass violence because there are "millions of sick people in the world" (Elkin 2015). Additionally, Trump goes on to say that these sick people are always going to "come through the cracks" (Vitali 2015) while arguing that further gun control measures or increased levels of institutionalization would not solve the problem (Elkin 2015). This discourse is stigmatizing for several reasons, but most importantly for its accusations that acts of mass violence are only committed by individuals experiencing mental health crises, or that individuals with mental health concerns are much more likely to commit violent acts. This has not been found to be the case by researchers. Appelbaum and Swanson (2010) describe that individuals experiencing a mental health crisis are much more likely to be the victims of violent crimes than they are to be the perpetrators of violent crimes. In fact, individuals experiencing significant mental health concerns are considerably less likely to engage in violent acts than the general population (2010). Additionally, this discourse provides a secondary message that individuals cannot be treated successfully for mental illness, even in an institutional or inpatient hospital setting as, according to Trump, hospitalization/inpatient treatment would not even work.

The next incident occurred after Trump was selected as the Republican nominee for the presidency. In a speech to veterans concerning increases in the rate of suicide among veterans, Trump included comments about post-traumatic stress disorder (PTSD): "When you talk about the mental health problems, when people come back from war and combat, they see things that maybe a lot of the folks in this room have seen many times over and you're strong and can handle it, but a lot of people can't handle it" (Waldman 2016). In this statement, Trump suggests that veterans who are diagnosed with PTSD lack the strength to endure what soldiers may experience on the battlefield. These comments are factually inaccurate and derogatory toward veterans, as the development of PTSD is not related to one's mental strength or grit (Cummings 2016). The claim that mental illness results from personal responsibility, as opposed to biological reasons or the experience of trauma, is highly stigmatizing (Cummings 2016; Holmes 2016). Thus, in using this language, Trump constructs an idea of mental illness as resulting from personal failings and weaknesses, and thus negatively depicts veterans who may have been traumatized during military deployment.

It is important to note one additional instance that was not directly related to Trump, but to his former chief strategist, Steve Bannon, who worked in close proximity to the President, while in that position. Following the announcement by the Trump transition team that Bannon was to become chief strategist, *The Hill* published email exchanges from 2015 concerning a piece of mental health legislation that was being supported by Paul Ryan, the current Republican Speaker of the House (Swan 2016). At this time, Bannon was the head of Breitbart news, a conservative editorial website. Other individuals at Breitbart wanted Bannon to consider a story on this piece of legislation, despite the fact that Bannon disliked Ryan. His response via email stated that he had a cure for mental illness that would not require a piece of legislation, namely that people should just "spank their children more" (Holmes and Marans 2016, para 5). In this response, we again see the attribution of personal responsibility, and even disobedience, to mental health concerns, despite research that has demonstrated that spanking children or performing other acts of corporal punishment have been linked to increases in the prevalence of mental illness in children and in adults, not decreases (American Academy of Pediatrics 2012). This is problematic in the way mental health concerns are described, and in that the statement advocates for behavior linked to the development of mental health concerns.

In the eight instances briefly described above, we see a preponderance of stigmatizing language used to describe mental health concerns. Oftentimes, these discursive practices are employed to personally attack other individuals. They all include the attribution of personal responsibility to the individual who may be experiencing a mental health concern, which is the type of messaging that anti-stigma mental health messaging campaigns seek to dispel. Also, it is important to note that some of this discourse discredits evidence-based treatment protocols, and includes factually inaccurate information regarding mental health disorders or symptomology, as can be seen in Trump's remarks on gun control.

Twitter Discourse

In order to analyze over 35,000 tweets that were generated from President Trump's Twitter account for potential discursive techniques involving the use of stigmatizing language about mental health concerns, an advanced search of the @realDonaldTrump verified account was conducted through the Twitter platform, using the following search terms: mental, crazy, insane, nutjob, wacko, basket case, breakdown, meltdown, and psycho. These terms were selected for their likelihood to be present in the Twitter account based on media coverage of President Trump's Twitter activity, as well as a common understanding of their use as being stigmatizing. This search resulted in 124 tweets from July 2011 through August 2017. Only the tweets that were written or retweeted by Trump were analyzed. Replies to Trump's tweets were not analyzed unless they were retweeted by Trump. Also, it must be noted that this may not represent the entirety of the account's tweets involving the search terms, as it has been reported that President Trump deletes some tweets (ProPublica n.d.).

We analyzed tweets with an iterative coding process where researchers read through the collected data multiple times, coding each tweet line by line, and then working to collapse the codes developed from this process into larger themes based on the discursive intent of Trump's tweets including negative and stigmatizing language involving mental health issues. Initial codes included the following: determining whether tweets attributed personal or external responsibility and control to mental illness symptomology; whether individuals with mental illness were perceived as dangerous, criminal, or in need of social distancing; whether the use of potentially stigmatizing language appeared to be an overt or casual act; and whether the use of potentially stigmatizing language was an attempt to disparage or discredit a political opponent.

Emergent codes included determining whether the tweet focused on Trump's involvement with the show *Celebrity Apprentice* ($n = 21$) or whether the tweets focused on politics and Trump's campaign ($n = 88$). Additionally, emergent coding included determining whether specific derogatory terms were used for specific populations, namely based on gender (male or female). Finally, there were a few tweets present ($n = 7$) that could not be coded due to either a lack of specificity within the tweet itself (e.g. "That was insane!") or because a different meaning was intended for the search term (e.g. the word meltdown being used to describe the financial meltdown and not a mental health concern).

The results of both initial and emergent coding were instrumental in theme generation. This process of iterative coding and theme generation is well-suited to exploratory empirical study of language selection and discursive practices. The themes identified through this iterative coding process are described in detail below.

Overtly Attacking Individuals

Our analysis demonstrated that Trump often employed stigmatizing terms concerning mental illness on Twitter to attack individuals he perceives to be a political threat, and that he does so overtly. Overt here is defined as directing a stigmatizing term or terms toward a person or policy, which Trump did in approximately 56% of the tweets. These individuals often included political opponents, journalists, and political pundits. For instance, Trump posted several tweets aimed at Megyn Kelly, then a Fox News television journalist, from March 15–19, 2016, for what he perceived to be negative coverage of his campaign on her show. This included tweets such as "If crazy @megynkelly didn't cover me so much on her terrible show, her ratings would totally tank. She is so average in so many ways!" (Trump March 19, 2016) and "Crazy @megynkelly says I don't (won't) go on her show and she still gets good ratings. But almost all of her shows are negative hits on me!" (Trump March 19, 2016).

Trump used the derogatory terms we searched for on a casual basis in tweets approximately 36% of the time. Casual use was not directed toward a person or policy. An example of casual use of a stigmatizing term in a tweet is "In order to try and deflect the horror and stupidity of the Wikileakes disaster, the Dems said maybe it is Russia dealing with Trump. Crazy!" (Trump July 26, 2016). In this tweet, the term "crazy" is not directed specifically to Democrats or an individual, and therefore was coded as casual use of the term.

The term "crazy" was used most often (63%) of all the terms searched in Trump's tweets. Men were more likely than women to be the recipient of Twitter attacks from Trump (40%–15%), but women were more likely than men to be described as crazy (78%–47%). A notable exception to this trend is Democratic presidential candidate Bernie Sanders, who Trump referred to as crazy in three of the four times he referenced him on Twitter. For example: "If Crooked Hillary Clinton can't close the deal on Crazy Bernie, how is she going to take on China, Russia, ISIS and all of the others?" (Trump May 13, 2016). It is interesting to note that an attempt to emasculate Bernie Sanders as a presidential candidate using the term crazy, which again, was more often used in reference to women, may be at play here.

All in all, President Trump employed the use of stigmatizing language surrounding issues of mental illness to attack those he perceived to be his opponents on Twitter. The next theme describes how the President did this in very specific ways.

Seeking to Discredit and Disparage

Trump appears to have sought to discredit and disparage his opponents with his stigmatizing language on Twitter, in an effort to make himself appear stronger. In the analyzed tweets, we found that attempts to discredit individuals or policies were present in approximately 54% of his tweets, whereas attempts to disparage opponents were present approximately 23% of the time. Discrediting was defined as the attempt to question or undermine the authority or reputation of an individual or policy, whereas disparaging was defined as categorical efforts to belittle or put down those with whom Trump did not agree. Examples of discrediting tweets include an attack against Ted Cruz: "Wow, Lyin' Ted Cruz really went wacko today. Made all sorts of crazy charges. Can't function under pressure - not very presidential. Sad!" [sic] (Trump May 3, 2016). Here, we can see how the use of the terms wacko and crazy aid Trump in questioning Cruz's ability to function, and how this undermines his viability as a candidate for the presidency. One example of Trump attempting to disparage an individual was "Dummy writer @tonyschwartz, who wanted to do a second book with me for years (I said no), is now a hostile basket case who feels jilted!" (Trump September 9, 2016). The name calling here was likely in response to critical remarks made by Swartz about his time working with Trump on a prior project and did not appear to be an attempt to question Schwartz's ability as a writer.

What is the purpose of using stigmatizing language to discredit or disparage individuals on Twitter? One clue can be found in some of the terms, such as "stupid," "dumb," "average," "disaster," and "lying," that were frequently coupled with stigmatizing terms in the analyzed tweets. These can be found in nearly all of the example tweets presented earlier in this chapter. The juxtaposition of words questioning the morals, strength, competence, and intelligence of individuals, along with their perceived mental state, occurred repeatedly in President Trump's tweets. Additional examples included the way Trump referred to Mika Brzezinski, co-host of the morning cable news show, *Morning Joe*. Tweets concerning Brzezinski include "Just heard that crazy and very dumb @morningmika had a mental breakdown while talking about me on the low ratings @Morning_Joe. Joe a mess!" (Trump September 2, 2016). Also, "I heard poorly rated @Morning_Joe speaks badly of me (don't watch anymore). Then how come low I.Q. Crazy Mika, along with Psycho Joe, came. (Trump June 29, 2017)...to Mar-a-Lago 3 nights in a row around New Year's Eve, and insisted on joining me. She was bleeding badly from a face-lift. I said no!"

(Trump June 29, 2017) [two-part tweet]. The final theme present in our analysis of Trump's tweets speaks to why mental health concerns are tied so closely to other perceived failings in his discourse.

Linking Mental Illness to Personal Failings

Trump linked mental illness to personal failings or a lack of control in his Twitter discourse. When coding tweets containing stigmatizing terms, our initial codes included determining whether personal control and responsibility or external control and responsibility were present in the tweets. Personal control and responsibility, or the idea that the symptomology of mental illness is well within a person's control and that they must do something to cause this symptomology, are described by Weiner's (1995) attribution theory as being highly stigmatizing. External responsibility, such as brain chemistry or environmental factors, and the perceived uncontrollability of the individual's symptoms are associated with lower levels of stigmatization. In our analysis, President Trump associated personal control and responsibility with stigmatizing language in approximately 68% of his tweets, often by coupling it with other negative personal characteristics. Put more simply, it appears that an individual would not be seen as "crazy" or "insane" if that individual had not lied, shown weakness, or most importantly, criticized Trump. In no tweets did Trump associate these terms with external responsibility or control.

Additionally, Trump coupled this association with personal control and responsibility with themes of dangerousness, criminality, or the need to be socially distanced in approximately 25% of the tweets. This is the type of language that has been identified as problematic in the past (see Wahl 1992) and that anti-stigma campaigns seek to disrupt. Examples include a tweet when President Trump equated President Obama's refusal to shut down all international flights during the height of the Ebola epidemic with the perceived mental instability of President Obama: "I am starting to think that there is something seriously wrong with President Obama's mental health. Why won't he stop the flights. Psycho!" (Trump October 16, 2014). Another example involves a tweet where Trump advocated for individuals to attack a woman on Twitter for what he perceived to be her role in a German man's suicide while piloting a plane full of passengers: "The girlfriend of Lubitz, the wacko co-pilot who took down the plane, knew he was insane and should have reported him. Put her through hell" (Trump March 29, 2015). Not only do we find evidence of Trump promoting discourse that incorrectly purports that the majority of individuals with mental health concerns are dangerous and criminal; in this instance, we see him calling for action to be taken against individuals associated with those who have experienced a mental health concern as a form of punishment.

In analyzing President Trump's Twitter account and its use of these stigmatizing words in the disparagement and discrediting of individuals with whom

Trump disagrees, it appears these terms are used as a discursive practice to delegitimize individuals by associating them with mental instability, danger-ousness, and incompetency. In the following discussion, we argue that this use of stigmatizing language presents threats to the progress made by anti-stigma campaign work since the 1990s.

Discussion and Conclusion

In summary, the analysis of both Trump's campaign and presidential discourse, as well as his language choices and discursive practices on Twitter demonstrate a level of discourse that is highly stigmatizing of mental health issues. Individ-uals whom Trump disagrees with are described as mentally ill or unstable in an effort to discredit or disparage them as political opponents and individuals. Trump used discourses of power to equate mental illness with individuals who do not agree with him as a means of dismissing those individuals and their stances. This pattern was most prevalent in President Trump's Twitter feed, where he often used derogatory terms associated with mental health concerns as a means of responding to individuals he may have perceived as having criti-cized him or his campaign.

Additionally, mental illness or mental health concerns, according to Trump's discourse, are based on personal shortcomings and responsibility instead of being attributed to biologically based causation or the experience of traumatic events. Individuals are to blame for their behaviors, as well as any other perceived weak-ness or shortcoming, according to Trump's discourse. Even when Trump was not personally attacking an individual or group on Twitter, this became evident in his comments to veterans concerning PTSD. In his estimation, some people aren't strong enough to handle things that may often be seen on the battlefield.

The idea that mental health concerns cannot or should not be treated with evidence-based practices fit with the belief that a mental illness can be at-tributed to personal responsibilities or shortcomings, as Weiner (1995) discussed in his attribution model. In some instances, such as Trump's feud with Rosie O'Donnell, Trump trivializes disorders, such as depression. In other instances, particularly in his discourse surrounding mass shootings and gun control, Trump embraces a discourse that states treatment does not work and that even intensive inpatient treatment is not effective. Coupled with Trump's support of the Republican party's recent attempt to repeal the Affordable Care Act—which included the proposed removal of many advances toward mental health parity, such as mandatory coverage for mental illness and substance abuse, and the expansion of Medicaid for those who are incapacitated by serious mental illness (Warnke 2017)—and a proposed budget that cuts many social safety net programs geared toward improved mental health and well-being for vulnerable populations, we see that Trump's campaign discourse appears closely related to his policy initiatives.

In essence, it seems that Trump believes individuals experiencing a mental health concern can only be socially distanced from others because of their perceived dangerousness, criminality, unpredictability, and incompetence. For instance, we see this most clearly in his handling of individuals like Stacie on *Celebrity Apprentice*, whom he eliminated as part of the televised contest because her behaviors were reported by other contestants to be "crazy."

In nearly every instance mentioned above, Trump's discourse undermines the work of anti-stigma mental health messaging campaigns. These campaigns routinely attempt to dispel myths about personal responsibility and controllability for mental illness. They seek to alert individuals to treatment options and the effectiveness of evidence-based treatment. They aim to share information that refutes false information regarding the dangerousness or criminality of individuals experiencing a mental health crisis, which, in turn, allows us as a society to view individuals with mental illness as something more than a trope or negative stereotype. They advocate for the understanding of individuals who have experienced mental health concerns as whole persons, and not simply defined by their disorder, but as individuals who can effectively seek treatment and subsequently lead successful lives (Hinshaw 2007; Corrigan 2012). Given that very few individuals have confronted Trump for his consistent use of stigmatizing language and the perpetuation of prejudicial beliefs concerning mental illness, we can see that not only is the use of such stigmatizing language still prevalent today, it appears it is still accepted in our society.

This illustrates the challenge that mental health communicators who are working on anti-stigma campaigns have in front of them in 2018. It may be that mental health communication professionals will need to develop different ways to combat stigma in their future campaigns, in order to break the cycle of stigmatized stereotypes, prejudicial beliefs, and discriminatory behaviors. They may also need to consider how best to counteract the stigmatizing narratives presented by persons in positions of significant power.

There are some limitations to this study. This research included a handful of discursive instances, as reported in the media, and from Twitter. Future studies should add further nuance to of our understanding of President Trump's discursive style when it comes to language involving mental illness. As President Trump's term continues, there are opportunities to add to the data corpus under study—both in his Twitter posts and official presidential communication. The discourse analysis presented here is a brief overview of Trump's discourse on mental illness. Additional analysis of his discursive practices is warranted, especially when it comes to discerning his intentionality; his use of stigmatizing language to discredit and disparage those he perceives as opponents, as well as his reliance on discursive measures to undermine and control his perceived opponents, occurs in a very Foucaultian sense (1998).

Also, this is just one small portion of much larger, overall concern when it comes to the status of anti-stigma campaigns and mental healthcare in the U.S.

While beyond the scope of this study, there are many other potential negative consequences for mental health policy and anti-stigma campaigns, including the reduction of funding for these initiatives, as mentioned earlier in this chapter, and the potential loss of mental healthcare if the Republican Party or Trump were to attempt to repeal or alter the Affordable Care Act again. If each of these items remain as they stand, as of January 2018, we could still expect to see substantial negative consequences through the increase of stigmatizing stereotypes, prejudicial beliefs, and discriminatory behaviors, solely based on the proliferation and acceptance of the discourses of power displayed by Trump when it comes to his use of derogatory language related to mental illness.

Bibliography

American Academy of Pediatrics. "Spanking Linked to Mental Illness." 2012, www.aap.org/en-us/about-the-aap/aap-press-room/pages/Spanking-Linked-toMental-Illness.aspx

Appelbaum, Paul S. and Jeffrey W. Swanson. "Law & Psychiatry: Gun Laws and Mental Illness: How Sensible are the Current Restrictions?" *Psychiatric Services* 61, no. 7 (2010): 652–54.

Apuzzo, Matt, Maggie Haberman, and Matthew Rosenberg. "Trump Told Russians that Firing 'Nut Job' Comey Eased Pressure from Investigation." *The New York Times*, May 19, 2017, www.nytimes.com/2017/05/19/us/politics/trump-russia-comey.html

Byrne, Peter. "Stigma of Mental Illness and Ways of Diminishing It." *Advances in Psychiatric Treatment* 6, no. 1 (2000): 65–72.

Clark, Joselyn. "Medicalization of Global Health 2: The Medicalization of Global Mental Health." *Global Health Action* 7, no. 1 (2014): 24000.

Corrigan, Patrick W. "Mental Health Stigma as Social Attribution: Implications for Research Methods and Attitude Change." *Clinical Psychology: Science and Practice* 7, no. 1 (2000): 48–67.

Corrigan, Patrick W. "Research and the Elimination of the Stigma of Mental Illness." *British Journal of Psychiatry* 201 (2012): 7–8.

Corrigan, Patrick W. "The Impact of Stigma on Severe Mental Illness." *Cognitive and Behavioral Practice* 5 (1998): 201–22.

Corrigan, Patrick W., Andrea B. Bink, J. Konadu Fokuo, and Annie Schmidt. "The Public Stigma of Mental Illness Means a Difference Between You and Me." *Psychiatry Research* 226, no. 1 (2015): 186–91.

Cummings, William. "Trump PTSD Comments Spark Emotional Debate." *USA Today*, October 3, 2016, www.usatoday.com/story/news/politics/onpolitics/2016/10/03/trump-ptsdcomments/91509626/

Elkin, Ali. "Donald Trump Says Mental Illness to Blame for Gun Violence." *Bloomberg*, October 4, 2015, www.bloomberg.com/politics/articles/2015-10-04/donald-trump-saysmental-illness-to-blame-for-gun-violence

Elliot, Stuart. "A New Campaign by Leo Burnett Will Try to Promote Prozac Directly to Consumers." *The New York Times*, July 1, 1997, www.nytimes.com/1997/07/01/business/a-new-campaign-by-leo-burnett-will-tryto-promote-prozac-directly-to-consumers.html

Foucault, Michel. *Madness and Civilization: A History of Insanity in the Age of Reason.* New York: Vintage, 1988.

Goffman, Erving. *Asylums: Essays on the Social Situation of Mental Patients and Other In-mates.* Chicago, IL: Aldine Transaction, 1968.

Hinshaw, Stephen P. *The Mark of Shame: Stigma of Mental Illness and an Agenda for Change.* New York: Oxford University Press, 2007.

Holmes, Lindsay. "Donald Trump's Comments on Veteran Suicide are Exactly Why There's PTSD Stigma." *Huffington Post*, October 3, 2016, www.huffingtonpost. com/entry/donald-trump-veterans-mentalhealth_us_57f280bbe4b082aad9bc4903

Holmes, Lindsay and Daniel Marans. "Steve Bannon's Cure for Mental Illness? 'Spank Your Children More.'" *Huffington Post*, November 15, 2016, www.huffingtonpost. com/entry/steve-bannon-mental health_us_582b39f4e4b060adb5706059

Horton, Richard. "Launching a New Movement for Mental Health." *Lancet* 370, no. 9590 (2007): 806.

Kaczynski, Andrew. "Donald Trump Viciously Mocked Rosie O'Donnell's Depression During their Public Feud." *Buzzfeed News*, March 28, 2016, www.buzzfeed.com/ andrewkaczynski/donald-trump-viciously-mocked-rosieodonnells-depression-dur?utm_term=.xkNLv0oEN#.ju52D9X80

Keith, Tamara. "Commander-in-Tweet: Trump's Social Media Use and Presidential Media Avoidance." *NPR*, November 18, 2016, www.npr.org/2016/11/18/502306687/ commander-in-tweet-trumps-social-media-use-and-presidential-media-avoidance

National Alliance on Mental Illness. "About NAMI." n.d., www.nami.org/About-NAMI.

National Alliance on Mental Illness. "National Alliance on Mental Illness Policy Plan." 2016, www.nami.org/getattachment/Learn-More/Mental-Health-Public-Policy/ Public-Policy-Platform-December-2016-(1).pdf

National Institute of Mental Health. "Any Mental Illness Among U.S. Adults." n.d., www.nimh.nih.gov/health/statistics/prevalence/any-mental-illness-ami-among-usadults.shtml

Nuzzi, Olivia. "Donald Trump to the Mentally Ill: You're Fired." *Daily Beast*, March 29, 2016, www.thedailybeast.com/articles/2016/03/29/donald-trump-to-the-mentally-ill-youre-fired.html

Parcesepe, Angela M. and Leopoldo J. Cabassa. "Public Stigma of Mental Illness in the United States: A Systematic Literature Review." *Administration and Policy in Mental Health and Mental Health Services Research* 40, no. 5 (2013): 384–99.

Payton, Andrew R. and Peggy A. Thoits. "Medicalization, Direct-to-Consumer Advertising, and Mental Illness Stigma." *Society and Mental Health* 1, no. 1 (2011): 55–70.

Pescosolido, Bernice A., Jack K. Martin, J. Scott Long, Tait R. Medina, Jo C. Phelan, and Bruce G. Link. "'A Disease Like Any Other'? A Decade of Change in Public Reactions to Schizophrenia, Depression, and Alcohol Dependence." *American Journal of Psychiatry* 167, no. 11 (2010): 1321–30.

ProPublica. "Deleted Tweets from Donald J. Trump, R-D.C." n.d., http://projects. propublica.org/politwoops/user/POTUS

Rüsch, Nicolas, Matthias C. Angermeyer, and Patrick W. Corrigan. "Mental Illness Stigma: Concepts, Consequences, and Initiatives to Reduce Stigma." *European Psychiatry* 20, no. 8 (2005): 529–39.

Sale, Elizabeth, Michelle Patterson, Carol Evans, Julie Kapp, and Ashley Taylor. "Telephone Survey of Missourians Regarding Attitudes toward People with Mental Illness." 2007.

Stuart, Heather. "Reducing the Stigma of Mental Illness." *Global Mental Health* 3 (2016): 1–14.

Substance Abuse and Mental Health Services Administration. "Leading the Change 2.0: Advancing the Behavioral Health of the Nation 2015–2018." 2014, http://store.

samhsa.gov/product/Leading-Change-2-0-Advancing-the-Behavioral-Healthof-the-Nation-2015-2018/PEP14-LEADCHANGE2

Summergrad, Paul. "Investing in Global Mental Health: The Time for Action is Now." *The Lancet Psychiatry* 3, no. 5 (2016): 390–91.

Swan, Jonathan. "Exclusive: Trump Campaign CEO Wanted to Destroy Ryan." 2016, http://thehill.com/blogs/ballot-box/presidential-races/300445-exclusive-trump-campaignceo-wanted-to-destroy-ryan

Team Up. "Style Guide: Reporting on Mental Health." 2012, www.eiconline.org/teamup/wp-content/files/mental-health-reporting-styleguide.pdf

Trump, Donald. Twitter Post. July 26, 2016, 3:47 P.M. https://twitter.com/realdonaldtrump/status/758071264128806912

Trump, Donald. Twitter Post. June 29, 2017, 5:52 A.M. https://twitter.com/realdonaldtrump/status/880408582310776832

Trump, Donald. Twitter Post. June 29, 2017, 5:58 A.M. https://twitter.com/realdonaldtrump/status/880410114456465411

Trump, Donald. Twitter Post. March 19, 2016, 8:14 A.M. https://twitter.com/realdonaldtrump/status/711209246419845120

Trump, Donald. Twitter Post. March 19, 2016, 8:16 A.M. https://twitter.com/realdonaldtrump/status/711209847702749184

Trump, Donald. Twitter Post. March 29, 2015, 4:24 P.M. https://twitter.com/realdonaldtrump/status/582322388097974272

Trump, Donald. Twitter Post. May 3, 2016, 4:02 P.M. https://twitter.com/realdonaldtrump/status/727634574298255361

Trump, Donald. Twitter Post. May 13, 2016, 6:03 P.M. https://twitter.com/realdonaldtrump/status/731288678451019776

Trump, Donald. Twitter Post. October 16, 2014, 1:23 A.M. https://twitter.com/realdonaldtrump/status/522664117438775296

Trump, Donald. Twitter Post. September 2, 2016, 5:28 A.M. https://twitter.com/realdonaldtrump/status/771686352438042624

Trump, Donald. Twitter Post. September 9, 2016, 10:47 P.M. https://twitter.com/realdonaldtrump/status/774484342030602240

United States Department of Labor. "Americans with Disabilities Act." 1990, www.dol.gov/general/topic/disability/ada

Vitali, Ali. "Trump: Mental Illness, Not Guns, to Blame for America's Mass Shooting Problem." *NBC News*, October 2, 2015, www.nbcnews.com/meet-the-press/trump-mental-illness-not-guns-blame-americas-mass-shooting-problem-n437901

Wahl, Otto F. "Mass Media Images of Mental Illness: A Review of the Literature." *Journal of Community Psychology* 20, no. 4 (1992): 343–52.

Waldman, Katy. "How to Talk about Mental Illness without Relying on Strength." *Slate*, October 31, 2016, www.slate.com/articles/health_and_science/medical_examiner/2016/10/donald_trump_s_comments_on_mental_illness_are_awful.html

Warnke, Melissa. "As Depression, Anxiety and Suicide Skyrocket, the GOP Wants to Gut Our Mental Health Coverage." *LA Times*, June 29, 2017, www.latimes.com/opinion/opinion-la/la-ol-trumpcare-mental-health-20170629story.html

Weiner, Bernard. *Judgments of Responsibility: A Foundation for a Theory of Social Conduct.* New York: Guilford Press, 1995.

World Health Organization. *A Mental Health Action Plan: 2013–2020.* Geneva, Switzerland: World Health Organization, 2013.

7

HABITAT FOR INHUMANITY

How Trolls Set the Stage for @realDonaldTrump

Erec Smith

Donald Trump: the Troll-made Man

Pierre Bourdieu, in *Language and Symbolic Power*, suggests that bullying is a form of social control, suggesting that certain ways of being are authorized while others are not. Bourdieu writes,

> Insults, like naming, belong to a class of more or less socially based acts of institution and destitution through which an individual, acting in his own name or in the name of a group that is more or less important in terms of its size and social significance, indicates to someone that he possess such and such a property, and indicates to him at the time that he must conduct himself in accordance with the social essence which is thereby assigned to him.
>
> *(Bourdieu 1999, 106)*

Although this behavior is often perpetrated by groups, Bourdieu mentions that a single person can embody the zeitgeist of many. The many, in fact, presuppose this person that Bourdieu calls the "group made man" who "personifies a fictitious person, which he lifts out of the state of a simple aggregate of separate individuals, enabling them to act and speak, through him, 'like a single person'" (106). According to Bourdieu, the presupposed "aggregate of separate individuals" provides the group made man with the ethos to speak for them. This person "receives the right to speak and act in the name of the group, to 'take himself for' the group he incarnates, to identify with the function to which 'he gives his body and soul,' thus giving a biological body to a constituted body" (106). People come to power as representations of an ideological community, putting into question the leader-follower relationship because, in a sense, the "leader" is "following" the group that made him and set the stage for his presence.

Bourdieu wrote of this dynamic long before the Internet and may not have imagined a habitus so anonymous and nebulous. The popular platform of Twitter, specifically, creates an alternative space in which the power dynamics of the real world are eclipsed by a space in which everyone has a voice and will be heard; one's Twitter handle and chosen hashtags are all one needs to hold forth in ways that can garner millions of "followers," that is, those fans and admirers of specific Twitter accounts. The nature of this space, the "Twitterverse," alters the concept of the "aggregate of separate individuals" (Bourdieu 1999, 106); in the "Twitterverse," individuals can come together to create and perpetuate the social capital that may elude them in real life. Those once deemed too cruel and ignoble to warrant any dignification in real-life society can find their community in the Twitterverse and create a leader that personifies the group's collective cruelty and ignobility. In Twitter, social capital derives from the unchecked ability to create a world, a habitus, where certain men can be endowed with power, rendering those who enjoy power in traditional, real-life circumstances utterly powerless and, often, victimized.

When taking this into consideration, Donald Trump's ubiquitous presence on Twitter is no surprise. However, many may mistakenly partake in a misleading case of cause and effect. Many believe that Trump supporters, especially those on Internet platforms like Twitter who are fond enough of Trump to share or reiterate his tweets, arose because Trump emboldened them to externalize sentiments of racism, sexism, and xenophobia. However, I argue that Trump's tweets have become rampant because the environment was already primed by Internet trolls: those that comment and debate for the sole purpose of agitation. Many of these trolls would become avid Trump supporters. Thus, I am keenly interested in those who blazed the path and, perhaps, created the Discourse community[1]—a habitus of trolls—that created a ready-made home for Trump's rhetoric. Twitter is more than just a social media platform, more than just a cesspool, as it is described by several in the American media.[2] Twitter is an institution that has called forth Donald Trump as the Troll in Chief. This chapter explores the relationship of Trump to the culture of trolling by explaining the rhetoric, ideology, and ritualistic actions of trolling, the ideology of hypermasculinity and authority that shape the troll community and Trump's role within it, and the possible influences of postmodern thought and anti-intellectualism on the rise of trolling. Ultimately, Internet trolls provided the rhetorical context in which Trump and his tweets could thrive. Donald Trump is a troll-made man.

Discourse of Trump Trolls in the Twitterverse

The online manifestations of the irreverent bullies commonly takes on the label 'troll,' a nebulous group that has been studied and theorized. I believe that many Trump supporters and trolls, in general, believe they are part of the same

Discourse community, that is, a community that shuns communication in its interpersonal sense, in favor of a complete annihilation of those who support or even marginally represent a more equitable and shared world. Trolls were here long before the 2016 presidential campaign, laying the groundwork on sites, such as 4chan and Reddit, that serve as forums for a variety of topics both staid and risqué, for the very possibility of a President Donald Trump. Trump tapped in to a communicative logic that was alive and well.

Primarily, we need to understand the logic of trolling; others take this on. Whitney Phillips' *This is Why We Can't Have Nice Things* aligns trolling with the Western affinity for agonistic rhetoric and a contemporary cultural logic that promotes one's right to be rude (Phillips 2015, 118). She cites Socrates as a proto-troll (many trolls do, as well) and cites Arthur Schopenhauer as a Godfather of trolling, who laid down a veritable but, perhaps, inadvertent 'how-to' for Trolling in *The Art of Controversy* (Phillips 2015, 124–26). When based on this understanding of Schopenhauer's work, the goal of trolling is not objective, agonistic debate for the sake of obtaining the truth. Instead, trolling's goal is a pseudo-objective, antagonistic debate for the sake of winning, whether right or wrong. Philosopher Richard Paul calls this "Sophistic Critical Thinking," which he defines as follows:

a   Thinking that meets epistemological demands insofar as they square with the vested interests of the thinker;
b   Skilled thinking that is heedless of assumptions, relevance, reasons, evidence, implications, and consistency only insofar as it is in the vested interest of the thinker to do so;
c   Skilled thinking that is motivated by vested interest, egocentrism, or ethnocentrism rather than by truth or objective reasonability. (Paul 2012, 47)

Trolling's telos is not virtuous in a traditional sense. It is the acquisition of power and the dismissal of inconvenient truths and ethics. Hence, the rise of alternative facts and the demonization of empirically based facts.

When it comes to Schopenhauer's *The Art of Controversy*, today's trolls can and, likely, have recognized a text in how to manipulate people and trick them so as to 'win' arguments they have no business winning. When Schopenhauer discusses how to stave off trolls, today's trolls may take the side of his hypothetical antagonist in hopes that their opponent has not read Schopenhauer or anyone else who has written about the proper detection of rhetorical fallacies.

However, to their defense, Schopenhauer has advice that can and has been taken by trolls for negative means. For example, Schopenhauer's advice to anger an opponent until he is too flustered to think clearly, meant to 'defend against' people hell-bent on winning instead of arriving at the truth, has been adopted by the latter's modern counterpart: trolls hell-bent on winning, as a way to fluster those in search of, or in defense of, the truth of a matter.

Trump, too, can manipulate *pathos* quite well; his rallies were prime examples. Yes, on Twitter he is talking to supporters instead of his opponents, who he is surely addressing indirectly, but he is also speaking to people he thinks are too uneducated to understand the fallacious reasoning and "sophistic" tactics he is using while seasoned and like-minded trolls wink in his direction. Both Donald Trump and trolls rely on the rhetorical ignorance of their supporters to acquire an argumentative "win," even if the victory is based on falsities.

Do trolls know what they are doing? According to Phillips, one can conclude that a troll's ultimate motivation is to maintain the illusion of superiority at all costs. Most trolls partake of a phallocentric attitude, taken as mere logic and reason, which shuns relational and contextual thought. Phillips writes, "For trolls, softness implies anything emotive, anything less than perfectly rational; they see strong negative emotions like sadness, frustration, or distress (referred to collectively as 'butthurt') as flashing neon target signs. Ironically, trolls court the very modes of thinking they subsequently attack" (Phillips 2015, 125–26). To the troll, relational and contextual thought, the kind that does not shun emotive language and considers empathy and personal situations, may come dangerously close to seeing the Other (racially, sexually, socio-economically, and physically) as an equal, and that cannot be tolerated. Thus, trolling is an antidote to equality, fairness, and respect; it is insurance that those who enjoy hegemonic supremacy may continue to enjoy it. Trolls are the storm troopers of a colonial and supremacist ideology, and Twitter is a battlefield as well as a home. So, when people do not fit this supremacist ideology, yet have the gall to carry themselves with pride, virtue, and a modicum of success, they are trolled.

When it comes to Donald Trump and his troll-like behavior and decision making, many citizens show clear disappointment.[3] However, trolls see an opportunity to double-down on the hypermasculinity described above. Other strategies existed that could address issues such as economic disparity, a concern often cited as the *raison d'etre* for Trump supporters. They chose the avenue lined with hypermasculinity and cruelty because it echoed a will to power that frequently shuns ethics and empathy while disparaging difference and inclusivity. *Logos*, in its true sense, is either shunned or bastardized in the names of power and supremacy.

This audience of Trump supporters is a community of sorts. As I've done many times, I recall James Gee's definition of Discourse when trying to understand the motivations of communities. According to Gee,

> Discourses are ways of being in the world, or forms of life which integrate words, acts, values, beliefs, attitudes, social identities, as well as gestures, glances, body positions and clothes…. Discourse is a sort of "identity kit"

which comes complete with the appropriate costume and instructions on how to act, talk, and often write, so as to take on a particular social role that others will recognize.

(Gee 1990, 142)

I would not dare suggest that all Trump supporters are the same, but is it fair to say that some were complicit in aspects of the "words, acts, values, beliefs, attitudes, social identities" of what can be called a Trump Discourse? These aspects manifest ritualistically—an expected phenomenon in maintaining a community—and are as follows, respectively: ad hominem attacks; aggressive and violent behavior; hypermasculinity, misogyny, extreme nationalism, anti-intellectuality, and, often, white supremacy[4]; and xenophobia, Islamophobia, and racism.[5] Frankly, focusing on all these aspects of Discourse may take more time than this chapter will allow. For now, as a microcosmic look into the Discourse, let us look at the issue of hypermasculinity, one could say that Trump's rhetoric abides by a terministic screen[6] of hypermasculinity and one could go as far as to say that "Trump supporter" Discourse is synonymous with a Discourse of hypermasculinity.

Hypermasculinity seems like both the driving force and the telos of Trump's online trolls. As mentioned, Internet trolls in general are not interested in substantial debate, facts, sound logic, or an aversion to fallacious reasoning. This online community seems to love the 'effects' of hypermasculinity—individuality, hierarchy, antagonism, separation, and exclusivity—to the downright dismissal of its intellectual and rhetorical *causes*. This hypermasculinity is seen by the members of this community as a necessary characteristic of proper leadership.

George Lakoff has suggested that this hypermasculinity is metonymous with the image of the strict father archetype. That is, if government is a metaphorical parent, than those who abide by the benefits of hypermasculinity would prefer a government that rules as such: the strict, take-no-guff patriarch as opposed to the nurturing parent model. Lakoff writes,

In the strict father family, father knows best. He knows right from wrong and has the ultimate authority to make sure his children and his spouse do what he says, which is taken to be what is right. Many conservative spouses accept this worldview, uphold the father's authority, and are strict in those realms of family life that they are in charge of. When his children disobey, it is his moral duty to punish them painfully enough so that, to avoid punishment, they will obey him (do what is right) and not just do what feels good. Through physical discipline they are supposed to become disciplined, internally strong, and able to prosper in the external world. What if they don't prosper? That means they are not disciplined, and therefore cannot be moral, and so deserve their poverty. This reasoning shows up in conservative politics in which the poor are seen as lazy and undeserving, and the rich as deserving their wealth.

("Understanding Trump" 2016)

Lakoff's description of the strict father extends to male superiority and, by extension, male chauvinism. This is clearly exemplified by the apologists for Trump's sexism and "hot mic" incident in which he was caught saying that women were objects to be man-handled by powerful men (*The New York Times* 2016). In the aftermath of the release of this information, Trump-supporting pundits were quick to dismiss the commentary from a 'boys will be boys' mindset. It was called "bad boy talk" by Michelle Bachman and "locker room talk" by Trump and several political pundits. Perhaps most telling is Trump surrogate Carl Paladino's statement that "gutter talk" is something "all men, do, at least all real men."[7] According to many Trump supporters and close allies, a real man, a strict patriarch, is inherently and appropriately sexist. I would also add to Lakoff's archetype the tendency to rule without justification. The hackneyed parental 'Because I said so,' usually follows a child's request for an explanation for decisions or demands. 'Because I said so,' connotes either no concern to explain oneself or no good answer to give. One could define Donald Trump similarly.

Not surprisingly, being female is a major characteristic of troll victims. Danielle Keats Citron, in *Hate Crimes in Cyberspace*, chronicles females victimized by sexist and sexually depraved trolls to the point of physical, emotional, and professional detriments (Cintron 2014, 13–14). According to Cintron, Cyberspace is "the next battleground for civil rights," and "the next stage of the women's rights movement should be focused on achieving equality in digital networks" (100). Sexual harassment is so deeply ingrained in American society, its amplified presence on the Internet is no real mystery (254).

Compare all this to Sociologist Anthony Giddens' concept of the democratization of intimacy, an idea similar to Lakoff's nurturing parent model. The democratization of intimacy is a negotiation of feelings, desires, and needs in relationships (Giddens 1998). This participatory take on "governing" interaction was becoming more acceptable in mainstream circles, especially with the inclusion of traditionally excluded groups. With a democratization of intimacy, everyone has a seat at the table. To extend the metaphor, the table is round; no one sits at the head.

The sharing inherent in the democratization of intimacy is diametrically opposed to the strict parent model in which the patriarch knows and does all. Thus, the very concept of diversity is anathema to those who abide by the strict parent ideology. In such an ideology and corresponding habitus, negotiation is a sign of weakness. Actions and words are unquestioned. *Ethos* and *pathos* push *logos* out of the equation. Might is right.

Further proof of this arises from the noted fact that many Trump supporters had and have forgone any concern for Trump's accuracy, which is a result of both a preference for a strict father figure and a desire to have their own beliefs reflected back to them. Several of Trump's supporters have no concern with whether or not he is lying. According to Jenna Johnson of the *Washington Post*, those Trump supporters who are aware of his fallacious rhetoric "view Trump's pledges more as malleable symbols than concrete promises, reflecting a willingness to shake things up and to be bold" (Johnson 2016). At best, Trump's words are a template on which his individual supporters paint pictures of a great America. Johnson continues, "Perhaps more than any other presidential candidate in history, Trump has mastered the art of putting forth a platform that is so vague — and so outlandish — that supporters can believe what they want to believe about his plans, even when it comes to something such as a concrete wall on the southern border" (Johnson). Vagueness is a tried and true rhetorical tactic especially effective and affective with audiences hungry for hope; that hope can be projected onto ambiguous and empty words.

Trump's vagueness is just one of the many tools used. In his essay "What the Media Can Do," George Lakoff identifies several tactics Trump uses—in speeches and in tweets—to further his agenda. According to Lakoff, repetition is the most systemic tactic; a constant flow of consistent messages strengthen neural links between words and meaning. Lakoff identifies repetition of the following messages: framing ("Crooked Hillary"), grammatical constructions (Radical Islamic Terrorists), metonymy of person and state (Trump is tough, so America is tough.), the family metaphor (a strict father protects his family), and exposure of the hidden (Hillary's "crooked" dealings). Generally, Internet trolls use these tactics as well. These messages round out the rhetorical tactics that populate Twitter (Lakoff 2017, 174–79). The rhetorical effect is the creation of a narrative that presents Trump and his Twitter trolls not as bullies and sadists, but as heroes and warriors. Lakoff suggests that the media should work to construct a new narrative that exposes Trump's tactics and shows people "how their brains can be used against them" (179). Twitter is not just social media, it is a very efficient tool for mind control.

This interpretation of Trump supporters is nothing new when it comes to politics heavily inspired by a strict-father ideology. In *The Origins of Totalitarianism*, Hannah Arendt writes about a regime's necessary manipulation of gullibility and cynicism to ensure that followers remain loyal despite an onslaught of blatant lies and contradictions.

> Mass propaganda discovered that its audience was ready at all times to believe the worst, no matter how absurd, and did not particularly object to being deceived because it held every statement to be a lie anyhow. The totalitarian mass leaders based their propaganda on the correct psychological assumption that, under such conditions, one could make people

> believe the most fantastic statements one day, and trust that if the next
> day they were given irrefutable proof of their falsehood, they would take
> refuge in cynicism; instead of deserting the leaders who had lied to them,
> they would protest that they had known all along that the statement was
> a lie and would admire the leaders for their superior tactical cleverness.
>
> *(1960, 382)*

So, deception, fallacy, and outright dishonesty are not deemed vices or ignoble
traits; they are seen as "superior tactical cleverness," that is, the necessary moves
to make sure power is taken back and maintained. Many Trump supporters fit
Arendt's description. They know Trump and his administration are wrong;
they simply do not care.

And herein lies my point. All this rounds out the logic of trolling, and all
this was already present before Trump used Twitter as one of his primary
campaign tools. Trump did not create the gullible and cynical. Such people
were already here and already found Twitter as a worthy habitus to perform
the concomitant post-truth that would ensure power or at least give a strong
illusion to their power. The ideology that dominates Twitter's hegemony is
worth exploring.

Although people have fit the description of trolls for quite some time, the
Internet has become an incubator and refuge for those who would not dare
behave this way in real life, unprotected by the Internet's anonymity. Twitter
has become a haven of such people. The anonymity has exacerbated fascist
cruelty replacing masks with made-up usernames and memes in place of profile
pictures. Thus, one could plausibly define the roots of "troll logic" as intense
insecurity, fear of a loss of power, and a fear of vulnerability. Phillips conveys
that much trolling is a kind of defense mechanism against a perceived angst and
hopelessness of society (Phillips 2015, 122–23). In *Precarious Life: The Powers of
Mourning and Violence*, Judith Butler cites vulnerability as the ultimate enemy
of hegemony, for it fosters a sense of empathy and compassion for marginalized
and oppressed people. But vulnerability has no place within the Discourse of
the strict father and the Discourse community of a place like Twitter. Twitter,
in fact, is a home, battlefield, and fort for trolls. Hegemony, *their* hegemony,
must remain. Thus, vulnerability must be avoided at all costs.

To trolls, the Others of society are not even recognized as people, for doing
so would induce a familiarity that, like vulnerability, would be detrimental to
supremacist thinking. Thus, as Butler explains, the Other is "derealized" and
deemed "neither alive nor dead, but interminably spectral" (Butler 2006, 33).
Trolls are especially cruel and relentless because they are not fighting a real,
"living" entity, but something so "Other" as to not fit the contours of humanity. How much stronger is this phenomenon when considering the Internet,
where identities are relegated to mere non-contextualized content, reductive
memes, and faceless words? Thus, it is no surprise that the most vicious trolls

are men carrying out a societal expectation to disassociate from their humanity with no consideration for context or the humanity involved in the particular subject matter (Butler 2006, 34–36). This is all to the detriment and demonization of commonplace morality. In fact, in places like the Twitterverse, this 'is' commonplace morality.

Perhaps the most telling aspect of the Twitterverse is one of its modes of architecture: the chat bot. A chat bot, an automated entity programmed to respond to and redistribute posts on particular topics, accounts for many Twitter troll accounts. Fake accounts have been around long before Trump, but have surged into the socio-political spaces, lately. According to Twitter Audit, a service created to detect bots and fake accounts, many of Trump's Twitter Trolls are actually fake accounts and bots (Bort 2017). Bots programmed to perpetuate "the Trump effect" and multiply the rituals that have come to define troll logic ensure a strong buttressing of Twitter's troll-centric landscape. Bot's helped construct, with computationally enhanced speed, a habitus that welcomed and emboldened those who would not have exposed themselves, otherwise. The biggest purpose of bots is to set the stage, secure a base, for trolls to thrive. The more public sentiment exuding a troll logic, the more legitimate—and seemingly hegemonic—it will appear (Riotta 2017). Bots exemplify the fact that there is power in numbers and, as Lakoff cited earlier, repetition.

Equally telling is the fact that Twitter seems to have no interest in policing its accounts and leaves the cleansing of its platform up to a user-centered honor code. According to CNN, "Twitter says its plan is to let its open forum service fix itself. The company encourages users who see falsehoods being posted to counter that message with the truth. Twitter says it will not screen accounts based on political content -- though it does shut down accounts tied to terrorism, hate-related violence, and child pornography" (Griffin and O'Sullivan 2017). The thought of relying on an honor code in a realm notorious for its lack, thereof, is an irony apparently lost on Twitter executives.

Troll Logic: Anti-intellectualism and Postmodernism

We come to an understanding of many Trump supporters through an approach to the Twitter troll, but we were warned. The phenomenon of anti-intellectualism, best and, perhaps, most famously articulated in Richard Hofstadter's 1963 work, *Anti-Intellectualism in American Life*, has found its latest breeding ground among Twitter-based Trump trolls. Anti-Intellectualism is used by Trump and Twitter trolls, alike. To be clear, anti-intellectualism is not a synonym for stupidity. Trolls can be considered intellectual terrorists, but intellectual, nonetheless. Anti-intellectuals either mistrust or fear experts and those who would do meticulous research before proving preferred viewpoints erroneous. So, as you may have already gleaned, anti-intellectuals and trolls, especially those of Twitter, share a common enemy—and so does Trump. Thinkers and intellectuals consider the viewpoints of others and delegitimize close-minded conclusions: two acts that are anathema in the Twitterverse. To consider viewpoints is to allow Others a seat at the table, to delegitimize close-mindedness is to flirt with the democratization of intimacy. Thus, intellectuality and fair-minded critical thinking must also be avoided at all costs. One can more certainly conclude that facts and critical thinking are unacknowledged, if not detrimental to supremacist goals.

This mistrust in intellectuals spreads to the mistrust of the media, at large, at least that part of the media that does not pertain to one's preconceived notions. The mistrust in the narratives delivered by the media, both local narratives and grand narratives, may be responsible for the age of post-truth. Conservative Pundit Charles Sykes wrote about this new age in *The New York Times* article titled "Why Nobody Cares the President is Lying." He writes, "the real threat is not merely that a large number of Americans have become accustomed to rejecting factual information, or even that they have become habituated to believing hoaxes. The real danger is that, inundated with 'alternative facts,' many voters will simply shrug, asking, 'What is truth?' — and not wait for an answer" (Sykes 2017). Unlike those aforementioned Trump supporters described by Johnson and Arendt, whose motivations were based in an acquisition of power, these followers have given up on truth, altogether.

Perhaps this is the natural conclusion of a decade-long embrace of what many inside and outside of academia would call postmodern relativism, as opposed to a less haphazard concept of anti-foundationalism. In my understanding, postmodernism was not supposed to carry forth without fair-minded critical thinking, but that was not always clear in its message. Lyotard's idea of postmodernism as "incredulity toward metanarratives" (1993, xxiv) opens the door to the embrace of preference instead of proof. In *The Postmodern Condition*, he writes about the power and attractiveness of narrative knowledge, as opposed to empirical knowledge, saying that scientific Discourse is just another metanarrative that also resorts to the same tricks as those deemed "savage, primitive, underdeveloped, backward, alienated, composed of opinions, customs, authority, prejudice, ignorance, ideology" (27). It would seem, then, that the emperor has no clothes. Citing Plato's original attempts to legitimize science, Lyotard notices a tragic irony, writing that science may be guilty of "stooping to what it condemns: begging the question, proceeding on prejudice. But does it not fall into the same trap by using narrative as its authority?" (29). This idea echoes Paul Feyerabend's controversial critique of scientific Discourse, as well. In his essay "How to Defend Society Against Science," he is even harsher on metanarrative, calling them "fairytales" of ideology (Feyerabend 1998, 55). He says that science was beneficial because it freed us from the oppressive hold of religion, but that science, itself, has become a religion of sorts, exempt from criticism and deemed objectively true by too many. Science was a great liberator, but it is not essentially liberating.

This following quote speaks volumes regarding our current situation (notice Feyerabend's choice to capitalize "Truth"):

> "Truth" is such a nicely neutral word. Nobody would deny that it is commendable to speak the truth and wicked to tell lies. Nobody would deny that—and yet nobody knows what such an attitude amounts to. So it is easy to twist matters and to change allegiance to truth in one's everyday affairs into allegiance to the Truth of an ideology which is nothing but the dogmatic defense of that ideology. And it is of course *not* true that we *have* to follow the truth. Human life is guided by many ideas. Truth is one of them. Freedom and mental independence are others. If Truth, as conceived by some ideologists, conflicts with freedom, then we have a *choice*. We may abandon freedom. But we may also abandon Truth.... My criticism of modern science is that it inhibits freedom of thought. If the reason is that it has found the truth and now follows it, then I would say that there are better things than first finding, and then following, such a monster.
>
> *(1998, 56–57)*

To be clear, I believe that attempts toward empirical and scientific data, although imperfect, are a more legitimate course of action than a self-interested adherence to a story of truth. However, Feyerabend's emphasis of freedom over an oppressive proof speaks to those who feel oppressed by societal forces meant to promote fairness, equality, and ethics. Although these are virtuous concepts to most, they do confine what we can and cannot do.

In fact, the dark side of postmodernism that many warned about and many ignored was laid out by Fredrick Jameson. In *Postmodernism, or The Cultural Logic of Late Capitalism*, Jameson believes that unchecked capitalism, often called neoliberalism today, breaks up what Lyotard would call a metanarrative into several realms of truth based on a Libertarian model of free trade and the legitimation/deification of Adam Smith's "invisible hand." This, in a sense, has a top-down effect on society, forcing people to make sense of a fragmented world. This had its positive effects: the validation of non-hegemonic viewpoints based on race, religion, sex, gender, and class. But it afforded the same to non-hegemonic views of morality and freedom. What's more, no one is special in such an inherently anti-hierarchical postmodern world: this includes scientists, academics, and experts of thought. Combining this with capitalism run amok and one comes across those who believe that power and money are all that matter. Therefore, the world has Donald Trump. Those without money go for the acquisition of power in any way they can muster, perhaps through racial, sexual, and educational (although sophistic) supremacy. Therefore, the world has Twitter trolls.

If we can't know truth but we desire power, the words, acts, and deeds of the potential leader who would give us that power are irrelevant; he can say whatever he wants as long as we maintain a status of superiority. This is why I find trolls' interpretation of Socrates as a culture hero, according to Phillips, ironic if not ridiculous. Socrates' tendency toward eristic was motivated by a desire to rid Athens of people who sought power because truth was unreachable. What Plato meant us to recognize as dialectical thinking, trolls may see as justified antagonism. Or maybe they don't but cite Socrates to add false ethos to their methods; this would be in line with troll logic.

Conclusion: Creating a Habitus of Resistance

We see the seeds of fake news and alternative facts. We see the Post-Truth era is, in effect, our postmodern chickens coming home to roost. *Logos*, the appeal to reason and fair-minded thought, has finally been debilitated, if not completely destroyed. Seeing this begin is sad. Speculating as to where it can lead is chilling.

In his book *Hegemony How-To: A Roadmap for Radicals*, Jonathan Smucker acknowledges that metanarratives are social constructions, but these social constructions work. Thus, recognizing how Trump and his trolls created a habitus of hate can give us similar tools to create a habitus of acceptance. Narrative is key.

> If we are serious about engaging in *the political*—if we are to build the collective power it will take to win meaningful change—we have to do more than merely deconstruct currently hegemonic metanarratives. We also have to construct our own novel metanarratives with different contents, in the service of a social justice agenda; *construct*, but also claim and contest meanings of popular symbols and elements of existing narratives. A compelling metanarrative—one that can realign society along different cleavages—is a fiction that we have to write.
>
> *(220)*

One may wonder if fighting fire with fire will do any good to people who knowingly construct false narratives to gain power. Indeed, Twitter is so overrun with trolls acting as agents of a hateful metanarrative that its efficacy as a media platform has been forever compromised. I am determining that Twitter is a sinking ship, a place that, according to writer Lindy West, is a "place unusable for anyone but trolls, robots, and dictators" (West 2017), a habitus where the "laws of social physics" (Bourdieu 1999, 111) are too different for progressive and equitable minds to function with any agency. An apt epigraph for the Twitterverse can be taken from Dante: "Abandon all hope ye who enter here."

Thus, we have to abandon what has become Trump's "natural habitat" and fight from a new one—one that must live mainly outside of social media. At the risk of sounding Luddite, the new narrative of inclusion must be constructed in analog. Real life, not social media, must be the habitus of resistance.

Notes

1 I capitalize "Discourse" based on the concept put forth by James Gee in which "Discourse" denotes a way of being as well as a way of communicating.
2 Several news outlets (*CNBC*, *Mother Jones*, *Salon*, and *Medium*, to name a few) describe Twitter as a cesspool because of its inundation of trolls. A salient example is Michael in October 2017, Kara Swisher, technology journalist and co-founder of Recode, said on CNBC that "Twitter has become somewhat of a cesspool in terms of how people treat each other, how people behave." "Cesspool" has become a popular nickname for Twitter.
3 According to Gallup, Trump's approval rating averaged 39% and sunk as low as 33% in 2017. "Presidential Approval Ratings," *Gallup News*, accessed January 5, 2018, http://news.gallup.com/poll/203198/presidential-approval-ratings-donald-trump.aspx
4 Instances of these behaviors abound. Trump's hypermasculinity and misogyny are apparent in his bragging about his ability to grope women without repercussion (Fahrenthold 2016). His mantra of "America First" conveyed an extreme nationalism throughout his campaign and beyond (Holland and Stephenson 2017). His anti-intellectuality may have been displayed best when stating that "he loves poorly educated," during Nevada caucus victory speech (Stevenson 2016). Trump's association with white supremacists is less conspicuous, but his equivocation of white nationalists with anti-racist protesters and his praise from prominent white nationalists for doing so, suggests a tolerance for such ideologies (Thrush and Haberman 2017).
5 Trump's xenophobia, Islamaphobia, and racism are commonly known. His speech about the inherent dangers of Mexican immigrants sparked his presidential campaign (Lee 2015). Trump's Islamaphobia may be best displayed by repetition of an incendiary and unsubstantiated story claiming an American General dipped bullets in pig's blood (deemed unholy in Islam) before executing Muslim terrorists, stoking further hate against the religion (Nakamura 2017). Trump's general racism, like his ties to white nationalists, is more apparent by his tolerance and lack of censure when it comes to those enacting and perpetuating racist ideologies (Thrush and Haberman 2017).
6 In *Language as Symbolic Action*, Kenneth Burke defines a terministic screen as term that serves as a lens through which we see the world. This lens, according to Burke, "must be a *selection* of reality; and to this extent it must function also as a *deflection* of reality" (Burke 1966, 45). So, one could say that Trump and Trump trolls abide by a terministic screen of hypermasculinity, which deflects other modes of reality but selects modes that move along with hypermasculinity, e.g., misogyny, authoritarianism, and supremacy.
7 Outlets, including *Washington Post* and *MSNBC*, report the comments made by Paladino, Bachman, and other Trump surrogates. The general theme is that locker room talk is not only acceptable but expected.

Bibliography

Arendt, Hannah. 1960. *The Origins of Totalitarianism*. New York: Meridian Books.
Associated Press. 2017. "Trump in Nevada: 'I Love the Poorly Educated.'" *Youtube*. Uploaded by Associated Press February 23, 2017. Video, 0:29. www.youtube.com/watch?v=Vpdt7omPoa0
Bort, Ryan. 2017. "Nearly Half of Donald Trump's Twitter Followers are Fake Accounts and Bots." *Newsweek*, accessed May 30, 2017, www.newsweek.com/donald-trump-twitter-followers-fake-617873
Bourdieu, Pierre. 1999. *Language and Symbolic Power*. Cambridge, MA: Harvard University Press.

Brodeur, Michael Andor. 2017. "Is Twitter Such a Cesspool that We Should Just Let It Go?" *Boston Globe*, Accessed January 6, 2017, www.bostonglobe.com/arts/2017/01/05/surrendering-twitterway/2TJebnIEuCrE7doawtPtuK/story.html

Burke, Kenneth. 1966. *Language as Symbolic Action*. Los Angeles, CA: University of California Press.

Butler, Judith. 2006. *Precarious Life: The Powers of Mourning and Violence*. 2nd ed. New York: Verso.

Citron, Danielle Keats. 2014. *Hate Crimes in Cyberspace*. Cambridge, MA: Harvard University Press.

Fahrenthold, David. (2016). "Trump Reported Having Extremely Lewd Conversation about Women in 2005." *Washington Post*. October 7, 2016. Accessed July 1, 2018. www.washingtonpost.com/politics/trump-recorded-having-extremely-lewd-conversation-about-women-in-2005/2016/10/07/3b9ce776-8cb4-11e6-bf8a-3d26847eeed4_story.html?utm_term=.a25541e35b97

Feyerabend, Paul. 1998. "How to Defend Society Against Science." In *Introductory Readings in the Philosophy of Science*. Eds. E.D. Klemke, Robert Hollinger, and David Wyss Rudge. Amherst, NY: Prometheus Books, 54–65. Print.

Frankfurt, Harry. 2005. *On Bullshit*. Princeton, NJ: Princeton University Press.

Gee, James Paul. 1990. *Social Linguistics and Literacies: Ideology and Discourses*. Bristol, PA: The Falmer Press. Print.

Giddens, Anthony and Christopher Pierson. 1998. "From the Transformation of Intimacy to the Life of Politics." In *Conversations with Anthony Giddens: Making Sense of Modernity*. Cambridge: Polity Press. Ebook.

Griffin, Drew and Donie O'Sullivan. 2017. "The Fake Tea Party Twitter Account Linked to Russia and Followed by Sebastian Gorka." *CNN*, accessed September 22, 2017, www.cnn.com/2017/09/21/politics/tpartynews-twitter-russia-link/index.html

Hofstadter, Richard. 1963. *Anti-Intellectualism in American Life*. New York: Alfred A. Knopf.

Holland, Steve and Emily Stephenson. "Trump, Now President, Pledges to Put 'America First' in Nationalist Speech." *Reuters*. January 20, 2017. Accessed July 1, 2018, www.reuters.com/article/us-usa-trump-inauguration/trump-now-president-pledges-to-put-america-first-in-nationalist-speech-idUSKBN1540I0

Jameson, Frederic. *Postmodernism, or the Cultural Logic of Late Capitalism*. Durham, NC: Duke University Press, 1995. Print.

Johnson, Jenna. 2016. "Many Trump Supporters Don't Believe His Wildest Promises— And they Don't Care." *Washington Post*, accessed June 7, 2016, www.washingtonpost.com/politics/many-trump-supporters-dont-believe-his-wildest-promises--and-they-dont-care/2016/06/06/05005210-28c4–11e6-b9894e5479715b54_story.html?utm_term=.b6ef6e37a4e5

Lakoff, George. 2017. "Understanding Trump." *George Lakoff*, accessed July 23, 2016, https://georgelakoff.com/2016/07/23/understanding-trump-2/

Lee, Michelle Ye Hee. 2015. "Donald Trump's False Comments Connecting Mexican Immigrants and Crime," accessed January 18, 2018, www.washingtonpost.com/news/fact-checker/wp/2015/07/08/donald-trumps-falsecomments-connecting-mexican-immigrants-and-crime/?utm_term=.9a94e03e5c77

Lyotard, Jean-Francois. 1993. *The Postmodern Condition" A Report on Knowledge*. Minneapolis, MN: University of Minnesota Press. Print.

Nakamura, David. "Trump Recycles Discredited Islamic Pig's Blood Tale after Terrorist Attack in Barcelona. *Washington Post*, 2017, accessed January 14, 2018, www.washingtonpost.com/news/post-politics/wp/2017/08/17/trump-recycles-discredited-islamic-pigs-blood-tale-after-terrorist-attack-inbarcelona/?utm_term=.6b1ea242f5c2

Paul, Richard. 2012. "Critical Thinking in North America." In *Critical Thinking: What Every Person Needs to Survive in a Rapidly Changing World.* Ed. A.J.A. Binker Tomales, CA: Foundation for Critical Thinking. Print.

Phillips, Whitney. 2015. *This is Why We Can't Have Nice Things: Mapping the Relationship Between Online Trolling and Mainstream Culture.* Cambridge, MA: MIT Press.

Riotta, Chris. 2017. "Donald Trump's Twitter Bots are Fake News Taking Over Facts." *Newsweek,* accessed June 5, 2017, www.newsweek.com/donald-trump-twitter-bots-fake-followers-trolls-army-white-house-propaganda-621018

Smucker, Jonathan. 2017. *Hegemony How-To: A Roadmap for Radicals.* Chico, CA: AK Press.

Squawk Alley. 2017. "Kara Swisher: Twitter Has Become a Cesspool in Terms of Behavior." CNBC, accessed January 14, 2018, www.cnbc.com/video/2017/10/13/kara-swisher- twitter- has-become-a-cesspool-in-terms-of-behavior.html

Stevenson, Peter W. 2016. "Trump Loves the 'Poorly Educated'—and Just About Everybody Else in Nevada." *Washington Post.* accessed July 1, 2018, www.washingtonpost.com/news/the-fix/wp/2016/02/24/donald-trump-loves-the-poorly-educated-and-just-about-everyone-else-in-nevada/?utm_term=.459c20bd0212

Sykes, Charles J. 2017. "Why No One Cares the President is Lying." *The New York Times,* accessed February 4, 2017, www.nytimes.com/2017/02/04/opinion/sunday/why-nobody-cares-the-president-is-lying.html?mcubz=0

Thrush, George and Maggie Haberman. 2017. "Trump Gives White Supremacist and Unequivocal Boost, accessed January 14, 2018, www.nytimes.com/2017/08/15/us/politics/trump-charlottesville-white- nationalists.html

The New York Times. 2016. "Transcript: Donald Trumps Taped Comments about Women." *The New York Times,* accessed October 6, 2016, www.nytimes.com/2016/10/08/us/donald-trump-tape-transcript.html?mcubz=0

"Understanding Trump." "What the Media Can do." In *What We Do Now: Standing Up for Your Values in Trump's America.* Eds. Dennis Johnson and Valerie Merians. Brooklyn, NY: Melville House Publishing, 2017.

West, Lindy. 2017. "I've Left Twitter: It is Unusable for Anyone but Trolls, Robots, and Dictators." *The Guardian,* January 3, 2017. www.theguardian.com/commentisfree/2017/jan/03/ive-left-twitter-unusableanyone-but-trolls-robots-dictators-lindy-west

PART III

"Fake News" and Madness

Read, Re-Tweet, and Teach All about It

8

TWEET THE PRESS

Effects of Donald Trump's "Fake News!" Epithet on Civics and Popular Culture

Dorian Hunter Davis and Aram Sinnreich

The meaning of "fake news" has undergone a profound evolution in the decades since Norm McDonald opened *Saturday Night Live's* Weekend Update segments with "Here's the fake news." From harmless satire in fake newspaper *The Onion* to misleading clickbait about the Pope's supposed endorsement of Donald Trump (Ritchie 2016), "fake news" has morphed from evoking mere laughter to evoking an existential threat to democracy. While other scholars have examined "fake news" stories as media artifacts (Bakir and McStay 2017; Horne and Adali 2017; Potthast et al. 2017), Donald Trump's appropriation of "fake news" as a rhetorical device for discrediting unfavorable coverage of his presidency, and the widespread adoption of the same tactic among Republicans and even foreign interests, calls out for more scholarship. This chapter takes up that challenge with an examination of "fake news" as a discursive weapon in Trump's tweets as president. Text mining, more than a thousand tweets from Trump's first six months in office, demonstrates the president's rebranding of the phrase for his own reputational management and examines civic and cultural effects of that rhetoric.

Defining "Fake News"

Before the 2016 presidential campaign made "fake news" notorious, the term was often used synonymously with the "comic journalism" Jon Stewart and Stephen Colbert produced on *The Daily Show* and *The Colbert Report*, respectively (Holt 2007; Amarasingam 2011; Balmas 2012). While the "fake" moniker also sometimes applied to inaccurate reporting, such as the "fake but accurate" documents on which *60 Minutes* based its 2004 Bush National Guard scoop (Balleza and Zernike 2004), "fake news" far more often described real news "cloaked" as entertainment (Zinser 2009, 366). This format, some scholars asserted, "contribute[s] more [than real news] to the type of deliberative discourse essential to a genuine democracy" (McBeth and Clemons 2011, 79), serving—for example—as a Fifth Estate, a watchdog of corporate media that comprise the Fourth Estate (Sotos 2009). For example, John Oliver's report on HBO's satirical *Last Week Tonight* about Sinclair Media's push to air conservative political messages on local newscasts (Oliver 2017) is one manifestation of that viewpoint.

Widespread circulation through Facebook and other social media of inaccurate stories produced to either drive traffic to ad-laden websites or influence the political preferences of low-information voters, however, resulted in a proliferation of new definitions tailored to that phenomenon, and few of them agree. Some scholars have redefined "fake news" as "intentional falsehoods that imitate journalistic facts...distributed via social media and, in some cases, mainstream media" (Himma-Kadakas 2017, 26), while others have made the distinction between real and fake news in terms of their modes of persuasion: "real news persuades through arguments while fake persuades through heuristics" (Horne and Adali 2017, 7). Others have sought to position the fraudulent stories disseminated on social media during the 2016 campaign as the latest incarnations of a much broader "fake news" tradition. In a review of "fake news" definitions from academic publications, for example, Tandoc Jr., Lim, and Ling identified six kinds of "fake news": news satire, news parody, fabrication, manipulation, advertising, and propaganda, and suggested each be considered along dimensions of facticity and intent to deceive (2017).

Anecdotal evidence, however, suggests that President Trump's use of "fake news" diverges from the definitions above. Trump first used the term "fake news" in a tweet on December 14, 2016, in response to a CNN report that he would continue in the role of executive producer on his NBC show *The Apprentice* as president (Byers 2016). After first tweeting that he planned to "[...] devote ZERO TIME!" to the upcoming season starring Arnold Schwarzenegger (Trump December 10, 2016), he followed up with another tweet labeling the CNN report "[...] ridiculous & untrue – FAKE NEWS!" (Trump December 10, 2016). The report, however, was true; Trump did serve as executive producer on Schwarzenegger's season of *The Apprentice*. The president-elect would use his Twitter account to denounce "fake news" eleven more times before Inauguration Day, most notably to rebut reports that the Federal Bureau of Investigation (FBI) had briefed him on a dossier of information the Russian government had supposedly collected on Trump for potential leverage on the incoming president. Those reports also turned out to be true, as FBI director James Comey later testified to Congress (Comey 2017). Trump's use of the "fake news" label in cases like these didn't denote infotainment in which "jokes and skits are based on, and peppered with, real news items and real stories" (Zinser 2009, 366), or "nefarious types intentionally sowing lies to influence [elections]" (Kurtzleben 2017). Rather it suggested "facts that contradict

Trump's version of reality" (*Los Angeles Times* Editorial Board 2017). As CNN's Jake Tapper observed, "Almost every single time he's used ['fake news'], the news has been accurate. It's just been news he doesn't like" (Tapper 2017).

"Fake News" in Trump's Tweets

To confirm empirically what the anecdotal evidence suggests—that President Trump often used his Twitter account to call real news fake—and to shed some light on the strategic purpose of that tactic, we text mined 1,011 @realDonaldTrump tweets published between January 20 and July 20, 2017, the first six months of Trump's presidency. This account was chosen rather than @POTUS because a previous analysis had demonstrated that @realDonaldTrump tweets took on the media twenty times more often than tweets from @POTUS (Taylor 2017). The search terms "fake news," #FakeNews, "fake," and "fraud" (Trump started labeling CNN "fraud news" in June) resulted in eighty-three relevant tweets. While the president tweeted other attacks on the media, such as personal insults about the hosts of MSNBC's *Morning Joe*, we confined our study to Trump's "fake news" tweets to focus the analysis on that particular rhetorical device. After collecting all references to "fake news" and its derivatives, we mined all tweets again for references to four issues that earned significant news coverage during the same time frame: the economy, with search terms to include, economy, jobs, employment, tax, stock, and trade; healthcare, with search terms to include health and ObamaCare; immigration, with search terms to include immigration, illegal, wall, and border; and terrorism, with search terms to include terror and Islamic State of Iraq and Syria (ISIS).

We found that 5.8% of @realDonaldTrump tweets used the phrase "fake news." 8.3% used "fake news" or variations on the phrase including "Fake Media" and "Fraud News." And 9% used "fake news," its derivatives, or inversions of the phrase, such as "real news" or "real story." Our numbers revealed that @realDonaldTrump tweeted more often about the relative fakeness of news than about the economy (8.7%), healthcare (7.5%), immigration (3.75%), or terrorism (2.2%) (see Figure 8.1). Because staffers sometimes tweet from the president's account, we then used the Trump or Not bot, an application that compares the syntax of Trump's recent tweets to that of his Twitter record (McGill 2017) to filter @realDonaldTrump tweets published between April 20 and July 20, 2017, to ones the bot told us Trump had a 50% or greater chance of having written. Because it had launched in March, the bot had not analyzed data for the first three months of Trump's presidency. We found that more than 15% of the tweets Trump or Not bot told us the president had written pushed the "fake news" narrative. The gap between numbers of "fake news" tweets and numbers of tweets about other salient issues was also much larger among tweets that Trump or Not bot alleges the president wrote himself. Of those,

11% were about the economy, 10% about healthcare, 4% about immigration, and 1% about terrorism.

What came as no surprise were the sources Trump labeled "fake news" most frequently (see Figure 8.2). CNN, a target of Trump's ire on Twitter since *The Apprentice* story in December 2016, took first place with thirteen mentions, followed by *The New York Times* and NBC News with eight mentions each.

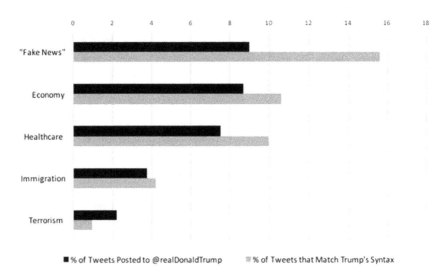

FIGURE 8.1 Prominence of "fake news" compared to four other topics in @real DonaldTrump tweets.

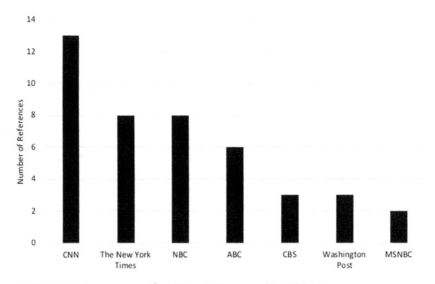

FIGURE 8.2 News sources @realDonaldTrump called "fake."

Part of Trump's frustration with CNN in particular might have been his contentious relationship with White House correspondent Jim Acosta, whom the president twice called "fake news" on camera (McKaskill 2017). *The New York Times* had frustrated Trump with stories based on White House leaks, and NBC had dared to publish unfavorable polls about the president's job performance. The source Trump name-checked the least often was MSNBC with just two mentions although he did launch regular personal attacks on *Morning Joe* hosts Joe Scarborough and Mika Brzezinski (Trump June 29, 2017), including one on Brzezinski's alleged cosmetic surgery (June 29, 2017).

From a temporal standpoint, Trump's use of the term ebbed and flowed between January and July 2017, with most of his "fake news" tweets accruing in the first, fourth, and sixth months of his presidency (Figure 8.3). While the targets of his ire were often unclear, responses to news coverage of his relationship to Russia accounted for at least sixteen of those tweets. And the months Trump tweeted most often about "fake news" happened to be ones in which major news events involving his administration and Russia took place. For example, in February, after fallout from publication of an alleged Russian dossier on Trump and National Security Advisor Michael Flynn's resignation, he tweeted, "The Democrats had to come up with a story as to why they lost the election, and so badly (306), so they made up a story - RUSSIA. Fake news!" (Trump February 16, 2017). In May, after James Comey's firing and the appointment of a special counsel for the probe into Russian election tampering, came Trump's assertion that "Russian officials must be laughing at the U.S. & how a lame excuse for why the Dems lost the election has taken over the Fake News." [*sic*] (May 30, 2017). And in July, after reports that Donald

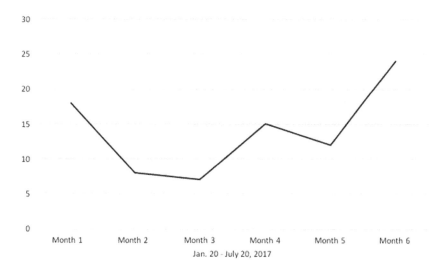

FIGURE 8.3   @realDonaldTrump's distribution of "fake news" tweets.

Trump Jr. had met during the presidential campaign with a Russian lawyer offering damaging information about Hillary Clinton, his father complained that "Hillary Clinton can illegally get the questions to the Debate & delete 33,000 emails but my son Don is being scorned by the Fake News Media?" [*sic*] (July 16, 2017).

To test our hypothesis that Trump used "fake news" in an effort to manage his reputation, we first eliminated what we considered the two likeliest alternatives: that Trump and the political media differed in their understanding of news values, the commercial and cultural factors that determine which stories make it to publication (Thurman 2015), and that Trump used "fake news" as a genuine critique of what he perceived to be inaccurate reporting. We thought the news values angle in particular was important to explore because "fake news" tweets lecturing the press for not covering issues that Trump thought were important did speak to a certain disconnect in perceptions of newsworthiness. For example, tweets blasted the media for their supposed failure to cover rising employment figures (Trump July 3, 2017) a record-high Dow Jones average (July 3, 2017), and other items on the administration's "long list of achievements" (April 29, 2017). The fact that Trump also bragged he could get his message out "[…] unfiltered […]" on Twitter further suggested he took issue with elements of the media's editorial process (June 6, 2017). Despite these examples, however, our analysis indicates that Trump's complaints about newsworthiness were infrequent, accounting for a negligible percentage the president's "fake news" rhetoric on Twitter.

The other possible motive we eliminated in our study was a genuine desire on President Trump's part to correct news he legitimately perceived as inaccurate. We thought this was an important angle to explore as well because some of the so-called "fake news" Trump decried on Twitter was in fact problematic. For example, a Russia-related CNN scoop published in June 2017 raised serious editorial questions and required a retraction (Stelter 2017). However, several factors led us to dismiss the possibility that Trump's "fake news" tweets sprang from a genuine concern about the veracity of news. For one thing, Trump himself has been an unapologetic peddler of fake news, from the fake Time magazine covers (Snider 2017) that hung in his golf clubs to the apocryphal story about General Pershing's treatment of Muslim terrorists (Yglesias 2017) that he kept presenting as a real historical incident long after the media had debunked it (Johnson and DelReal 2017). For another, Trump's attitude toward sources he characterizes as "fake news" tends to be one of convenience rather than principle. While the president made a habit of calling the *Washington Post* "fake news," for example, he praised the paper in summer 2017 for one "well-reported" story on the Obama administration's failure to take effective action on Russian meddling in the 2016 election (Wemple 2017). Trump demonstrated a similar fair-weather friendship with *The New York Times* (Bauder 2017). That CNN accepted the resignations of three employees as a result of the only story yet to be retracted among those Trump deemed "fake news" also suggests a high standard for accuracy at the entity Trump called "fake news" most frequently.

Ultimately, we were able to conclude that Trump's "fake news" epithet is an effort at what Lakoff in his taxonomy of Trump tweets calls "deflection," or attacks on bearers of bad news for the president meant to undermine public faith in the messenger (Lakoff 2017) and protect the president's reputation. Trump's tweets calling Russia coverage "fake news," for example, framed allegations of Russian interference in the presidential election as a Democratic excuse for Trump's victory (Trump February 16, 2017). Rather than addressing it as a national security issue, Trump's tweets depicted it as slight to the president's image as a perennial winner. Self-aggrandizement was also the theme of a tweet complaining that "FAKE NEWS" refused to mention "[...] Big crowds of enthusiastic supporters lining the road [...]" for him in Florida (February 12, 2017). Many other "fake news" tweets responded to perceived attacks on Trump's personal qualities or on those of his family. For example, Trump affirmed in one tweet, meant to debunk reports of Steve Bannon's disproportionate influence over the president, that he makes his own decisions: "I call my own shots, largely based on an accumulation of data, and everyone knows it. Some FAKE NEWS media, in order to marginalize, lies!" (February 6, 2017). Other tweets defended the activities of his children. When his daughter Ivanka raised eyebrows by taking Trump's seat at the G-20 summit, for instance, he tweeted that "If Chelsea Clinton were asked to hold the seat for her mother, as her mother gave our country away, the Fake News would say CHELSEA FOR PRES!" [*sic*] (July 10, 2016). Even tweets that alluded to policy debates almost inevitably veered toward reputation management. For example, Trump tweeted in the middle of a June 2017 GOP push to repeal and replace the Affordable Care Act: "Some of the Fake News Media like to say that I am not totally engaged in healthcare. Wrong, I know the subject well & want victory for U.S." (June 28, 2017). Almost all of the president's "fake news" tweets appear to serve that public relations function.

"Fake News" in Popular Culture

We believe that two factors account for the deep cultural penetration of Trump's "fake news" epithet, which has sparked a "sematic shift" around the term "fake news" (Gendrau 2017). One has been Trump's proficient use of repetition on Twitter in particular for branding, or establishing mental associations (Walvis 2008), between "fake news" and mainstream media. Trump's attacks on media institutions as "fake" have been so sustained since *The Apprentice* tweet in December 2016 that one reporter asked White House spokesman Sean Spicer if the president's "fake news" refrain were an effort to "brand" the media like he'd branded Marco Rubio as "Little Marco" during the Republican primaries

(King 2017). To be sure, those efforts have yielded mixed results. For example, one summer 2017 poll showed more Americans trust CNN than Trump (Chavez 2017). However, there is no question that Trump's appropriation of "fake news" as an epithet for traditional media has entered the vernacular of the president's supporters and detractors alike. The hosts of *Fox & Friends* have used the phrase to dismiss stories critical of Trump, and others from John McCain (Page Six 2017) to *Morning Joe* host Joe Scarborough (Scarborough 2017) have used it ironically. At one point, the president even claimed to have coined the term (Cillizza 2017). The associations Trump has created around "fake news" that 70% of Americans in a summer 2017 Fox News poll thought Trump disliked the media more than he disliked white supremacists (Fox News 2017), and one unnamed CNN employee wondered to *Vanity Fair* whether Trump's war on the media could change CNN's centrist brand, driving the network's reporting further to the left (Ellison 2017).

Another reason for the cultural penetration of Trump's anti-media rhetoric is the help it gets from the affordances of Twitter, the platform on which the president most often deploys it. Because Twitter "disallows the communication of detailed and sophisticated messages" (Ott 2016, 60), for instance, Trump's "fake news" tweets during his first six months as president exuded completeness at 140 characters, the platform's character limit until November 2017, negating the need to include evidence to support even his broadest assertions. For example, one February 2017 tweet insisting "[…] The White House is running VERY WELL. […]" and that Trump "[…] inherited a MESS […]" reached the platform's character limit without the burden of elaborating on either term Trump had emphasized in capital letters (Trump February 18, 2017). Like "Lyin' Ted" and other truncated syllogisms Trump used in the presidential primaries, which connected to voters' assumptions about the ideal qualities of a candidate without making explicit arguments about his targets (DiSanza and Legge 2016), "fake news" functions as rhetorical shorthand, connecting to people's inherent suspicions about media bias (Swift 2016) without presenting a persuasive argument about the accuracy of any particular story. This effect squares with Levinson's invocation of McLuhan in describing Trump's tweets as "cool" media, messages that invite interpretation because of their situation in the text-constrained environment of Twitter (Levinson 2016). In other words, Trump's tweets blasting real stories as "fake news"—the lack of evidence for which would be conspicuous on a platform without a character limit—can pass on Twitter for more compelling assertions.

What these two factors have in common is their appeal to people with differing amounts of trust in mainstream media. For those who believe Trump over traditional news, Twitter's structural preference for brevity helps obscure the complete lack of evidence in Trump's tweets blasting adversarial media as "fake." Trump's calling negative stories "fake news" also provides skeptics of professional journalism with a circular argument against stories that contradict their world view: the stories must be fake because their sources are fake; their sources must be fake because the stories are fake. For those who trust news media over Trump, on the other hand, that same "fake news" branding effort is the manifestation of Trump's dishonesty (Wang 2017), unpresidential demeanor (Ibid), or even authoritarian tendency (Collinson 2017). From the two million retweets his "fake news" posts have generated from supporters and detractors alike to the endless coverage and satire of his penchant for tweeting out aggression at reporters, Trump's "fake news" rhetoric has become a notable part of the cultural conversation, and where and how he delivers that rhetoric has been integral to its success.

Rhetorical Implications

Perhaps the most immediate consequence of the president's "fake news" epithet has been a fundamental change in our use and understanding of the term "fake news." Among the semantic implications of that rhetoric have been confusion in Trump's own inner circle about the meaning of the phrase from one moment to another, the adoption of "fake news" as epistrophe in emulations of Trump's syntax throughout popular culture, and the politicization of the phrase among Trump's supporters and critics. Taken together, these represent substantial shift in how Americans think and speak about news and politics.

End of "White House" Metonymy

One result of Trump's "fake news" tweets is the end of "White House" metonymy. While "White House" once served as rhetorical shorthand for "the president and his staff," Trump's own spokespeople have contradicted both the substance and authority of the president's tweets more than once, resulting in mixed messages from the White House itself. For example, White House spokesman Sean Spicer contradicted a Trump tweet in July 2017 defending Donald Trump Jr.'s decision to accept opposition research on Clinton from a Russian lawyer, claiming instead that Don Jr. had thought the meeting was about adoptions (Collins 2017). And Sarah Huckabee Sanders claimed to reporters the same month that Trump had talked sanctions during a meeting with Russian President Vladimir Putin after Trump had tweeted he hadn't (McLaughlin 2017). On other occasions, Spicer maintained that Trump's tweets were official White House statements (Le Miere 2017), while other Trump aides scolded the media for taking Trump's tweets too seriously (Nussbaum 2017).

Trump's "fake news" epithets have put that disconnect between the president and his staff into even starker relief. For example, at one February 2017 White House briefing Spicer seemed to confirm leaks suggesting that Trump's call with the Australian prime minister had been tense although Trump himself tweeted that "FAKE NEWS media lied" about a "very civil conversation" (Black 2017). A week later, White House advisor Kellyanne Conway declined to call CNN "fake news" although her boss had called the network fake on both TV and Twitter (Fabian 2017). And a month after that, Trump muddled White House messaging on "fake news" even more when he contradicted himself, seeking a security clearance for daughter Ivanka after tweeting in November 2016 that reports he planned to obtain one for her were "typically false" (Gilmer 2017).

The administration's spin on "fake news" became so confusing at one point that Spicer seemed unsure which of Trump's definitions of the term he was supposed to be defending, and of how to articulate the president's view of "fake news" coherently (Fussell 2017). For example, when Spicer dismissed a report that Jared Kushner had tried to set up backchannel communications with the Russian government because of the story's anonymous sourcing, which Trump had previously deemed a "fake news" tactic, reporters pointed out that Trump had just retweeted an anonymously sourced story favorable to Kushner (Ibid). Spicer's efforts to defend Trump's differing stances on the trustworthiness of unnamed sources further undermined the cohesion of White House messaging in Trump's war on the media. One cabinet member's statement in a different context that "The president speaks for himself" (Manchester 2017) further illustrated the lack of message discipline at the Trump White House even beyond the issue of "fake news."

"Fake News!" Epistrophe

Another consequence of Trump's anti-media tweets has been the rise of "Fake news!" as epistrophe. Trump, a master of picking a message and sticking to it (Hearn 2016), is no stranger to repetition. During the GOP primaries, one of the most predictable (and parodied) qualities of Trump's tweets blasting rivals was the likelihood that he'd punctuate whatever insult he tweeted out with "Sad!" That construction repeated itself in several of Trump "fake news" tweets: an insult punctuated with the "Fake news!" epithet: "The failing @nytimes has been wrong about me from the beginning. Said I would lose the primaries, then the general election. FAKE NEWS!" (Trump January 28, 2017). While the phrase appears just once in each of Trump's tweets attacking the media, the cumulative effect of the president's sporadic repetition of this construction is that "Fake news!" takes on an epistrophic function similar to that of the oft-repeated phrase "Believe me" in Trump's speeches (Sclafani 2017).

If scare quotes around "fake news," "alt-right" and other emerging concepts are the defining punctuation marks of 2016 (Garber 2016), the matter-of-fact dismissiveness of "Fake news!" as a verdict on whatever statement precedes it is one of the defining rhetorical innovations of Trump's tweets, the influence of which is evident in popular culture. Snapchat's "FAKE NEWS" Bitmoji (Paresh 2017), which functions as either a response to or punctuation of a previous statement, for example, appears to satirize Trump's anti-media tweets rather than his TV appearances, where "fake news" more often serves as an adjective following a linking verb in phrasing such as "Russia is fake news" (Office of the Press Secretary 2017) and "You are fake news" (Savransky 2017). Trump's use of "Fake news!" to punctuate those tweets became such a recognizable trope in 2017 that one observer on Twitter compared the practice to Will Ferrell's Robert Goulet impression from *Saturday Night Live*, in which Ferrell ends every sentence with "Goulet!"

Politicization of "Fake News"

While scholars differ on a working definition of "fake news," most of the literature does agree that real and fake news stories can be distinguished from each other based on their intrinsic qualities. Trump's appropriation of "fake news," however, has contributed to politicization of the phrase, blurring that distinction for the public. Tweets proclaiming that "Any negative polls are fake news, [...]" (Trump February 6, 2017), for example, demonstrate the president's rhetorical unmooring of that term from its use in describing clickbait meant to imitate journalism. In Trump's conceptualization, it's not the source, presentation, or accuracy that distinguish real and fake news stories; it's the impact those stories have on his own reputation. As a result, Lakoff observes that we now have to distinguish between "real fake news" and "fake fake news" (Kurtzleben 2017), the former exemplified in erroneous claims that thousands of fraudulent Clinton votes had been found in an Ohio warehouse (Shane 2017) and the latter in Trump's characterizations of unfavorable reporting.

Widespread adoption among Trump's supporters and anti-Trump Republicans alike of "fake news" as an epithet for critical reporting has also contributed to a partisan divide on the meaning of "fake news." One June 2017 Economist/YouGov poll showed that 64% of Republicans saw "fake news" as inaccurate reporting, while 84% of Democrats saw it as spin for news some people just don't like (Frankovic 2017). And that same poll found an even larger partisan split on perceptions of Trump's rationale for calling news stories fake. 66% of Republicans said Trump called out fake news when he believes the reporting is inaccurate; 87% of Democrats thought he used the term as a form of political spin. That sharp partisan split on the definition of "fake news," and on the president's motive for using the term, squares with prior research showing a relationship between "fake news" and political polarization (Ribiero et. al. 2017), and lends credence to the finding that views of "fake news" depend in part on views of the larger news media environment (Nielsen and Graves 2017).

Against this partisan backdrop, even dictionaries disagree on the definition of "fake news." Citing its neutrality in the "fake news" debate, Dictionary.com defined the term in September 2017 as "false news stories, often of a sensational nature, created to be widely shared online for the purpose of generating ad revenue via Web traffic or discrediting a public figure..." (Steinmetz 2017). Merriam-Webster, on the other hand, deemed a "fake news" entry unnecessary on the grounds that "fake news" is self-explanatory, and the Oxford English Dictionary opted to hold off on defining the term because its meaning, which had been obvious since "fake news" was coined in the nineteenth century, is now evolving (Ibid).

Journalistic Implications

Because so much attention has been paid to Trump's use of Twitter to circumvent the news media gatekeeping process, it's easy to forget that "traditional media outlets continue to play a large role in amplifying and spreading" elements of Trump's political brand (Oates and Moe 2016, 1), including his claim that unflattering coverage is "fake news." One obvious reason for covering Trump's anti-media tweets is the inherent newsworthiness of the president's blistering and sometimes bizarre attacks on reporters and news organizations. Another is that Trump's tweets, unlike President Obama's, have been characterized and disseminated as official statements from the president (Landers 2017) and tend to break more news. But a third and more concerning reason news outlets are eager to pounce on Trump's tweets is the economics of journalism. Covering tweets is quick and inexpensive, and because time constraints dominate news production, a strong preference can develop for accessible content (Himma-Kadakas 2017). Trump's tweets are the low-hanging fruits that disrupt news coverage of other issues and "attract an irrationally large amount of attention" (Oates and Moe 2016, 22). That "covfefe" was the third-most-searched term on Google during the first six months of Trump's presidency (Kight 2017) speaks to that point.

While CNN anchor Don Lemon has called for a "blackout" on news coverage of Trump's tweets (Lemon 2017), other journalists have recognized the practical benefits of reporting on the president's Twitter account. Apart from being economical to cover, Trump's tweets, which are unpredictable in both their timing and content, encourage TV and web news consumers in particular to keep coming back for the latest updates (Novak 2016). One morning America wakes up to "covfefe"; another to a surprise ban on transgender troops in the military. This perpetual spring of low-cost content provides news outlets a financial incentive to cover Trump's tweets, extending the reach and influence of the president's Twitter account and reducing available time and space for coverage of other topics.

The convergence of newsworthiness and economical content that Trump's tweets represent contributed to coverage of one of the president's most controversial tweet—a.gif ripped from old WWE footage of Trump tackling a WWE official with a CNN logo superimposed on the official's head, and hash tagged "#FraudNewsCNN #FNN" (Trump July 2, 2017). The culmination of tensions that had metastasized ever since Trump had first labeled CNN "fake news" over its *The Apprentice* reporting, that July 2 tweet, which was seen as an incitement to violence, prompted CNN to beef up newsroom security, and resulted in a full week of coverage, including investigative reporting into the origin of the.gif itself (Kaczynski 2017). When CNN reporter Andrew Kaczynski identified the Reddit user who'd created the.gif and threatened to "dox"—or out—him if he continued to publish vile content about CNN personalities online, a vigorous Twitter debate ensued about the ethics of doxing under the hash tag #CNNBlackmail, and Kaczynski revealed that both his wife and mother had gotten threatening calls as a result of his reporting on the tweet (Thomsen 2017). Trump's tweet and its fallout at CNN also provided fodder for competing news outlets. *The New York Times*, for example, published four separate stories: one about the tweet itself (Grynbaum 2017a), two about the backlash to CNN's coverage (Roose 2017; Victor 2017), and a profile of CNN president Jeffrey Zucker pegged to the tweet controversy (Grynbaum 2017b).

Political Implications

While the influence of Trump's "fake news" epithet is most evident through its pervasiveness in popular culture, as previous sections of this chapter have illustrated, the long-term civic impact of the president's penchant for labeling negative news coverage "fake" is also worth a brief discussion. Trump's attacks on the press have put into starker relief, and perhaps even deepened, the partisan divide on trust in news media. For example, "fake news" is now so heavily associated with Trump that Republicans and Democrats can't agree on what it means, or on what the president means when he uses it (Frankovic 2017). Furthermore, Trump's distain for professional journalism has prompted him to promote dubious counter-programming options that are more favorable to the administration, such as "Real News of the Week," a series he launched on his Facebook page in August 2017 (Hains 2017). The president's "fake news" talk and vaulting of alternative facts and sources has political implications as well because it undermines the reach and influence of critical reporting.

Partisan Divide on Media Trust

One of the most alarming consequences of Trump's "fake news" tweets has been a mainstreaming of hostile media effect, in which news consumers see media presentations that challenge their own perceptions of the issues as biased and infer malice on the parts of those responsible (Vallone et. al. 1985). Trump's suggestion, for instance, that stories requiring correction are "fake" attributes nefarious motives to professional journalists. Writes *Washington Post*'s Callum Borchers: "Such an overly broad definition [of fake news] unfairly attaches malicious intent to the kinds of mistakes that inevitably appear in good faith journalism" (Borchers 2017). To be sure, the antagonistic relationship between the Executive Branch and the mainstream media is nothing new. Long before Trump advisor Steve Bannon called the media an "opposition party" (Quigley 2017), President Richard Nixon called the political press "the enemy" (Maer 2003), and his vice president Spiro Agnew dismissed the media as "hostile critics" who "read the same newspapers and draw their political views from the same sources" (Lippman 2006). Nixon, like Trump, believed that "[g]etting a fair hearing from the public…required discrediting the media" (Greenberg 2016, 398). While the Nixon administration promoted the view that news media were biased against Republicans in the tone of their reporting (Hemmer 2014), however, Trump's tweets labeling the news media "[…] FAKE […]" paint a much more sinister picture of "dishonest" (Trump February 17, 2017) newsrooms engaging in "[…] fraudulent reporting, […]" (July 16, 2017) and peddling "[…] Purposefully incorrect stories […]" (June 13, 2017). Sowing distrust in the character of journalism, Trump's vitriolic anti-media rhetoric on Twitter has contributed to such a sharp partisan divide on media trust that it made news when Republican Senate Majority Leader Mitch McConnell stated the obvious: that most news isn't fake (Stelter August 21, 2017).

Alternative Facts

From a theoretical standpoint, Trump's assault on traditional mainstream media institutions could also have detrimental consequences for the public sphere. As Habermas observed, "newspapers and magazines, radio and television are the media of the public sphere" (Habermas et al. 1974, 49), the deliberative realm where public opinion on issues of civic importance foments. When Trump characterizes *The New York Times*, NBC, ABC, CBS, and CNN as "[…] the enemy of the American People!" (Trump February 17, 2017), he undermines public confidence in the organizations whose news gathering and reporting help drive the deliberative discussion at the heart of functioning democracy. Brzenzinski echoed that concern once on *Morning Joe*, positing that Trump "is trying to undermine the media and trying to make up his own facts," and wondering whether his efforts could "undermine the messaging" of mainstream media on issues of national importance (Brzezinski 2017).

A weakened role for traditional news media in the public sphere could have negative implications for the fomentation of public opinion that drives the development and implementation of policy. If Carey is correct that "We create, express, and convey our knowledge of and attitudes toward reality" in part through the practice of journalism (2009, 13), then Trump's relentless assault on the picture of his administration that political news media have constructed is in effect also an assault on political reality. This is exemplified in Kellyanne Conway's infamous coinage of the term "alternative facts" to describe spin, the White House spokesman put forward to counter mainstream media reports about the crowd size at Trump's inauguration (Bradner 2017).

That media shape public perceptions of reality (Lippmann 1922; Carey 2009; Moy and Hussein 2011) makes a poll showing some Americans see Trump as more truthful than political news media (Concha 2017) all the more sobering. This view of the president as more credible than his own watchdogs is problematic because, as Dearing and Rogers (1996) point out, the media agenda informs the public agenda which, in turn, informs the political agenda. A president whose own media streams, from Twitter to "Real News of the Week," supplant adversarial journalism for a large swath of the public has much more power over the formation of public opinion and therefore over the development of public policy. That shift in the balance of agenda-setting power has the potential to affect our national character. As Gans observed, "there is, underlying the news, a picture of nation and society as it ought to be" (1980, 39). To the extent that news helps guide our assessments and understanding of both present and past, the sidelining of professional journalism—our "membrane of social memory" (Schudson 2014, 85)—could have repercussions long after Trump leaves the White House.

Trump's Fake "Fake News"

This chapter has examined "fake news" as a rhetorical device in Donald Trump's tweets as president. First, we compared previous definitions of the term to anecdotal evidence that Trump's use diverges from our prior understandings of "fake news." Analyzing the term's prevalence and use among more than a thousand tweets during the first six months of Trump's presidency, we then demonstrated that Trump often labeled real news "fake," and that his use of that misnomer was not a product of differing news values nor of questions about the veracity of reporting, but rather of his bruised own ego: a discursive weapon in Trump's reputation management arsenal. After establishing the nature of its use, we identified two aspects of Trump's "Fake News" device that have enabled it to enter the vocabularies of the president's supporters and detractors alike, and considered implications of its prevalence in popular culture. This chapter has also shown that Trump's dismissal of real news as "fake" poses certain challenges and even dangers for American democracy, including the prospect of a president who once tweeted fake quotes from both himself (Chandler 2014) and Abraham Lincoln (Shelbourne 2017) becoming an arbiter for some Americans of what's real and what's fake.

Bibliography

Amarasingam, Amarnath (Ed.). *The Stewart/Colbert Effect: Essays on the Real Impacts of Fake News*. North Carolina: McFarland & Company, 2011.

Bachl, Marco. "Selective Exposure and Hostile Media Perceptions During Election Campaigns." *International Journal of Public Opinion Research* 29, no. 2 (2016): 352–62. https://doi.org/10.1093/ijpor/edw014

Bakir, Vian and Andrew McStay. "Fake News and the Economy of Emotions: Problems, Causes, Solutions." *Digital Journalism* (published online July 2017). https://doi.org/10.1080/21670811.2017.1345645

Balleza, Maureen and Kate Zernike. "Memos Are Fake But Accurate, Typist Says." *The New York Times*, September 5, 2004.

Balmas, Meital. "When Fake News Becomes Real: Combined Exposure to Multiple News Sources and Political Attitudes of Inefficacy, Alienation, and Cynicism." *Communication Research* 41, no. 3 (2012): 430–54. https://doi.org/10.1177/0093650212453600

Bauder, David. "The New York Times is a Favorite Trump Target – and Interview Venue." *The Boston Globe*, July 20 2017.

Black, Aaron. "9 Times the Trump Team Denied Something – and Then Confirmed It." *Washington Post*, August 3, 2017.

Borchers, Callum. "'Fake News' Has Now Lost All Meaning." *Washington Post*, February 9, 2017.

Bradner, Eric. "Conway: Trump White House Offered 'Alternative Facts' on Crowd Size." *CNN*, January 23, 2017.

Brzezinski, Mika. *Morning Joe*. MSNBC, February 22, 2017.

Byers, Dylan. "Donald Trump Will Remain EP On 'Celebrity Apprentice.'" *CNN*, December 8, 2016.

Carey, James W. *Communication as Culture, Revised Edition: Essays on Media and Society*. New York: Routledge, 2009.

Chandler, Adam. "Donald Trump Retweets Fake Donald Trump Quote Making Fun of Donald Trump." *The Atlantic*, June 10, 2014.

Chavez, Aida. "Poll: More Americans Trust CNN than Trump." *The Hill*, July 4, 2017.

Cillizza, Chris. "Donald Trump Just Claimed He Invented Fake News." *CNN*, October 26, 2017.

Collins, Kaitlan. "Spicer Contradicts Emails, President on Trump Jr. Meeting." *CNN*, July 18, 2017.

Collinson, Stephen "Trump's Authoritarian Streak." *CNN*, October 12, 2017.

Comey, James. "Ex-FBI Director's Prepared Testimony for Senate Panel," June 2, 2017. www.reuters.com/article/us-usa-trump-russia-comey-text/text-ex-fbi-director-comeys-prepared-testimony-to-senate-panel-idUSKBN18Y2X8

Concha, Joe. "Trump Administration Seen as More Truthful than News Media: Poll." *The Hill*, February 8, 2017.

de Bruijn, Hans. "Donald Trump's Rhetoric: An Analysis of His Frames." Delft University of Technology, 2016.

Dearing James W. and Everett Rogers. *Agenda-Setting*. Thousand Oaks, CA: Sage, 1996.

DiSanza, James R. and Nancy J. Legge. "The Rhetoric of Persuasive Attack: Continuing the Development of a Taxonomy of Attack Strategies and Tactics." *Relevant Rhetoric* 7 (2016): 1–16.

Ellison, Sarah. "Has Trump Turned CNN into a House of Existential Dread?" *Vanity Fair*, July 18, 2017.

Fabian, Jordan. "Conway: 'I Don't Think CNN is Fake News.'" *The Hill*, February 7, 2017.

Fox News, "Fox News Poll," August 30, 2017. www.foxnews.com/politics/interactive/2017/08/30/fox-news-poll-results-830.html.

Frankovic, Kathy. "What Is Fake News? Often Just Something People Don't Like." *YouGov*, June 7, 2017.

Fussell, Sidney. "Sean Spicer Was Weirdly Unprepared to Talk about Trump's Favorite Subject: Fake News." *Gizmodo*, May 30, 2017.

Gans, Herbert. *Deciding What's News: A Study of CBS Evening News, NBC Nightly News, Newsweek and Time.* New York: Random House, 1980.

Garber, Megan. "The Scare Quote: 2016 in a Punctuation Mark." *The Atlantic*, December 23, 2016.

Gendrau, Henri. "The Internet Made 'Fake News' a Thing – Then Made It Nothing." *Wired*, February 25, 2017.

Gilmer, Marcus. "Once Again, Trump Makes One of His Old Tweets 'Fake News.'" *Mashable*, March 22, 2017.

Greenberg, David. *Republic of Spin: An Inside History of the American Presidency.* New York: W.W. Norton and Company, 2016.

Grynbaum, Michael M. "Trump Tweets a Video of Him Wrestling 'CNN' to the Ground." *The New York Times*, July 2, 2017.

Grynbaum, Michael M. "The Network Against the Leader of the Free World." *The New York Times*, July 5, 2017.

Habermas, Jurgen, Sara Lennox, and Frank Lennox. "The Public Sphere: An Encyclopedia Article." *New German Critique* 3 (1974): 49–55.

Hains, Tim. "Ex-CNNer Kayleigh McEnany Anchors Official 'Real News of the Week' from Trump Tower." *Real Clear Politics*, August 6, 2017.

Hearn, Alison. "Trump's 'Reality' Hustle." *Television & News Media* 17, no. 7 (2016): 656–59.

Hemmer, Nicole. "The Conservative War on Liberal Media Has a Long History." *The Atlantic*, January 17, 2014.

Himma-Kadakas, Marju. "Alternative Facts and Fake News Entering Journalistic Content and Production Cycle." *Cosmopolitan Civil Societies* 9, no. 2 (2017). https://doi.org/10.5130/CCS.V9I2.5469

Holt, Jason (Ed.). The Daily Show and Philosophy: Moments of Zen in the Art of Fake News. Malden, MA: Blackwell Publishing, 2007

Horne, Benjamin D. and Sibel Adali. "This Just In: Fake News Packs a Lot in Title, Uses Simpler, Repetitive Content in Text Body, More Similar to Satire Than Real News." *International AAAI Conference on Web and Social Media*, 2017.

Howard, Daniel J. "Familiar Phrases as Peripheral Persuasion." *Journal of Experimental Social Psychology* 33 (1997): 231–43.

Johnson, Jenna and Jose A. DelReal. "Trump Tells Story about Killing Terrorists with Bullets Dipped in Pigs' Blood, Though There's No Proof of It." *Washington Post*, February 20, 2017.

Kaczynski, Andrew. "How CNN Found the Reddit User Behind the Trump Wrestling GIF." *CNN*, July 5, 2017.

Kight, Stef W. "The Insane News Cycle of Trump's Presidency in 1 Chart." *Axios*, September 22, 2017.

King James. "Trump Camp Doubles Down on Attacks against Media." *Vocative*, February 23, 2017.

Kurtzleben, Danielle. "With 'Fake News,' Trump Moves from Alternative Facts to Alternative Language." *NPR*, February 17, 2017.

Lakoff, George, "A Taxonomy of Trump's Tweets," interview by Brooke Gladstone and Bob Garfield, *On the Media. WNYC*, January 13, 2017.

Landers, Elizabeth. "White House: Trump Tweets Are Official Statements." *CNN*, June 6, 2017.

Le Miere, Jason. "Trump's Tweets Are Official Statements, Spicer Says, Completely Contradicting White House Aides." *Newsweek*, June 6, 2017.

Lemon, Don. *New Day. CNN*, December 27, 2016.

Levinson, Paul. *McLuhan in the Age of Social Media*, 2015. Kindle.

Lin Mei-Chen, Paul M. Haridakis, and Gary Hanson. "The Role of Political Identity and Media Selection on Perceptions of Hostile Media Bias during the 2012 Presidential Campaign." *Journal of Broadcasting and Electronic Media* 60, no. 3 (2016): 425–47. https://doi.org/10.1080/08838151.2016.1203316

Lippman Jr., Theo. "Attacks on Press Recall Agnew's Ire." *Baltimore Sun*, July 9, 2006.

Lippmann, Walter. *Public Opinion*. New York: Free Press, 1922.

Los Angeles Times Editorial Board. "Trump's War on Journalism." *The Los Angeles Times*, April 5, 2017.

Maer, Peter. "Nixon's Gift That Keeps on Giving." *CBS News*, December 8, 2003.

Manchester, Julia. "Tillerson on Trump's Values: 'The President Speaks for Himself.'" *The Hill*, August 27, 2017.

McBeth, Mark K. and Randy S. Clemons. "Is Fake News the Real News? In *The Stewart/ Colbert Effect: Essays on the Real Impacts of Fake News*. Ed. Amarnath Amarasingam. Jefferson, NC: McFarland & Company, 2011, 79–98.

McGill, Andrew. "A Bot That Can Tell When It's Really Donald Trump Who's Tweeting." *The Atlantic*, March 28, 2017.

McKaskill, Nolan D. "Trump Lashes Out at 'Fake News' When Pressed about Failure to Hold News Conference." *Politico*, August 14, 2017.

McLaughlin, Aidan. "Sarah Huckabee Sanders Contradicts Trump's Claim that He Didn't Talk Sanctions with Putin." *Mediaite*, July 10, 2017.

Mitchell, Amy, Jeffrey Gottfried, Jocelyn Kiley, and Katerina Eva Matsa. "Political Polarization and Media Habits." Pew Research Center, October 21, 2014.

Moy, Patricia and Muzammil M. Hussein. "Media Influences on Political Trust and Engagement." In *The Oxford Handbook of American Public Opinion and the Media*. Eds. George C. Edwards III, Lawrence R. Jacobs, and Robert Y. Shapiro. Oxford: Oxford University Press, 2011, 220–35.

Nielsen, Rasmus Kleis; and Lucas Graves. "'News You Don't Believe': Audience Perspectives on Fake News." Reuters Institute for the Study of Journalism, 2017.

Novak, Jake. "Sorry, the Media Can Never Stop Covering Trump's Tweets." CNBC, December 28, 2016.

Nussbaum, Matthew. "Trump Wants You to Take His Tweets Seriously. His Aides Don't." *Politico*, June 5, 2017.

Oates, Sarah; and Moe, Wendy W. "Donald Trump and the 'Oxygen of Publicity': Branding, Social Media, and Mass Media in the 2016 Presidential Primary Elections." American Political Science Association Annual Meeting, Political Communication Section, 2016.

Office of the Press Secretary. "Remarks by President Trump in Press Conference." The White House, February 16, 2017.

Oliver, John. *Last Week Tonight with John Oliver*. HBO, July 2, 2017.

Ott, Brian L (2016) The Age of Twitter: Donald J. Trump and the Politics of Debasement. *Critical Studies in Media Communication* 37, no. 1 (2016): 59–68. https://doi.org/10.1080/15295036.2016.1266686

Page Six. "John McCain Salutes 'Morning Joe' for 10 Years of Fake News.'" *The New York Post*, September 19, 2017.

Paresh, Dave. "People's Bitmoji Obsession Gives Snapchat a Quiet Edge in Augmented Reality." *The Los Angeles Times*, September 14, 2017.

Potthast, Martin, Johannes Kiesel, Kevin Reinhartz, Janek Bevendorff, and Benno Stein. "A Stylometric Inquiry into Hyperpartisan and Fake News," 2017. arXiv: 1702.05638

Quigley, Aidan. "Trump Aide Bannon Calls Media the 'Opposition Party.'" *Politico*, January 26, 2017.

Ribeiro, Manoel Horta, Pedro H. Calais, Virgilio A.F. Almeida, and Wagner Meira Jr. "Everything I Disagree with is '#FakeNews': Correlating Political Polarization and Spread of Misinformation." In *Proceedings of Data Science & Journalism*, 2017.

Ritchie, Hannah. "Read All about It: The Biggest Fake News Stories of 2016." CNBC, December 30, 2016.

Roose, Kevin. "How a CNN Investigation Set Off an Internet Meme War." *The New York Times*, July 5, 2017.

Savransky, Rebecca. "Trump Berates CNN Reporter: 'You Are Fake News.'" *The Hill*, January 11, 2017.

Scarborough, Joe. *Morning Joe*. MSNBC, September 22, 2017.

Schudson, Michael. "Journalism as a Vehicle of non-Commemorative Cultural Memory." In *Journalism and Memory*. Eds. Barbie Zelizer and Karen Tenenboim-Weinblatt. New York: Palgrave Macmillan, 2014, 86–96.

Sclafani, Jennifer *Talking Donald Trump: A Sociolinguistic Study of Style, Metadiscourse, and Political Identity*. New York: Routledge, 2017.

Shane, Scott. "From Headline to Photograph, a Fake News Masterpiece." *The New York Times*, January 18, 2017.

Shelbourne Mallory. "Trump posts fake Lincoln quote on Instagram." *The Hill*, February 12, 2017.

Snider, Mike. "Time Asks Trump to Take Down Fake Magazine Covers." *USA Today*, June 28, 2017.

Spinney, Laura. "The Shared Past that Wasn't: How Facebook, Fake News and Friends Are Altering Memories and Changing History." *Nature* 543 (2017): 168–70. https://doi.org/10.1038/543168a

Steinmetz, Kathy. "The Dictionary is Adding an Entry for 'Fake News.'" *Time*, September 27, 2017.

Stelter, Brian. Twitter Post. August 21, 2017, 1:50 P.M. https://twitter.com/brianstelter/status/899735376809668608

Stelter, Brian. "Three Journalists Leaving CNN After Retracted Article." CNN, June 27, 2017.

Swift, Art. "Six in Ten See Partisan Bias in News Media." Gallup, April 5, 2017.

Tapper, Jake. *The Lead with Jake Tapper*. CNN, August 7, 2017.

Tandoc Jr., Edson C., Zheng Wei Lim, and Richard Ling. "Defining 'Fake News': A Typology of Scholarly Definitions." *Digital Journalism* (published online August 2017). https://doi.org/10.1080/21670811.2017.1360143

Taylor, Jessica. "Official White House Twitter Accounts Stay on Message While Trump Strays." NPR, July 4, 2017.

Thomsen, Jacqueline. "CNN Reporter's Family Getting Dozens of Harassing Calls over Reddit Report." *The Hill*, July 6, 2017.

Thurman, Neil "Journalism, Gatekeeping, and Interactivity." In *The Handbook of Digital Politics*. Ed. Stephen Coleman and Deen Freelon. Northampton, MA: Edward Elgar Publishing, 2015, 357–74.

Trump, Donald. Twitter Post. April 29, 2017, 10:39 A.M. https://twitter.com/realdonaldtrump/status/858375278686613504

Trump, Donald. Twitter Post. December 10, 2016, 3:27 A.M. https://twitter.com/realdonaldtrump/status/807547249681166336

Trump, Donald. Twitter Post. December 10, 2016, 6:11 A.M. https://twitter.com/realdonaldtrump/status/807588632877998081

Trump, Donald. Twitter Post. February 6, 2017, 4:01 A.M. https://twitter.com/realdonaldtrump/status/828574430800539648

Trump, Donald. Twitter Post. February 6, 2017, 4:07 A.M. https://twitter.com/realdonaldtrump/status/828575949268606977

Trump, Donald. Twitter Post. February 12, 2017, 2:19 P.M. https://twitter.com/realdonaldtrump/status/830904083519242241

Trump, Donald. Twitter Post. February 16, 2017, 6:39 A.M. https://twitter.com/realdonaldtrump/status/832238070460186625

Trump, Donald. Twitter Post. February 17, 2017, 1:48 P.M. https://twitter.com/realdonaldtrump/status/832708293516632065

Trump, Donald. Twitter Post. February 17, 2017, 3:15 P.M. https://twitter.com/realdonaldtrump/status/832730328108134402

Trump, Donald. Twitter Post. February 18, 2017, 5:31 A.M. https://twitter.com/realdonaldtrump/status/832945737625387008

Trump, Donald. Twitter Post. January 28, 2017, 5:04 A.M. https://twitter.com/realdonaldtrump/status/825328817833123840

Trump, Donald. Twitter Post. July 2, 2017, 6:21 A.M. https://twitter.com/realdonaldtrump/status/881503147168071680

Trump, Donald. Twitter Post. July 3, 2017, 5:10 A.M. https://twitter.com/realdonaldtrump/status/881847676232503297

Trump, Donald. Twitter Post. July 3, 2017, 2:10 P.M. https://twitter.com/realdonaldtrump/status/881983493533822976

Trump, Donald. Twitter Post. June 6, 2017, 4:58 A.M. https://twitter.com/realdonaldtrump/status/872059997429022722

Trump, Donald. Twitter Post. June 13, 2017, 3:35 A.M. https://twitter.com/realdonaldtrump/status/874576057579565056

Trump, Donald. Twitter Post. June 28, 2017, 3:58 A.M. https://twitter.com/realdonaldtrump/status/880017678978736129

Trump, Donald. Twitter Post. June 29, 2017, 5:52 A.M. https://twitter.com/realdonaldtrump/status/880408582310776832

Trump, Donald. Twitter Post. June 29, 2017, 5:58 A.M. https://twitter.com/realdonaldtrump/status/880410114456465411

Trump, Donald. Twitter Post. July 10, 2017, 4:47 A.M. https://twitter.com/realdonaldtrump/status/884378624660582405

Trump, Donald. Twitter Post. July 16, 2017, 3:35 A.M. https://twitter.com/realdonaldtrump/status/886534810575020032

Trump, Donald. Twitter Post. July 16, 2017, 4:15 A.M. https://twitter.com/realdonaldtrump/status/886544734788997125

Trump, Donald. Twitter Post. May 30, 2017, 4:04 A.M. https://twitter.com/realdonaldtrump/status/869509894688387072

Vallone Robert P., Lee Ross, and Mark R. Leper. "The Hostile Media Phenomenon: Biased Perception and Perceptions of Media Bias in Coverage of the Beirut Massacre." *Journal of Personality and Social Psychology* 49, no. 3 (1985): 577–85.

Victor, Daniel. "CNN Story About Source of Trump Wrestling Video Draws Backlash." *The New York Times*, July 5, 2017.

Walvis, Tjaco. "Three Laws of Branding: Neuroscience Foundations of Effective Brand Building." *Brand Management* 16, no. 3 (2008): 176–94. https://doi.org10.1057/palgrave.bm.2550139

Wang, Amy B. "Lawmakers Blast Trump's 'Crude, False, and Unpresidential' CNN Tweet." *Washington Post*, July 2, 2017.

Wemple, Erik. "Trump on Washington Post: 'Fake News.' Trump on Helpful Washington Post Story: 'Well Reported.'" *Washington Post*, July 6, 2017.

Yglesias, Matthew. "Trump Calls for the United States to Imitate Fake War Crimes to Fight Terrorism." *Vox*, August 17, 2017.

Zinser, James "The Good, the Bad, and The Daily Show." In *The Daily Show and Philosophy: Moments of Zen in the Art of Fake News.* Ed. Jason Holt. Hoboken, NJ: Wiley-Blackwell, 2009. Kindle.

9

SETTING THE "FAKE NEWS" AGENDA

Trump's Use of Twitter and the Agenda-building Effect

Rod Carveth

Perhaps no president or presidential candidate has engaged in what Kellyanne Conway labeled as "alternative facts" as Donald J. Trump. Be it claiming that his inaugural crowd was the largest in history, or that he graduated at the top of his class at Wharton Business School, Trump has had a rather tenuous (often disconnected) relationship with the truth. Yet, despite the frequency with which Trump has played fast-and-loose with the facts—Daniel Dale wrote in *Politico* that from September 15 to October 18 Trump stated 253 "inaccuracies"—he pulled off the election win.

One would think that as President, Donald Trump might be more careful about his claims, many of which he disseminates on Twitter. Perhaps the most outrageous claims occurred on Saturday, March 4, 2017, when he tweeted that while he was President, Barack Obama had wiretapped his phones in Trump Tower. Trump provided no evidence for the charge, instead doubling down on his claim by requesting the Congress to investigate his charges. Federal Bureau of Investigation (FBI) Director James Comey later testified before Congress about Trump's claims on March 20, 2017, and refuted those claims.

How can we understand why Trump would make such bold claims about a former U.S. president? In the 1960s, historian Richard Hofstadter wrote about the "paranoid style" in American politics. Hofstadter proposed that the "paranoid style" consisted of individuals as feeling persecuted, and often engaging in conspiracy theories. Trump exhibits both characteristics. For example, Trump has suggested that the media are "out to get him" by engaging in "fake news"—stories that are either highly distorted or made up. In addition to feeling persecuted by the media, Trump has promoted various conspiracy theories, such as the claim that 3–5 million individuals cast their ballots fraudulently, which is why he lost the popular vote by 2.86 million votes.

This chapter first reviews Hofstadter's thesis about the paranoid style in American politics. The next section reviews some of the evidence of Trump's feelings of persecution and engaging in conspiracy theories both during his presidential campaign and his early presidency. The third section examines the genesis and outcome of Trump's "ultimate alternative fact" of his being wiretapped. The chapter ends by exploring what this incident means for this emerging era of alternative facts in the age of Trump.

Hofstadter and the Paranoid Style in American Politics

Richard Hofstadter's essay, "The Paranoid Style in American Politics," was originally published in *Harper's* in 1964 at the height of the Cold War. Much of Hofstadter's essay outlined the history of U.S. conspiracy movements, focusing on the recurring themes present in these movements. A chief theme that Hofstadter identified was the notion of the paranoid style, which he defined as "a way of seeing the world and expressing oneself" (Hofstadter 1964, 4).

According to Hofstadter, a paranoid style is characterized by the person espousing it feeling persecuted. In addition, those characterized as having a paranoid style see the world around them as being changed in a negative fashion from the way it used to be. This perception unleashes both fear and anger in individuals in such a way that their discussion about the world tends to be characterized by rhetoric that is "overheated, oversuspicious [sic], overaggressive, grandiose, and apocalyptic" (4). It is not surprising, therefore, that this rhetorical style lends itself to conspiracy theories—"the existence of a vast, insidious, preternaturally effective international conspiratorial network designed to perpetrate acts of the most fiendish character" (4). Consequently, since "what is at stake is always a conflict between absolute good and absolute evil, the quality needed is not a willingness to compromise, but the will to fight things out to a finish" (31).

Social Identity Theory and the Paranoid Style

Social identity theory was developed by Henri Tajfel and John Turner in 1979 (Tajfel and Turner 1979) and expanded upon by others (e.g. Brown and Turner 1981; Abrams and Hogg 1990). Social identity is defined as an individual's self-conception as a member of desired social groups (Tajfel 1974). In other words, the social identity is constructed by how people define themselves according to the characteristics of the social group to which they belong.

According to social identity theory, when an individual joins a group, her sense of self-identity is extended to incorporate the group identity. The "social identity" of the group then becomes part of the group member's personal identity. Individuals see themselves part of a group rather than just connected to individuals in the group. Consequently, much of the sense of who we are derives from our connections with social groups.

One key assumption of social identity theory is that society is made up of social categories that contribute "a system of orientation for self-reference; they create and define the individual's place in society" (Tajfel and Turner 1979, 33). As a result of this system of orientation, a person develops the perception that she shares the same social reality with other members of her category (Hogg and Abrams 1988). Thus, members of a social category believe that they have some characteristic, or characteristics, that set them apart them from other groups. The result is that those members compare themselves as members of an "in-group" in opposition to "out-groups." Such comparisons increase the social identity of the in-group, leading to an enhancement of an individual member's sense of well-being, self-worth, and self-esteem (Tajfel and Turner 1986; Hogg and Abrams 1988; Abrams and Hogg 1990).

Communication between members of an in-group and an out-group is marked not only by cognitive processes—such as the knowledge of group membership—but also by affective processes such as "shared feelings of acceptance-rejection, trust-distrust, and liking-disliking that characterize attitudes toward specific groups in a social system" (Brewer and Kramer 1985, 230). As a result, in-group members are viewed in favorable terms, whereas those in the out-group are perceived negatively because they are perceived to possess more undesirable traits.

Importantly, in-group members also tend to perceive out-group members as all alike, a phenomenon known as "out-group homogeneity bias" (Linville et al. 1989, 166). The flip side of this process is known as the "in-group differentiation" hypothesis, or the view that individuals tend to perceive members of their own groups as showing much larger differences from each other than those of other groups. To sum up, in social identity theory, the group membership is not something foreign which is tacked onto the person, but is a real, true, and vital part of the person.

Trump and the Paranoid Style

It is clear that from the outset that the Trump campaign for the presidency adopted the paranoid style. Trump, whose previous political experience was being a leader of the conspiracy-driven "birther movement"—the attempt to delegitimize the presidency of Barack Obama by alleging that he was not born in the U.S.—made the primary goal of his campaign to win again. This is evident from his opening statement announcing his presidential run:

> Our country is in serious trouble. We don't have victories anymore. We used to have victories, but we don't have them. … When do we beat Mexico at the border? They're laughing at us, at our stupidity. And now they are beating us economically. They are not our friend, believe me. But they're killing us economically. … When Mexico sends its people,

they're not sending their best. They're not sending you. They're not sending you. They're sending people that have lots of problems, and they're
bringing those problems with us. They're bringing drugs. They're bringing crime. They're rapists. And some, I assume, are good people. ...

(Time 2015, para. 10)

Sadly, the American dream is dead.
But if I get elected president I will bring it back bigger and better and
stronger than ever before, and we will make America great again

(para. 76)

As you can see here, Trump has adopted important themes in his announcement that not only define his campaign but also illustrate his use of the paranoid
style.

The first element of the use of the paranoid style is Trump's reference to the
forces out there ("them") who are undermining the American way of life ("us")
as evidenced by Trump's assertions that "We don't have victories anymore." In
other words, the American way of life symbolized by capitalism and competition is under assault.

Trump then needs to identify the 'them.' Trump first describes the enemies
outside of the U.S., such as the Mexicans, who are portrayed as rapists and
criminals. Trump then makes reference to the enemies within the country,
who are the politicians "controlled fully by the lobbyists, by the donors, and
by the special interests, fully" (*Time* 2015, June 16). Trump thus asserts that
there is a major attack on the U.S. way of life and there is only one way to
combat it.

"Now, our country needs— our country needs a truly great leader, and we
need a truly great leader now. We need a leader that wrote 'The Art of the
Deal'" (para. 39). In other words, America used to be great, but both internal
and external forces have lessened its greatness, to the extent that only a person
not part of either system can Make America Great Again: Donald Trump.

The problem with such a conspiracy theory, however, is that those who don't
believe Trump can make America great again are necessarily part of the attempt
to destroy America, and, thus, they must be at least symbolically destroyed. For
example, after Trump won, he interviewed former GOP presidential contender
Mitt Romney for the position of Secretary of State. Romney had been a firm
and vocal critic of Trump during the presidential campaign, so his being under consideration for the Secretary of State position generated a lot of national
attention. While under consideration, Romney appeared to repudiate many of
the things he had said about Trump during the campaign when he stated after
a dinner with Trump that the president-elect had "a message of inclusion and
bringing people together, and his vision is something which obviously connected
with the American people in a very powerful way" (Collins 2016, para. 10).

Ultimately, Trump did not pick Romney as Secretary of State, but not before letting Romney twist in the wind for about two weeks, a move seen by many as a form of payback for Romney's disloyalty (Collins).

Trump versus the Press

During his last day of campaigning, Donald Trump declared, "We're not running against Crooked Hillary. We're running against the crooked media." He argued that the "corrupt media never shows the crowds" at his rallies as a method the media used to diminish the impact of his campaign. What Trump mostly referred to is the fact that at all rallies there is a "pool" camera for the national media. The goal of the cameraperson in charge of the head-on pool camera is to shoot the candidate walking onto the stage, shoot the candidate while he or she is presenting the speech, and to shoot the candidate leaving the stage. But, Trump also ignored the fact that many national and local media disseminated videos and pictures of the crowd sizes, as well as reported on them (Graves 2016). The fact that the media did show the crowds, however, did not deter Trump from continuing to level the charge.

These attacks against the media had been building during the course of his campaign. After being asked a question about his past misogynistic comments by then Fox News anchor Megyn Kelly during the first GOP debate, Trump later commented in an interview, "There was blood coming out of her eyes, blood coming out of her ... whatever" (Yan 2015, para. 4). In another example of his assault on the media, a couple of months later Trump physically mocked *The New York Times* reporter, Serge Kovaleski, who has arthrogryposis, a congenital condition affecting the joints. Trump denied he mocked Kovaleski, saying he never met Kovaleski. Kovaleski refuted the claim, noting he had interviewed Trump numerous times (Haberman 2015). The most troubling of Trump's attacks against the media occurred during a rally in which he targeted NBC reporter Katy Tur. After assessing the increasingly hostile crowd reaction, the Secret Service escorted Tur to her car (Bellstrom 2016).

For a person who had achieved virtual 100% name recognition because of his past as a media celebrity, including his long stint as host of *The Apprentice* and *Celebrity Apprentice*, Trump's choice to attack the media as an enemy of America was a clever strategic choice. Attacking politicians was an issue given that he would need to work with Republicans to get legislation passed. To go to war with lobbyists was somewhat problematic as Trump himself had lobbyists working for him. Engaging in a battle with business would almost be doing battle with himself.

But, Trump was quite familiar with the media landscape, and knew that the news media were highly competitive. That allowed him to exploit the media in two ways. First, the news media increasingly had been splitting along ideological lines, with Fox News and *The Wall Street Journal* on the right and MSNBC and *The New York Times* on the left. Trump could exploit that ideological rift by siding with the conservative media and then charging other media with being biased, a charge continually repeated by conservatives since the Nixon Administration.

Second, as Patterson and McClure (1976) and Patterson (1980) have documented, the news media have continually focused on the "horse race" aspect of political campaigns—that is, who is ahead and who is behind. Toward that end, the media spend a great deal of resources on polling, and then continually report on the findings of those polls. The horse race coverage of politics drowns out coverage of other aspects of the campaign, such as issues and character. This was important to Trump because while he had a memorable campaign slogan—Make America Great Again—his positions on issues lacked the kind of depth Hillary Clinton had.

Patterson (2016) found 41% of all coverage of the 2016 presidential campaign focused on the horse race, whereas only 10% focused on issues. Another 17% focused on controversies such as the Hillary Clinton email scandal and the *Access Hollywood* tape demonstrating Donald Trump making misogynistic remarks about women. Consequently, issues got very little coverage in the campaign.

By employing an "us" (the people and conservative media) versus "them" (special interests and liberal media) strategy, and knowing that the media would be focusing more on process (who was ahead and who was behind) versus content (campaign issues), Trump was able to at least somewhat neutralize the power of the press during the 2016 election. For example, as much as Trump complained that the news media were trying to "rig" the election in Clinton's favor, Clinton actually received 62% negative coverage over the course of the election versus 38% positive. By contrast, Trump received 56% negative coverage versus 44% positive (Patterson 2016).

The election of Trump, therefore, became a repudiation of the "crooked media." His supporters delighted at how the "fake news media" had been wrong in their election polling projections—actually, the polls had been fairly accurate on a national basis although off on some state polls. Despite the reality of his receiving less negative campaign coverage than Clinton, Trump kept portraying the press as an enemy that was keeping Trump from making America great again. It was a campaign theme that continued to resonate with his followers.

The media represent important sources of information on which to base this social comparison process. Media research has suggested that being exposed to frequent and positive media portrayals of in-group members is one way of positively comparing the in-group with the out-group. As a result, individuals will (i) actively seek out media portrayals of in-group members, and actively avoid portrayals of out-group members; (ii) seek out positive media portrayals of in-group members; and (iii) avoid negative media portrayals of in-group members. Seeing positively portrayed in-group characters will increase identification with the in-group, enhance personal self-esteem, and exacerbate negative assessments of the out-group. When individuals do not find appropriate in-group representations in the media, they may seek out alternative sources of social identity support or demand increased representation.

The Pew Research Center has conducted research on news consumption and political ideology finds that viewers tend to consume news media in line with their political perspectives. Conservatives will get their news from Fox News, talk radio, and conservative publications like *The Wall Street Journal*. By contrast, liberal news consumers received their news from CNN, National Public Radio (NPR), and *The New York Times*.

Conservatives and liberals are different in other ways in terms of their news consumption behavior. Conservatives were more tightly clustered around a small number of news sources, particularly Fox News. In addition, 66% said their close friends share their conservative political views. By contrast, liberals got their news from a greater variety of news sources. In addition, liberals were more likely to follow issue-based groups, rather than political parties or candidates, on social media, and more likely than conservatives to block or "defriend" someone on a social network because of politics (Mitchell et al. 2014).

In the 2016 election, a full 40% of Trump voters relied on Fox News for their information about the campaign. Clinton voters got their information from a greater variety of sources with CNN at 18%, MSNBC at 9%, and Facebook at 8%. On social media, conservatives relied on the Drudge Report and Breitbart, whereas liberal went to the Huffington Post and *BuzzFeed News* (Gottfried et al. 2017). What these findings show is that Trump voters were in more of a conservative news 'echo chamber' than Clinton voters were in a liberal news 'echo chamber.'

Perhaps one of the most striking findings from Pew is that there is a significant gap between Democrats and Republicans over the statement that news media criticism helps keep leaders in line. Nearly, nine of ten Democrats (89%) agreed with that statement, whereas only 42% of Republicans did, a 47-point difference. What is striking about that finding is that a similar Pew poll conducted in January 2016 found 74% of Democrats and 77% of Republicans agreed with the same statement (Barthel and Mitchell 2017). While the constant attack by Trump that the media were dishonest or 'fake news' may not have been the sole cause of this gap, it strains credulity to suggest that it wasn't a major factor.

Trump, Obama, and Tweeting about the "Deep State"

As indicated earlier, the twin objectives of the paranoid style are to frame a perspective in line with the desired interpretation of that perspective and then to silence the opposition. During the course of the campaign, and ramping up after the election, Trump furthered what is known as the "deep state" controversy—the notion that there exist clandestine networks within the government that is seeking to undermine and de-stabilize the Trump Administration. As proof of the "deep state," Trump and his allies point to the number of leaks that have appeared, which have embarrassed the president and his administration.

The notion of the deep state has been generally applied to foreign governments, such as Turkey and Egypt. Loren DeJonge Schulman, former official in President Obama's National Security Council and senior fellow at the Center for a New American Security, objected to the use of the term "deep state" applied to U.S. politics: "A deep state, when you're talking about Turkey or Egypt or other countries, that's part of government or people outside of government that are literally controlling the direction of the country no matter who's actually in charge, and probably engaging in murder and other corrupt practices" (Davis 2017, para. 14). Thus, the deep state theme suggests a dangerous conspiracy, perhaps one designed to overthrow a legitimately elected government.

Almost as soon as Trump became inaugurated, the conservative media, led by Fox News host Sean Hannity and conservative radio hosts Rush Limbaugh and Alex Jones began to fan the flames of the "deep state" theory—that "Obama holdovers" were secretly gathering information on, and leaking that information to, a news media whose purpose was to bring down the Trump administration. These conservative critics charged as evidence of such a deep state conspiracy information that suggested that there was collusion between the Trump campaign and Russian efforts to influence the presidential election. By early March, just six weeks into the Trump administration, Donald Trump himself engaged in perpetuating the "deep state" theory.

In the early morning hours of March 4, 2017, while away at his Mar-a-Lago Club in Florida, Donald Trump posted a series of tweets accusing his predecessor, former President Barack Obama, of wiretapping him during the 2016 elections. Trump tweeted that he "just found out that Obama had my 'wires tapped' in Trump Tower just before the victory. Nothing found. This is McCarthyism!" (Diamond et al. 2017, para. 2). Trump then posted three more tweets which linked Obama's 'wiretapping' to President Nixon and the Watergate scandal, an incident that cost Nixon the presidency.

Trump did not provide evidence to support his tweets—in fact, *Politifact* would later claim Trump's assertion rated a "pants on fire" falsehood—but that did not stop the story from spreading quickly on social media. Within hours of the tweets, stories began to emerge that a warrant had been issued for President Obama's arrest. The story was false, of course, but it illustrates three important things about Trump's base: (i) it is very social media savvy; (ii) it hates President Obama; and (iii) it does not let facts get in the way of telling a good story.

Though the White House staff kept quiet during the day, President Obama managed to issue a statement through his spokesperson Kevin Lewis that "No White House official ever interfered with any independent investigation led by the Department of Justice (DOJ). Neither President Obama nor any White House official ever ordered surveillance on any U.S. citizen. Any suggestion otherwise is simply false" (Levy 2017a, para. 8). Clearly, the former president was not going to let the charge by Trump stand unanswered.

The next day, White House press secretary Sean Spicer issued a statement Trump requested that congressional intelligence committees look into whether the Obama administration illegally investigated anyone in the Trump campaign and that "neither the White House nor the president" would comment further until congressional intelligence committees finished those investigations.

Another White House spokesperson, Sarah Huckabee Sanders, appeared on ABC's *This Week* to affirm the president's position. Sanders stated that she thought Trump based his allegations on sources "that have led him to believe there was potential." About the notion that former President Barack Obama had ordered Trump to be wiretapped, Sanders declared, "Everybody acts like President Trump is the one that came up with this idea.... There are multiple news outlets that have reported this" (ABC News 2017, para. 111) although she left unclear as to what those sources actually were. *Politifact* was also rated Sanders claim about multiple news sources reporting the claim as being false.

While Spicer was issuing this statement, *The New York Times* reported that James Comey was asking the Justice Department to publicly deny Trump's accusations out of concern that the president's tweets might make it look as though the bureau itself had acted improperly. Meanwhile, on NBC's program *Meet the Press*, former Director of National Intelligence James Clapper appeared and declared that no wiretap activity was mounted against Trump while Clapper oversaw the national security apparatus, which was until January 20, 2017.

During the following day's press briefing (Tuesday, March 7), reporters asked Spicer whether he had personally seen any evidence whether Trump Tower had been wiretapped. Spicer deflected the question by stating, "That's probably above my pay grade." He then asserted what would become a common refrain: "The president believes that the appropriate place for this to be adjudicated is for the House and Senate Intelligence Committees." Spicer did reveal that James Comey had not been asked by Trump if Trump Tower had been wiretapped. When asked if Trump had "any regrets" about making the accusation, Spicer quickly retorted, "No. Absolutely not" (Thrush and Haberman 2017, para. 19).

On March 10, 2017, the House Intelligence Committee formally requested that the Justice Department turn over any documentary evidence by Monday, March 13 related to possible instances of the Obama administration electronically eavesdropping on Donald Trump. In the White House briefing following the committee announcement, ABC News reporter Jonathan Karl asked Spicer whether President Trump would apologize to President Obama if his wiretapping accusation proves to be unfounded. Spicer pushed back on the question stating, "I'm not getting into a series of hypotheticals, prejudging the outcome of a report or an investigation that hasn't occurred yet. I think once it's done, we'll respond appropriately" (Smith 2017, paras. 5–6).

The story began to change a bit the next Monday, March 13, when during the White House press briefing, Spicer suggests that Trump didn't mean that Obama literally wiretapped him: "If you look at the president's tweet, he said very clearly quote – 'wiretapping' – end quote" (Hains 2017, para. 18). Spicer suggested the media about reading too literally into Trump's claim of Obama's involvement: "He doesn't really think that President Obama went up and tapped his phone personally" (Hains 2017, para. 17). Spicer added, "The president used the word wiretap in quotes to mean broadly surveillance and other activities during that. There is no question that the Obama administration, that there were actions about surveillance and other activities that occurred in the 2016 elections" (Diamond 2017, para. 6). In other words, Spicer declared that Trump didn't necessarily mean there was a physical tap on his phones. Belying that interpretation by Spicer is that two out of Trump's four tweets on the subject do not include the quotation marks. Furthermore, in one tweet, Trump made specific reference to his "phones" (Diamond 2017, para. 8).

That same day, the DOJ requested more time from the House Intelligence Committee to provide possible evidence related to Trump's wiretapping claim. The Committee granted the DOJ until March 20 to comply with the request. Two days later, Trump appeared as a guest on Fox News' *Tucker Carlson Tonight*, where Carlson questioned Trump about the wiretap investigation. One of the questions Carlson asked Trump was how Trump found out that Trump Tower was wiretapped. Trump responded, "Well, I've been reading about things. I think it was January 20, a *New York Times* article where they were talking about wiretapping." Trump added, "I think you're going to find some very interesting items coming to the forefront over the next two weeks" (Levy 2017b, para. 4). As this interview shows, when pressed on details, Trump deflected and promised new revelations to come. In this way, Trump attempted to change the news agenda.

The problem for Trump was that, as *Politifact* noted, *The New York Times* article did not report that President Obama ordered that Trump be wiretapped. What the article did say is that there had been intelligence investigations into some of the people in Trump's circle. In addition, that day, the leaders of the House Intelligence Committee—Devin Nunes, a Republican from California, and Adam Schiff, a Democrat from California—proclaimed that there was no evidence that Trump Tower had been wiretapped by anyone in the Obama administration. Nunes announced, "I don't think there was an actual tap of Trump Tower" (Cillizza 2017b, para. 3). Nunes did go on to say,

> So now you have to decide… are you going to take the tweets literally? And if you are, then clearly the president was wrong. But if you're not

going to take the tweets literally, and if there's a concern that the president has about other people, other surveillance activities looking at him or his associates, either appropriately or inappropriately, we want to find that out.

(para. 4)

Nunes was furthering the narrative proposed by Spicer two days earlier that Trump should not be taken literally in terms of his tweets—that President Obama did not wiretap Trump, but had Trump and Trump's friends, family and associates surveilled.

The leaders of the Senate Intelligence Committee—Richard Burr, a Republican from North Carolina and Mark Warner, a Democrat from Virginia—released a joint statement which asserted, "Based on the information available to us, we see no indications that Trump Tower was the subject of surveillance by any element of the United States government either before or after Election Day 2016" (Johnson et al. 2017, para. 2). Spicer pushed back during that day's press briefing, dismissing the statements of the two committee chairs as not being based on investigative work (Baker and Savage 2017). Warner countered after the press briefing through his spokeswoman that "The bipartisan leaders of the Intelligence Committee would not have made the statement they made without having been fully briefed by the appropriate authorities" (para. 21). Spicer, who would not have made such statements without the approval of the president, was calling into doubt the bipartisan conclusion of the Senate Intelligence Committee. It appears that Spicer once again was presenting alternative facts.

Spicer further claimed that Trump believed he had been wiretapped based on Fox News commentator Andrew Napolitano's suggestion that President Obama used Britain's Government Communications Headquarters (GCHQ) to spy on Trump (Baker and Erlanger 2017). Using GCHQ, President Obama "was able to get it and there's no American fingerprints on this" (Miller 2017, para. 7). Spicer's charge set off a firestorm of activity. Fox News anchor Shepard Smith stated, "Fox News knows of no evidence of any kind that the now president of the U.S. was surveilled at any time, in any way. Full stop" (Sterne 2017, para. 5). Clearly, Fox News was distancing itself from the British spy link as far as possible. Furthermore, GCHQ called Spicer's comment "utterly ridiculous" and "nonsense." A spokesperson for British Prime Minister Theresa May proclaimed that the British government received assurance from the White House that these allegations would not be repeated. The United Kingdom's newspaper, the *Telegraph*, reported that the White House apologized to the United Kingdom.

Yet, the same day at a joint press conference with visiting German chancellor, Angela Merkel, Trump joked, "as far as wiretapping, I guess, by this past administration, at least we have something in common" (Delaney and Turkel 2017, para. 4). Merkel did not appear to be amused, as the episode echoed memories of past revelations that European Union heads of state had been surveilled by U.S. intelligence agencies. In 2013, a German newsmagazine revealed that a document apparently from a U.S. National Security Agency database indicated Merkel's cellphone was first listed as a target as far back as 2002.

March 21 featured a pivotal moment in the investigation by the House Intelligence Committee when chairperson Nunes went to the White House to meet a source at a secure location to view information regarding possible "incidental" surveillance of Trump associates. "Incidental" surveillance occurs when people are observed during the surveillance of a targeted individual. The problem with incidental surveillance is that the names of those non-target individuals might be revealed, a process called "unmasking," and leaked to the press. Nunes was concerned that members of the Trump team may have been mentioned in surveillance of targeted Russian officials. The unusual thing about Nunes' behavior is that he went to the White House to view the information that the source was providing. Congress has its own secure sites. Consequently, speculation emerged that Nunes was possibly giving advance warning to the White House about findings in the investigation (Barrett 2017).

The next day, Nunes held a solo news conference where he proclaimed that he had credible information that the U.S. intelligence community incidentally collected the personal communications of Trump transition team members, and possibly the president. Nunes then charged that the intelligence community widely disseminated that information among the intelligence community although he refused to disclose the source of the information. He disclosed that he had informed the president of the discovery (Barrett 2017). Nunes stressed that the communications were unrelated to Russia. He also said he believed the surveillance was conducted legally through the employment of a Foreign Intelligence Surveillance Act (FISA) warrant. Nunes added that information collected was not related to Russia. Nunes held his news conference without consulting with his committee's ranking member, Adam Schiff. Schiff then held his own news conference to declare that Nunes' actions were inappropriate. Schiff added, "[Nunes] will need to decide whether he is the chairman of an independent investigation into conduct which includes allegations of potential coordination between the Trump campaign and the Russians, or he is going to act as a surrogate of the White House, because he cannot do both" (Memoli 2017, para. 4).

When Nunes' office was asked about the reason why he went to the White House and not to a secure location at Congress, Nunes spokesperson Jack Langer issues a forceful reply:

> Chairman Nunes met with his source at the White House grounds in order to have proximity to a secure location where he could view the information provided by the source. The chairman is extremely concerned

by the possible improper unmasking of names of U.S. citizens, and he began looking into this issue even before President Trump tweeted his assertion that Trump Tower had been wiretapped.

(Wright 2017, para. 3)

But, perhaps the most important event of the day occurred when Trump was asked whether he felt "vindicated by Chairman Nunes." Trump replied, "I somewhat do. I must tell you I somewhat do. I very much appreciated the fact that they found what they found. But I somewhat do" (Miller et al. 2017, para. 5). This statement is critical because it represents a turning point in the controversy. From that point forward, Trump moved off the charge that President Obama had wiretapped him.

By March 30, after nearly a month of focus on his tweets about President Obama, Trump shifted his focus to the broader investigation about Russian interference in the U.S. election. That day, Trump called FBI Director Comey to ask if Comey could "lift the cloud" of the Russian investigation because it was hampering his ability to "make deals for the country" (Apuzzo and Schmidt 2017, para. 6). Comey responded that the investigation was proceeding as quickly as possible. Trump pressed Comey as to whether Trump himself was under investigation. Comey informed Trump that the FBI was not "personally investigating" Trump. The president replied, "We need to get that fact out," urging Comey to make a public statement clearing Trump, an action that Comey did not subsequently do (Apuzzo and Schmidt 2017, para. 21). Six weeks later, Trump would fire Comey because he would not back away from the Russian investigation. Ironically, that action resulted in a special prosecutor, former FBI Director, Robert Mueller, being appointed.

Nunes soon faced ethics complaints filed against him because of his visit to the White House and subsequent news conference. He originally dismissed them, stating the multiple "left-wing activist groups have filed accusations against me with the Office of Congressional Ethic, charges Nunes claimed were 'entirely false and politically motivated'" (Cillizza 2017a, para. 6). By April 6, however, Nunes announced that he was stepping down as leading the House Intelligence Committee's investigation. Rep. Mike Conaway, R–Texas, was then elevated to being chair of the investigation. For all intents and purposes, the Obama–Trump wiretap controversy faded into the background (Barrett 2017).

In the end, Donald Trump had an accusation about the behavior of his predecessor, an accusation that had no basis in fact. To Trump's followers, the accusation sounded as if it could be true. Comedian Stephen Colbert coined the term "truthiness" to refer to false assertions that had the characteristics of being 'truthy' in that the assertions felt true. Given that to many Trump supporters, President Obama was capable of almost anything criminal or unethical, charging him with illegal surveilling a political rival felt right.

Trump then was able to reinforce the "truthiness" of his claim with the help of Sean Spicer and Devin Nunes. When Nunes announced that Trump associates *could have been incidentally mentioned* (emphasis added) in surveillance of Russian targets, Trump announced he was vindicated and moved on. He had "proved" he was right—*without any evidence to support his position* (emphasis added). Furthermore, since Trump had already established that the news media were "fake news" and not to be believed, then no one could tell his followers anything differently. Therefore, when the DOJ later revealed that no evidence existed that President Obama had "wiretapped" Trump, Trump and his followers had so bought into the bogus charge that its lack of truth had no effect.

Agenda Building

The events we see as news stories in the mass media representations of the events, not the events themselves. These representations (news) are selected, constructed, and evaluated by journalists and their editors. Lippmann observed, "the news is not a mirror of social conditions, but the report of an aspect that has obtruded itself" (Lippmann 1922, 341). McCombs and Shaw hypothesized that the issues on media agenda determines, to some degree, the issues on the public agenda. Media coverage provides "salience cues" to the audience which issues are important. For example, issues receiving extensive news coverage are considered more important than those issues receiving less coverage (McCombs and Shaw 1972).

Early agenda-setting research largely adopted a "mirror-image" perspective about media effects focusing on the overall match between the relative frequency of the news media's coverage of a set of issues, on one hand, and the relative salience of the same set of issues among the public, on the other (1972).

The results of these studies have generally supported this perspective (McLeod et al. 1974; McCombs and Stone 1976; Shaw and McCombs 1977). Initial studies of agenda setting examined how the media agenda affected the public agenda in the voting process. Later work began exploring the agenda-setting function on other issues. For example, Shoemaker et al. (1989) found that the more the media emphasized the negative aspects of drug use, the more the public considered drugs as a problem. Researchers also found that the relationship of the media and the public could be interactive. Gonzenbach (1992), in exploring the drug issue between 1985 and 1990, found that the press mirrored and had an immediate impact on the public agenda, but that the public agenda also filtered back into the press agenda which, in turn, reinforced subsequent public opinion.

The thirty-plus years of agenda-setting research has revealed the agenda-setting process to be far more complex than originally conceptualized. Media usage patterns, the nature of the issues involved, and audience characteristics have all mediated the impact of agenda setting. Consequently, researchers have sought out other concepts that complement or supplant the theory. For example, there are times in which the media themselves create issues that would not naturally be part of the public agenda. This process is known as agenda building. Agenda building goes beyond agenda setting, occurring when news stories rivet attention on a problem and make it seem important to the public. As one example, Lang and Lang applied the concept of 'agenda building' to their study of the news coverage of the Watergate crisis. They said, "agenda building is a collective process in which media, government, and citizenry reciprocally influence one another in at least some respect" (Lang and Lang 1983).

Two central concepts of agenda building are *scarcity* and *subjectivity*. Scarcity refers to the limits that news organizations have to cover the news—the amount of space in the newspapers, the amount of time in a newscast, the number of personnel an organization can devote to news gathering, etc. Therefore, in order to gain a place on a scarce news agenda, issues must "compete" with one another for coverage. Subjectivity refers to the fact that the importance of issues is not inherent in the issue itself, but how groups and the media define its importance, oftentimes in terms of its being "marketable."

An issue usually becomes part of the agenda-building process when it is at the center of some conflict, especially when it involves some policy differences. These conflicts contain three aspects to them: scope, intensity, and visibility (Cobb and Elder 1983). Scope refers to the number of people involved in the conflict. Intensity is characterized by how involved the participants are in the conflict. Visibility refers to how many people become aware of the conflict.

Two final integral concepts to agenda building are *triggers* and *initiators*. Triggers are unforeseen event that initiators use to connect to the conflict to get the issue on the media agenda. Cobb and Elder note that some of the most noteworthy issues on the public agenda began as a small or even local conflict that was skillfully redefined to become a conflict of national importance (1983). As was seen in the episode about the "wiretap" charges, Trump was able to masterfully build his agenda on to the media's agenda.

What Trump has done is to control with agenda-building process with his use of Twitter. When Trump issues a tweet, often early in the day, the media will cover it. At first, the media covered Trump's tweets because Trump is the first president to utilize Twitter for making public statements. In essence, Trump's using Twitter was a novelty. But, as both Trump and the news media learned, the tweets became a method by which issues could be built as part of the public agenda. The difference from the process that Lang and Lang (1981) described is that while it took months for an event such as Watergate to get built onto the public agenda, in an era characterized by the prevalence of social media, getting an item to be built onto the public agenda takes a matter of minutes.

Conclusion

In July 2017, several political polls assessed President Trump's approval rating. Across the polls, his approval was between 36% and 40%. On July 16, Trump issued the following tweet: "The ABC/Washington Post Poll, even though almost 40% is not bad at this time, was just about the most inaccurate poll around election time!" (Morin 2017, July 16, para. 2) This tweet was illustrative of both Trump's attitudes toward the press and his loose relationship with facts. First, the ABC/Washington Post poll had Trump's approval rating at 36%, not almost 40%. More important, the ABC/Washington Post poll was no more inaccurate than other polls at election time. Other polls, such as NBC/Wall Street Journal, had Clinton winning by 3–4 points over Trump (Abramson 2017, July 16). The ABC News/Washington Post poll also noted that there was a loss of voter enthusiasm for Clinton after FBI Director Comey's reopening of an investigation into Clinton's personal email server. The poll noted, "The change in strong enthusiasm for Clinton is not statistically significant and could reflect night-to-night variability. Still, it bears watching" (ABC October 31, 2016). The poll may have missed an important trend in the election although it should be noted that by the end of a political campaign, most people have made up their minds. Swings in enthusiasm among undecided voters are more difficult to assess.

Trump put out a tweet that was factually wrong on two counts—how his approval number was almost 40% and how the ABC/Washington Post poll was the most inaccurate poll in the election. But, the inaccuracies of the tweet are less important than the attack against the media. The poll number was low, but, Trump argues, it's an *inaccurate poll* (emphasis added) and, thus should be ignored, though, all polls at the time—except for the highly unreliable Rasmussen poll—had Trump's approval rating at no higher than 42%. In case people missed Trump's point, Trump followed with the following tweet: "With all of its phony unnamed sources & highly slanted & even fraudulent reporting, #Fake News is DISTORTING DEMOCRACY in our country!" (Rucker 2017, July 16, para. 5). The argument has now shifted from (i) the poll number is bad, but it is from an inaccurate poll and it is being reported by the "fake" news media to (ii) the news media that is "distorting" democracy in the U.S.

A July 25, 2017 Reuters' poll demonstrated that Trump's strategy was playing with his base—the Trump voter in-group. In terms of job performance, overall 58% disapproved of Trump's performance, while 35% approved. Among Independent voters were similar results—57% disapproved and 32% approved. But there were stark differences in terms of political ideology. Republicans recorded 74% approval and 23% disapproval, while the numbers were nearly reversed for Democrats, 85% disapprove and 12% approve. An even more marked contrast came from Trump versus Clinton voters. Those who voted for Clinton gave Trump a 93% disapproval rating versus only 5% approval. On the other hand, those who voted for Trump rated him at 84% approval and only 13% disapproval (Reuters 2017, July 24). Thus, Trump clearly has been able to cement the approval of his base. That may have come at some cost, though, as Clinton voters are at least as polarized in terms of their disapproval of Trump. Furthermore, the attacks against the media have further divided Republicans and Democrats.

A July 2017 NPR/PBS News Hour/Marist poll showed that 91% of Republicans trusted the media either not much or not at all, whereas 56% of Democrats trusted media a good amount or a great deal (Taylor 2017, July 3).

What Trump has done through his paranoid style is to attract a significant loyal base of people who believe that Trump is leading a charge to restore America to the way it was before—when it was great, and when it was winning—but is being hampered by a "deep state." In addition, although there is no evidence of such a conspiracy, the media reports demonstrating that fact are ignored because it is "fake news."

Thus, Trump has crafted a stunningly effective strategy to mobilize his electoral base. No matter how wild his claims, Trump's base stubbornly believes him. That base also rejects any attempt to criticize "their" president, agreeing with Trump that it is a deep state conspiracy to subvert a democratically elected president. Unfortunately, it may be Trump himself who is distorting democracy in the process.

Bibliography

ABC. *Deep Unfavorability for Clinton, Trump Marks the Election's Sharp Divisions. ABC/ Washington Post Poll,* October 31, 2016, www.langerresearch.com/wp-content/uploads/1184a92016ElectionTrackingNo9.pdf

ABC News. "This Week" Transcript 3–5–17: Sarah Huckabee Sanders, Josh Earnest, and Sen. Al Franken. March 5, 2017, http://abcnews.go.com/Politics/week-transcript-17-sarah-huckabee-sanders-josh-earnest/story?id=45911284

Abrams, D., & Hogg, M. A. (Eds.). (1990). Social identity theory: Constructive and critical advances. Hemel Hempstead, England: Harvester Wheatsheaf.

Abramson, Alana. "President Trump Just Said This Poll Was the 'Most Inaccurate' Around the Election. It Wasn't." *Time,* July 2017, http://time.com/4860080/donald-trump-approval-ratings-poll-twitter-response/

Apuzzo, Matt and Michael Schmidt. "Comey Says Trump Pressured Him to 'Lift the Cloud' of Inquiry." *The New York Times,* June 7, 2017, www.nytimes.com/2017/06/07/us/politics/james-comey-statement-testimony.html?mtrref=www.google.com

Baker, Peter and Stephen Erlanger. "Trump Offers No Apology for Claim on British Spying." *The New York Times,* March 17, 2017, www.nytimes.com/2017/03/17/world/europe/trump-britain-obama-wiretap-gchq.html

Baker, Peter and Charlie Savage. "Trump Digs In on Wiretap, No Matter Who Says Differently." *The New York Times,* March 16, 2017, www.nytimes.com/2017/03/16/us/politics/richard-burr-mark-warner-trump-wiretap.html

Barrett, Brian. "Devin Nunes: A Running Timeless of His Surveillance Claims and White House Ties." *Wired,* April 12, 2017, www.wired.com/2017/04/devin-nunes-white-house-trump-surveillance/

Barthel, Michael and Amy Mitchell. "Americans' Attitudes About the News Media Deeply Divided Along Partisan Lines." 2017, www.journalism.org/2017/05/10/americans-attitudes-about-the-news-media-deeply-divided-along-partisan-lines/

Bellstrom, Kristen. "What Is Donald Trump's Beef with NBC Reporter Katy Tur? Here's the Backstory." November 3, 2016, http://fortune.com/2016/11/03/donald-trump-katy-tur/

Brewer, M. and Kramer, R. (1985). The psychology of intergroup attitudes and behavior. *Annual Review of Psychology*, vol. 36, pp. 219–243.

Brown, R. J., and Turner, J. (1981). Interpersonal and intergroup behavior. In J. Turner and H. Giles (Eds.). Intergroup behavior. Oxford: Basil Blackford.

Cillizza, Chris. "Devin Nunes Confirms it: The Evidence of Trump Tower being Wiretapped Just Doesn't Seem to Exist." *Washington Post*, March 15, 2017a, www.washingtonpost.com/news/the-fix/wp/2017/03/15/the-evidence-of-trump-tower-being-wire-tapped-just-does-not-exist/?utm_term=.77291c27db7d

Cillizza, Chris. "Why Devin Nunes is Bowing Out of the Russia Investigation." *CNN*, April 6, 2017b, www.cnn.com/2017/04/06/politics/devin-nunes-russia/index.html

Cobb, R. W., and Elder, C. D. (1983). Participation in American politics: The dynamics of agenda-building. 2d ed. Baltimore, MD: The Johns Hopkins University Press.

Collins, Gail. For Mitt Romney, Dinner and a Kiss-Off. *The New York Times*, December 15, 2016, www.nytimes.com/2016/12/15/opinion/for-mitt-romney-dinner-and-a-kiss-off.html

Davis, Julia Hirschfeld. "Rumblings of a 'Deep State' Undermining Trump? It Was Once a Foreign Concept." *The New York Times*, March 6, 2017, www.nytimes.com/2017/03/06/us/politics/deep-state-trump.html

Delaney, Arthur and Amanda Turkel. "Donald Trump Says He and Angela Merkel 'Have Something In Common' On Wiretapping." *The Huffington Post*, March 17, 2017, www.huffingtonpost.com/entry/trump-merkel-wiretapping_us_58cc2ca4e4b00705db4f5894

Diamond, Jeremy. "Spicer: Trump didn't Mean Wiretapping When He Tweeted about Wiretapping." *CNN*, March 14, 2017, www.cnn.com/2017/03/13/politics/sean-spicer-donald-trump-wiretapping/index.html

Diamond, Jeremy, Jeremy Zeleny, and Shimon Prokupecz. "Trump's Baseless Wiretap Claim." *CNN*, March 5, 2017, www.cnn.com/2017/03/04/politics/trump-obama-wiretap-tweet/index.html

Gonzenbach, W. (1992). A tine-series analysis of the drug issue, 1985-1990: The press, the president and public opinion. *International Journal of Public Opinion Research*, vol. 4, no. 2, pp. 126–147.

Gottfried, Jeffrey, Michael Barthel, and Amy Mitchell. "Trump, Clinton Voters Divided in Their Main Source for Election News." Pew Research Center, 2017, www.journalism.org/2017/01/18/trump-clinton-voters-divided-in-their-main-source-for-election-news/

Graves, Allison. "Trump Says the Media Doesn't Show His Crowds at Rallies. He's Wrong." *Politifact*, November 3, 2016, www.politifact.com/truth-o-meter/statements/2016/nov/03/donald-trump/trump-says-media-doesnt-show-his-crowds-rallies-he/

Haberman, Maggie. "Donald Trump Says His Mocking of New York Times Reporter Was Misread." *The New York Times*, November 26, 2015, www.nytimes.com/2015/11/27/us/politics/donald-trump-says-his-mocking-of-new-york-times-reporter-was-misread.html

Hains, Tim. "Spicer On Spying: Trump Used 'Wiretapped' In Quotes To Mean Broad Surveillance And Other Activities." *RealClearPolitics*, March 13, 2017, www.realclearpolitics.com/video/2017/03/13/spicer_on_spying_trump_used_wiretap_in_quotes_to_mean_broad_surveillance_and_other_activities.html

Hofstadter, Richard. "The Paranoid Style of American Politics." *Harper's Magazine*, 1964, 77–86.

Hogg, M. A., and Abrams, D. (1988). Social identifications: A social psychology of intergroup relations and group processes. London: Routledge.

Johnson, Kevin, Erin Kelly, and David Jackson. "Senate Intelligence Committee Finds 'No Indications that Trump Tower was the Subject of Surveillance.'" *USA Today*, March 16, 2017, www.usatoday.com/story/news/politics/2017/03/16/senate-intelligence-committee-finds-no-indications-trump-tower-subject-surveillance/99258506/

Lang, G. and Lang, K. (1981). Watergate: An exploration of the agenda-building process. In G. Wilhoit and H. de Bock (eds.). *Mass Communication Review Yearbook*, Vol. 2, pp. 447–468. Beverly Hills, CA: Sage.

Levy, Gabrielle. "Obama 'Livid,' in 'Disbelief' Over Wiretapping Allegations." *U.S. News and World Reports*, March 8, 2017a, www.usnews.com/news/politics/articles/2017-03-08/obama-livid-in-disbelief-over-trump-wiretapping-accusations-reports-say

Levy, Gabrielle. "Trump Says NYT, Fox News Sources for Wiretapping Claims." *U.S. News and World Reports*, March 16, 2017b, www.usnews.com/news/national-news/articles/2017-03-16/donald-trump-tells-tucker-carlson-source-of-wiretapping-claim-was-new-york-times-and-fox-news

Linville, Patricia, Gregory Fischer, and Peter Salovey. (1989). "Perceived Distributions of the Characteristics of In-Group and Out-Group Members: Empirical Evidence and a Computer Simulation." *Journal of Personality and Social Psychology* vol. 57, no. 2, pp. 165–88.

Lippmann, W. (1922). Public opinion. New York: Macmillan.

McCombs, M. and Shaw, D. (1972). The agenda-setting function of mass media. *Public Opinion Quarterly*, vol. 36, pp. 176–87.

McCombs, M. and Stone, G. (1976). Studies in agenda-setting. Syracuse, NY: Newhouse Communication Research Center, Syracuse University.

McLeod, J., Becker L., and Byrnes J. (1974). Another look at the agenda-setting function of the press, *Communication Research*, vol. 12, pp. 131–66.

Memoli, Michael. "Schiff Says Nunes Can't Lead Russia Inquiry and be a Trump Surrogate." *Los Angeles Times*, March 22, 2017, www.latimes.com/politics/washington/la-na-essential-washington-updates-schiff-nunes-can-t-lead-russia-probe-1490218818-htmlstory.html

Miller, Greg, Karoun Demirjian, and Devlin Barrett. "House Intelligence Chair Says Trump Campaign Officials Were Ensnared in Surveillance Operations." *Washington Post*, March 22, 2017, www.washingtonpost.com/powerpost/house-intelligence-chair-says-its-possible-trumps-communications-were-intercepted/2017/03/22/f45e18ba-0f2d-11e7-9b0d-d27c98455440_story.html?utm_term=.fb17a1712af7

Miller, Zeke. "British Spy Service Says Claim That It Wiretapped President Trump Is 'Utterly Ridiculous.'" *Time*, March 17, 2017, http://time.com/4704774/donald-trump-barack-obama-gchq/

Mitchell, A., Jeffrey Gottfried, Jocelyn Kiley, and Katerina Matsa. "Political Polarization & Media Habits." Pew Research Center, 2014, www.journalism.org/2014/10/21/political-polarization-media-habits/

Morin, Rebecca. "Trump Calls ABC/Washington Post Poll 'Most Inaccurate Poll Around Election Time.'" *Politico*, July 16, 2017, www.politico.com/story/2017/07/16/trump-criticizes-abc-washington-post-polls-240602

Patterson, T. E. (1980). The mass media election: How Americans choose their president. New York: Praeger.

Patterson, Thomas. "News Coverage of the 2016 General Election: How the Press Failed the Voters." Shorenstein Center on Media, Politics and Public Policy, December 7, 2016, https://shorensteincenter.org/news-coverage-2016-general-election/

Patterson, T. E., and McClure, R. D. (1976). The unseeing eye. New York: Putnam.

Reuters. "Trump Approval." *Reuters/Ipsos*, July 24, 2017, http://polling.reuters.com/#poll/CP3_2/filters/AB7_2016: 2

Rucker, Philip. "Trump Defends His Son—Drawing a Contrast with Clinton—And Says Media are 'Distorting Democracy.'" *Washington Post*, July 16, 2017, www.washingtonpost.com/news/post-politics/wp/2017/07/16/trump-defends-his-son-drawing-a-contrast-with-clinton-and-says-media-are-distorting-democracy/?utm_term=.5e543c676573

Shaw, D. and McCombs, M. (1977). The emergence of American political issues. St. Paul, MN: West.

Shoemaker, P., Wanta, W. and Leggett, D. (1989). Communication campaigns about drugs: Government, media, and the public. In P. Shoemaker (Ed.). Communication campaigns about drugs, pp. 67-80. Hillsdale, NJ: Lawrence Erlbaum.

Smith, Allan. "Sean Spicer Angrily Defends Trump's Wiretap Claims in Wild, Contentious Press Briefing." *Business Insider*, March 16, 2017, www.businessinsider.com/sean-spicer-trump-wiretapping-claims-2017-3

Stelter, Brian. "Donald Trump Says Media is Out to Get Him." *CNN*, August 8, 2016, http://money.cnn.com/2016/08/14/media/donald-trump-media-bias-first-amendment/index.html

Sterne, Peter. "Fox News: 'No Evidence of any Kind' that Obama Wiretapped Trump." *Politico*, March 17, 2017, www.politico.com/blogs/on-media/2017/03/fox-news-no-evidence-trump-obama-wiretapping-236186

Tajfel, H. (1974). Social identity and intergroup behaviour. *Social Science Information*, vol. 13, pp. 65–93.

Tajfel, H., & Turner, J. C. (1979). An integrative theory of intergroup conflict. In W. G. Austin & S. Worchel (Eds.), The social psychology of intergroup relations (pp. 33-47). Monterey, CA: Brooks/Cole.

Tajfel, H. and Turner, J.C. (1986) The social identity theory of intergroup behavior. *Psychology of Intergroup Relations*, vol. 5, pp. 7–24.

Taylor, Jessica. "Americans Say Civility Has Worsened Under Trump; Trust In Institutions Down." *NPR*, July 3, 2017, www.npr.org/2017/07/03/535044005/americans-say-civility-has-worsened-under-trump-trust-in-institutions-down

Thrush, Glen and Maggie Haberman. "Trump Aides Address His Wiretap Claims: 'That's Above My Pay Grade.'" *The New York Times*, March 7, 2017, www.nytimes.com/2017/03/07/us/politics/trump-wiretap-claim-obama.html

Time. Here's Donald Trump's Presidential Announcement Speech. *Time*, June 16, 2015, http://time.com/3923128/donald-trump-announcement-speech/

Turner, John C., Michael Hogg, Penelope Oakes, Stephen Reicher, and Margaret Wetherell. Rediscovering the social group: A self-categorization theory. Oxford: Blackwell, 1987.

Wright, Austin. "Nunes on White House Grounds before Monitoring Claim." *Politico.com*, March 31, 2017, www.politico.com/story/2017/03/devin-nunes-white-house-monitoring-claim-236541

Yan, Holly. "Donald Trump's 'Blood' Comment about Megyn Kelly Draws Outrage." *CNN Politics*, August 8, 2015, www.cnn.com/2015/08/08/politics/donald-trump-cnn-megyn-kelly-comment/index.html

10

DIGITAL SOPHISTRY

Trump, Twitter, and Teaching about Fake News

Bryan A. Lutz

While media pundits debate the hows and whys of Donald Trump's election to the American presidency, a growing number suggest that Trump's rise was made possible by fake news shared on Twitter and other social networking sites. Fake news could be, as one managing editor for *U.S. News & World Report* put it, "fabricated stories which are either wholly not grounded in fact, or work in enough falsehoods as to be misleading" (Schlesinger 2017). But if fake news is simply a fabricated story, there is no need to neologize such phenomena. Tabloid media and other intentional forms of misinformation have long been studied. So how is fake news different? What are the effects of fake news? And urgently, what should be done to attenuate its negative effects? These questions are of increasing importance because America's current president, Donald Trump, has played a significant role in proliferating dubious information via Twitter. In the last decade, Trump has tweeted numerous stories that have been proven false, such as Barack Obama being born in Kenya, or that Senator Ted Cruz's father was involved in President Kennedy's assassination, or that Anthony Scalia was murdered (Farley 2016; Struyk 2016; Yilek 2016; Carrol 2017; Halloway 2017). These sensationalized and self-serving stories gain added legitimacy when shared through social media by the president elect, prompting demands for congressional inquiries, legal actions and, in rare cases, citizen vigilantes. Moreover, Trump spreads dubious information while labeling more established news outlets as "fake." Within such a tense context, scholars and educators must learn new ways of teaching students how to respond to fake news, especially when the term seems interchangeable with accusations of bias, or outright lying.

This chapter explores the phenomenon of fake news and offers ways to teach students about its definition, its forms, its functions, and its effects. First, this chapter discusses competing definitions of fake news contextualized within the history of tabloid media. This history can be useful for students because it shows how fake news has the characteristics of older forms of misinformation. Second, it discusses the Sophists and formulates neo-sophistic criticism as a lens for analyzing fake news. The Sophists further elucidate fake news in ways that both complement and conflict with how fake news is understood. Third, the chapter demonstrates how students can apply neo-sophistic criticism to online texts as a means for understanding the forms and effects of fake news and the digital Sophists that produce them. Suitable for this volume about Trump's tweets, two news stories are analyzed: #Pizzagate and paid protestors. These stories were chosen because they are prolific fake news stories endorsed by Donald Trump via Twitter. To conclude, the chapter contributes to scholarship in the social sciences, where scholars are charting the ecosystems that produce fake news (Mihailidis and Viotty 2017; Wardle 2017) and examining how peoples' subconscious biases play a role in internalizing fake news as legitimate reporting (Allcott and Gentzkow 2017; Frimer et al. 2017).

Misinformation, Tabloid Media, and Fake News

Misinformation is not a new phenomenon. From state-run propaganda to partisan reporting, the power of media has long been used either to stretch truths or to lie outright for the benefit of various interests. But of all forms of misinformation, we might consider tabloid media as the closest precursor to fake news. In *Panic Attacks* (2004), sociologist Robert Bartholomew argues that the "Great Moon Hoax" was the first twentieth-century example of tabloid media publishing an intentionally fabricated story as news in the U.S. Reported in *The New York Sun* in 1835, the story cited a prominent scientist, Sir John Herschel, and claimed that Herschel had discovered 'bat-men' living in colonies on the moon. The Great Moon Hoax was not intended to be read as real news, and yet if proved convincing for two reasons. First, the authors wrote the story in ways that mimicked a real newspaper. Second, the writing mimicked Herschel's style and his proclivity for using technical jargon. The Great Moon Hoax proved so convincing that the story unintentionally provoked a mass panic among citizens of New York, who feared that alien life was a threat to their own.

While the Great Moon Hoax was an intentionally fabricated story with unintended consequences, scholars chronicling the history of tabloid journalism cite the 1874 Central Park Zoo Escape as *exemplum optimi* of intentional misinformation (Wallace 2000; Bartholomew and Radford 2011). Published in the *New York Herald*, the Zoo Escape story likewise panicked the people of New York by reporting that dangerous animals had escaped the Central Park Zoo. Unlike the Great Moon Hoax, the story was written to be hyperbole rather than falsehood. Outlined by then editor Thomas B. Connery and authored by Joseph I. C. Clarke, Clarke had witnessed the mishandling of the animals at the Central Park Zoo and embellished a story far more serious than the events he had observed. Connery's intentions for publishing the fabricated story were not to deceive, but to, in his words, serve the "public good." He wished "to warn the public and the authorities of an impending danger" based on his observations of the zoo (Connery 1893). For Connery and Clarke, while the story was fake, using a fabricated story to warn the public against a threat was true enough to warrant publication. True or not, with sensationalism and controversy came significant financial success. Bartholomew shows that such stories launched a new 'penny press,' a kind of paper that would better appeal to the American Middle Class by replacing the mundane and dry prose of traditional media with more vibrant and sensational writing. Tabloid journalism grew to prominence, and the terms "tabloid media" and "yellow journalism" were coined to distinguish such media from more factual reporting (McKerns 1976).

Both the Great Moon Hoax and The Central Park Zoo Escape are useful for teaching students about the precursors to fake news. First, they exist as alternative media that is distinct from legitimate news sources. Second, they are purposed toward generating revenue by being entertaining and sensational rather than wholly accurate. Third, particularly in the case of the Great Moon Hoax, the authors purposefully wrote the story in ways that made it seem credible. Fourth, particularly in the case of The Central Park Zoo Escape, the authors may justify embellishment as a means to elucidate a legitimate threat. Fifth, the authors' motivations were linked to profit and to sustaining alternative publications. When taken in sum, this short history provides a precedent for why fake news exists.

But how is fake news different from other forms of tabloid media? Claire Wardle at the John F. Kennedy School of Government at Harvard University has called fake news an ecosystem facilitated largely by social media. The fake news ecosystem, she argues, has three elements: the different types of contents that are being created and shared, the motivations of those who create this content, and the ways this content is distributed (Wardle 2017). Within the first element, Wardle identifies seven different types of content: satire or parody; misleading content; imposter content; fabricated content; false connection, where the headline does not match the content; false context, genuine content with false contextual information; and manipulated content. The trouble with these criteria is that all of the above are applicable to tabloid media; what makes fake news truly distinguishable is Wardle's final element, social media and other free chat applications as the primary means of distributing fake news.

Fake news 'requires' the participation of its readership through social media as an essential element of its success. Paul Mihailidis and Samantha Viotty demonstrate this element more fully in their study "Spreadable Spectacle in Digital Culture: Civic Expression, Fake News, and the Role of Media Literacies in 'Post-Fact' Society" (2017). They examine the story of #Pizzagate as an example of fake news, and argue that social or "spreadable media" is what makes fake news possible because the ecosystem of information bypasses editorial gatekeeping and displays the information with equal emphasis and recognition as more legitimate news outlets. As a form of spreadable media, social media affords users more control over their content, making a digital space for increased interaction among like-minded people within its own ecosystem. Fake news' power to spread is directly linked to its audience's capability to republish the story across multiple social media channels.

Because fake news is powered by social media, fake news poses a real challenge for educators, particularly with regard to digital literacy. Social media largely exists outside the checks and balances of convention media. There are no editors or fact checkers between the production and proliferation of fake news. Any interventions, such as from fact-checking sites, happen only after the media is produced. It is for this reason that Michelle Ciulla Lipkin, director of the National Association for Media Literacy Education (NAMLE), cautions that in "every step of the [media] chain from content creator to social media platform to user must be held more accountable" than they are now. Lipkin further argues that students cannot be insulated from the dangers of fake news; instead, "we need to embrace technology and media and empower students to use it. We need to stop trying to protect kids and start preparing them" (Padgett 2017, 6). However, Mihailidis and Viotty argue that "the positioning of media literacy as a solution simplifies the problem to what is at best an unhelpful context, and at worst a red herring that exacerbates the current uproar over fake news and misinformation online" (449). They further argue that if literacy is to be a solution, it must "respond directly to the emerging spreadable ecosystem for information, created and propagated by homophilius networks, [and] lack of trust in gatekeeping" (450). Later, this chapter demonstrates how to map these emerging spreadable ecosystems and assess the means and intents of fake news authors.

The issues discussed by Wardle, Lipkin, and Mihailidis and Viotty are similar to the concerns of Rhetoric and Composition studies since its inception. The disciplined has long explored the available means and media for persuasion and theorized about the motivations behind the need to persuade. In this tradition, this chapter responds directly to the spreadable ecosystems of misinformation by teaching students ways to become their own gatekeepers. Another goal is to posit the Sophists and neo-sophistic criticism as a way to further elucidate definitions of fake news and to name fake news authors and their motivations. By invoking the visage of the Sophists will not only further elucidate fake news but also serve to better chart the means and motivations of digital Sophists and the fake news they produce.

Sophists, Sophistry, and Neo-sophistic Criticism

Since the late 1980s and early 1990s, rhetoric and composition scholars have examined the Sophists and how their philosophies might shape how we teach persuasion. Edward Schiappa (1990) cautioned against such study because very few of the Sophists' works survived to the present and thus much of what we know about the Sophists we know through the diatribes against them authored by philosophers like Plato, Aristotle, and Isocrates (1990, 213). Despite his contention, Schiappa agrees that "Sophist" can be *neo*-Sophist, an approximation of sophistic philosophy as a concept for examining contemporary rhetorical phenomenon. Schiappa maintains that the application of neo-sophistic concepts can be productive some twenty-five years later after his initial publication (2015, 4–8). Scott Consigny made the Sophist/neo-Sophist distinction clear, discerning between "the construction of neo-sophistic rhetorical theory and criticism and the historical reconstruction of specific sophistic doctrines concerning discourse" (Consigny 1996, 214). This chapter embraces the neo-sophistic not to make definitive claims about who the Sophists were, but to demonstrate how adopting a visage of the Sophists can be a method for defining fake news and understanding how fake news is authored.

To truly understand fake news, three units of analysis for neo-sophistic criticism are needed: (i) dissoi logoi, (ii) différend, and (iii) means and media. Each unit of analysis approximately represents one facet, or building block, of the Sophist's philosophy of argumentation and persuasion. First, the dissoi logoi was the sophistic exercise for teaching students about argument. The Sophist Protagoras, for example, "can be remembered for maintaining that there are two opposing arguments about everything, and as teachers the Sophists encouraged students to try arguing for the weaker side" (Gibson 1993, 286). This practice teaches students to "juxtapose competing arguments, to imagine the merits of either side," and practice arguing a position regardless of whether or not they agree with it (Bizzell and Herzburg 1990, 23).

When wearing the visage of the Sophist, a teacher can encourage students to construct arguments "on both sides of an issue [and] consider how they are both like and unlike" (McKiharan 1994, 192). Teaching Dissoi logoi serves two fundamental objectives: first, investigating sites where humans compete to make meaning and deliberate over 'truth'; and second, developing enough proficiency in argumentation to effectively argue a point, whether they believe what they are saying is true in any absolute sense, or not. The Sophists' philosophy rejected capital 'T' truth as a way to foreground how a skilled rhetor could use communication to make reality by swaying audiences toward the speaker's point of view. In contemporary classroom practice, the dissoi logoi may call to mind not only the pedagogical utility of critical engagement in the classroom but also the utility of university debate teams, or instructor-led mock trials for teaching students proficiency with argument.

Sophistic study also concerns the motivations of speakers and how their motivations might make competing positions irreconcilable. Victor Vitanza, in his article, "The Sophists? Negation, Subjectivity, and The History of Rhetoric," argues that the conflict between Sophists and Rhetoricians produced a *différend* (from Jean-Francois Lyotard), or the incommensurable and irreconcilable positions between two or more parties in tension. The différend emerges when two parties hold competing criterion for credibility and truth, and when their investment in their respective positions is tied to their identity. This identity is defined in relationship to an Other, or the representation of an opposing view where that the Other is unable to represent themselves. Vitanza demonstrates how the différend emerges by making explicit parallels between how the Sophists were represented in the works of Aristotle and Plato rather than preserved in the works of the actual Sophists. In this way, the Sophists have always posed a problem because their presence in the rhetorical canon could be interpreted as a silenced Other, the marginalized and the oppressed. For Vitanza, it was Plato and Aristotle who enjoy the privilege of being established, whereas the Sophists are "rootless," having their history purposefully forgotten in the same ways as "the Jews, with the Gypsies, the Queers" and others that represent "that-which-cannot-be-represented." In this way, the différend is not only what, but whom cannot be reconciled, because their perspectives were (mis)represented and silenced by dominant discourses (Vitanza 1996, 27). In naming the différend, Vitanza envisions the Sophists as a cautionary tale for when any speaker, writer, or scholar attempts to represent a position unlike their own and in the absence of the Other's voice.

The final unit of analysis is to examine the means and media available for successful argumentation. For the Sophists, the means the power of one's voice combined with artfully crafted words, rhythms, and gestures. Success was measured by how many people could be persuaded of the argument. In this way, the Sophists subscribed to a sort marketplace of ideas within their own schools. Sophists cultivated rivalries among skilled students and measured students' success by their ability to refute another's views, devise new theories, and attract new audiences (McKiharan 1994, 403). The Sophists claimed success by teaching students how to argue effectively rather than honestly, and, as Gibson argues, "No doubt their very success invited envy and criticism, especially their financial success" (Gibson 1999, 284). In this history, we might hear echoes the conservative ideology of the marketplace as being the impartial arbiter of all things. If an author can be successful both financially and by generating a following, then the argument is true, or at least true enough.

Demonstration of Neo-sophistic Criticism: Fake News as Digital Sophistry

This section demonstrates how neo-sophistic criticism can add precision to definitions of fake news, thereby empowering students with a conceptual frame for responding directly to emerging ecosystems of misinformation. This demonstration involves the application of neo-sophistic criticism to texts coupled with teaching students a base literacy in how websites and social media work. To understand fake news, then, is to understand the confluence between the technologies used to author and proliferate fake news and the philosophy that drive its production. Neo-sophistic criticism has three units of analysis:

1 *Dissoi logoi*: does the author seek to strengthen a less plausible or implausible position? Does the author seek to make a weaker argument stronger?
2 *Différend*: does the author take a tense and irreconcilable position in response to an Other, and does the author actively name an identity or opponent that personifies that position?
3 *Means and media*: does the author demonstrate an effort to circumvent traditional media channels? Is the author situated to profit from their claim through advertising, and gain a following through likes, clicks, or shares?

When formulated into a concept, neo-sophistic criticism enables students to define fake news and analyze its forms and effects. As a method, the three primary units of analysis can be applied to specific texts. 'Texts' in this case can be any electronic news item found online. To teach sophistry as a concept is to wear the visage of the Sophist to teach how fake news communicates in ways that correspond with the neo-sophistic philosophy of communication. Understood in this way, fake news is a form of digital sophistry, where digital Sophists utilize social media to circumvent traditional media channels; name an irreconcilable position that the author opposes; and argue for the expressed purpose of strengthening an implausible position. The questions above are the conceptual framework for determining whether a text is indeed fake news.

As an example of classroom practice, this chapter demonstrates here how to analyze two stories widely regarded as fake news. The first is the story of "#Pizzagate." After the publication of emails written by Clinton's campaign manager, John Podesta, by the whistleblowing site WikiLeaks, rumors began on the social media sites Twitter, Facebook, Reddit, and 4chan that Clinton's team was running a pedophile ring out of Comet Pizza, an establishment owned by openly gay James Alefantis (Alefantis 2016; Gillin 2016; Wade 2017). The rumor began with a single tweet from the Twitter account @DavidGoldbergNYC, which turned out to be a white supremacist group posing as a Jewish lawyer (Gillin 2016). The tweet suggested that Trump's opponent, Hillary Clinton, along with the recently resigned congressman Anthony Weiner, was involved in a child-trafficking ring from the bottom of the Washington D.C. pizza restaurant. The tweet gained legitimacy within online forums on Reddit and 4chan, and an article posted on aceloewgold.com, culminating into several online several texts. So powerful was the fake news story that it motivated a man to drive from his home in North Carolina to the restaurant in Washington D.C. to self-investigate the story while armed with an AR-15 (Slotkin 2017). The story began as a complete fabrication, offering no evidence other than photos of the restaurant juxtaposed with a composite photo of Anthony Weiner's head on a man's exposed chest. But in the hands of fake news authors, the story took on a life of its own.

The second is the story of Eric Tucker, a 35-year-old co-founder of a marketing company in Austin, Texas. Through his participation on Twitter, Tucker heard stories that billionaire George Soros was paying to transport protestors to different locations to discredit Trump's campaign and presidency. While observing one such protest, Tucker saw a parade of buses parked at a hotel close by. Tucker deduced that he had found evidence that the protestors had been bused to Austin (Maheshwari 2016). He photographed the buses and tweeted his claim, and then president-elect Trump boosted the message by tweeting, "Just had a very open and successful presidential election. Now professional protesters, incited by the media, are protesting. Very unfair!" (Trump November 10, 2016). According to *The New York Times*, Trump's endorsement of Tucker's tweet started a "frenzy" where the tweet was reported as news on the conservative discussion forum The Free Republic, a multiple-thread discussion forum on the social networking site Reddit (Maheshwari 2016). Tucker deleted the tweet after learning that the buses he photographed were for attendees of a local conference. He even tried to clarify that what he was wrong via a second tweet, but that tweet generated far less attention (2016). There is evidence suggesting that the story had a significant impact on the 2016 Presidential election. Shortly after the election, an online poll found that "73% of Trump voters thought the billionaire financier George Soros paid protesters to disrupt the Republican candidate's rallies" (Hunt 2017).

Dissoi Logoi: Strengthening the Weaker Argument

Beginning with the first unit of analysis, the dissoi logoi brings into view how the author can make a weaker argument stronger. Consider how applying the sophistic concept of dissoi logoi explains how both the #Pizzagate story and Eric Tucker's busing story should qualify as fake news. Generally speaking, Clinton was positioned as the stronger candidate while positioning Donald Trump as the weaker one. The dominant media narrative placed Hilary Clinton as the likely winner of the presidency. She was far more experienced than Trump and thus the more qualified presidential candidate. By contrast, Trump is viewed by his supporters as the anti-establishment candidate, the underdog in the fight against a powerful establishment and thus a weaker side of a simple, dichotomous debate. Trump himself has claimed that he is a power separate from the politicians in Washington and one at odds with a 'liberal' media. So, to defend against the hegemony of politicians and media, the goal is not to preoccupy oneself with any capital "T" truth, but instead to strengthen Trump's positions and his candidacy. Two of Trump's primary arguments against Clinton's candidacy were that she is a corrupt criminal (Lock her up!), and that Clinton should be suspected of illegal activities including human trafficking and rigging elections. Both claims were made by Trump via Twitter in November 2016.

#Pizzagate began with a claim that Clinton and Podesta were running a child sex trafficking out of the basement of Comet Pizza (Alefantis 2016; Gillin 2016; Wade 2017). But since there was no evidence of trafficking, and since traditional media channels were not reporting the story, supporters of Trump put considerable effort into piecing together evidence in support of the rumor using Reddit and 4chan as a forum for discussion. On those forums, users shared alleged photos of the basement where the children were kept; they 'decoded' Podesta's repeated use of the word 'pizza' in his emails as a signal for sexual activity with minors; and they similarly 'decoded' the branding of the surrounding buildings as containing sexual imagery and symbols used by pedophiles. While the photos of the basement were determined to be fabrications (Gillin 2016; Ritchie 2016), the forum users were able to identify some resemblances between symbols used by Comet Pizza and surrounding businesses and actual symbols used by child traffickers. Their source was legitimate, as they used the Federal Bureau of Investigation's (FBI) database to support their claims, even if their assessments were loose. But key here is that it was the users, more so than any one author or news source, that worked to make the implausible seem plausible—the weaker argument now made stronger.

By sharing photo evidence and citing WikiLeaks cables as evidence, social media users sought to strengthen the rumor that protestors were being paid to visit Trump's campaign stops. These reports inspired Tucker to look for evidence that buses were driving protestors to campaign events. Tucker contributed evidence to the story by tweeting pictures of buses and claiming he observed protestors walking from the bus to Trump's campaign rally. Tuckers original tweet then garnered over 300,000 shares on Facebook (Maheshwari 2016). For comparison, CNBC compared this story and others to the top performing Facebook story for *The New York Times* the same month, which racked up just around 370,000 engagements (Ritchie 2016). Stories claiming that protestors were bused from site to site by Soros began on alternative media sites rather than legitimate news sources. Like tabloid media, the story of paid protestors was more entertaining and sensational than accurate, and the story also generated significant hysteria. But unlike the Great Moon Hoax or The Central Park Zoo Escape, this story was neither confined to any single news source nor was it confined to New York State. In the absence of evidence for paid protestors, Trump's supporters sought ways to make weaker arguments stronger. In the sphere of social media, this scant evidence was taken as definitive proof, thereby gaining the attention of Trump, who likewise used his position to boost the credibility of the fake news stories. User participation was key in spreading this misinformation, and Tucker made the weaker argument stronger by playing the role of witness to the story.

Différend: Naming the Other and Soliciting Prejudice

Considering now the différend as the second facet of neo-sophistic criticism and as lens for analyzing fake news. The différend is the incommensurable and irreconcilable position embodied by an Other. In the case of #Pizzagate, articles repeatedly and explicitly refer to Clinton and Alefantis in derogatory terms and use loaded language although many of those articles have been scrubbed from the Internet.[1] This move solicited the prejudices of its audience by denoting Clinton and Alefantis as antithetical to their own political and social allegiances. The différend in this case was liberals: Clinton, a woman and Democratic nominee, and an openly gay owner of a pizza restaurant who was once in a relationship with a member of Clinton's campaign. Moreover, the distrust of conventional media sources is also embedded within the liberal différend, as "mainstream" media is portrayed as having a liberal bias that allegedly blinds them to seeing the legitimacy of the story. The liberal différend, then, was consubstantial with women and with Lesbian, Gay, Bisexual, and Transgender (LGBT) individuals, and all of whom are embedded within the connotation of both criminal and political opponent advantaged by traditional media.

Likewise in the case of Tucker, the liberal différend was George Soros and his alleged affiliations with left-wing political interests. Soros is an outspoken Democrat with verifiable ties to the Democratic Party. But within texts on Reddit and 4chan, Soros is more than a supporter. The users accused Soros of paying individuals to protest for progressive causes. Specifically, Soros' supposed influence extends beyond protestors against Donald Trump's campaign to include the Black Lives Matter protests in Ferguson and the Women's March in Washington (Mikkelson 2015; Greenburg 2017). This claim gained further legitimacy when it was boosted by Trump's campaign manager, Corey Lwandowski, who shared a fake news article claiming that Clinton, Soros, and Democrats, and specifically people of Middle Eastern descent comprised the large constituency of paid performers working to start riots and discredit Trump.[2] The term "liberal" is never clearly defined in these online texts apart from either its political allegiances to the Democratic Party or its allegiances to a number of minoritized populations in the U.S. In this broadly generalizing move, the liberal différend is then consubstantial with Soros' affiliation with the Democratic Party, with Black Lives Matter, and with Muslims. Tucker and others heard these stories and through prejudice reasoned that Soros was behind the buses Tucker had photographed.

This acute attention to individuals suggests that authors of fake news view information about said individuals as consubstantial with the identities they oppose. In addition to fake news' participatory nature, the différend seems to be an important component that distinguishes fake news from other forms of tabloid media. #Pizzagate and the story of paid protestors are like conventional tabloid media in that both are sensationalized stories that have little or no factual evidence for support. But contrary to the Great Moon Hoax or The Central Park Zoo Escape, fake news stories are not about aliens or zoo animals; instead, they name an opposition with which any reconciliation as truth or credibility is impossible. As Wardle (2016) has noted, fake news often serves the purpose of galvanizing partisan allegiances. Moreover, fake news sites demonstrate a preoccupation with naming the people involved in the story and likewise naming their opponents as simultaneously liberal, woman, black, gay, and Muslim. The liberal identity as the différend, or an irreconcilable position that conflates "liberal" with other marginalized social positions, works beyond partisanship to solicit prejudice. If we consider that Trump has proven a certain affinity for dog whistle politics, and that he has no compunction about denouncing or degrading people of marginalized identities (Vega 2016; López 2018), then we see why digital Sophists may adopt a similar strategy.

Means and Media: Social Media, Open-source Websites, and the Ecosystems of Fake News

The final unit of analysis is to consider the means and media used to produce fake news beginning first by discussing social media. It is social media sites like Twitter that add a new participatory dimension to fake news. Since social media enables users to share information so quickly through its channels, the users themselves become publishers of misinformation. Since users can act so quickly and in haste, fake news has added pressure on journalists to respond quickly, and this haste has had consequences. For example, Fox News had to issue an on-air apology after reporting that Hillary Clinton had called Bernie Sanders' supporters "a bucket of losers" at a speaking engagement. Like the Great Moon Hoax, the story was authored in a way that appeared factual: it cited a recent release of Clinton's emails by WikiLeaks, and the story's key quote echoed Clinton's earlier statements about Trump supporters as a "basket of deplorables." But in addition, the story gained significant traction due in part to Donald Trump tweeting about the email release. In addition, then Fox News anchor Megyn Kelly also boosted the story by tweeting about it; however, while the story sounded believable, both the quote and the details of where it was supposedly uttered were fabricated. Marco Chacon wrote this story for his satire news site RealTrueNews.org, and Chacon later expressed regret that his story was believed and reported as legitimate news (Chang et al. 2016; Greenwald 2016).

In addition to social media, websites authored with open-source tools are an equally important aspect of fake news. In the past decade, there has been a boom of websites authored with WordPress software and hosted on for-pay hosting sites, such as Cloudflare, GoDaddy, and Dreamhost. It is increasingly common for authors both nationally and internationally to use for-profit hosting services to host *WordPress* installations. While these services are suited for the typical small business owner or casual writer to gain a web presence, the purpose of fake news sites is to provide the veneer of legitimate news while making advertising revenue by sharing alternative, often sensationalized media stories that gain clicks, likes, and shares. Writing for *BuzzFeed News*, Silverman and Alexander (2016) show how teenagers in Macedonia created fake news websites that appear to be separate websites created by different people, but that are in fact either one author or small group of authors using several WordPress sites to report the same misinformation. Their findings have important implications for understanding fake news. It is possible for one person or a small group of people to build multiple websites that work in tandem with social media, and through the interactions among these different channels of media, boost each site's rankings within search engines. This implication is significant for two reasons. First, there is no limit to how one person or one group of authors can amplify their voice using complex networks of open-source websites; second, while tabloid print media can be confined to supermarket checkout lanes, fake news articles are aggregated by search engines right alongside *The New York Times*, *The Associated Press*, and other well-established and edited news outlets, affording them a certain veneer of legitimacy to the untrained eye. Working in tandem, social media and open-source websites combined are the two major aspects of the ecosystems of fake news, and charting the means and media empowers students and instructors to name and to map these aspects.

The story of paid protestors illustrates how social media and open-source websites are essential parts of fake news ecosystems. Tucker and Trump's tweets seemed to function as surrogates to news outlets. After tweeting a picture of buses in Austin, Tucker used the hastags #fakeprotests #trump2016 #austin. Shortly after, the headline "They Found the Buses!" appeared on Reddit with the same hashtags, and the conservative forum site freerepublic.com hosted a vibrant conversation where users claimed to have also seen buses unloading protestors at Trump's campaign sites (Maheshwari 2016). Later, Trump's campaign manager, Corey Lwandowski, boosted the story via Twitter by sharing an article from ABCNews.com.co, a WordPress installation that is a facsimile of the website for ABC News and authored by the late Paul Horner, a self-identified fake news writer. Inspired by reports, Horner created a fake ad on *Craigslist* soliciting protestors before writing the story endorsed by Lwandowski. Paul Horner offers his account of the story's virality, "[Trump's] campaign manager posted my story about a protester getting paid $3,500 as fact. Like, I made that up. I posted a fake ad on Craigslist" (Dewey 2016). Here, social media and open-source software worked to boost each other's message while circumventing traditional media and strengthening a weakened position with little to no factual basis. Tucker, who had only forty followers before the story broke, had a following that grew to the thousands after obtaining the endorsement of Trump (Maheshwari 2016), each existing all over the country and the world. More than simply a false story, users of social media gave eyewitness testimony confirming the fabricated narratives.

ACELOEWGOLD   ABOUT   CONTACT   SUPPORT ACELOEWGOLD   --BECAUSE REALITY IS ONLY WHAT WE'RE TOLD.

"It is dangerous to be right in matters on which the established authorities
are wrong." – Voltaire

#PIZZAGATE, CLINTON, & PODESTA: WHAT IS IT, AND IS IT CREDIBLE?

CONTRIBUTE TO THIS BLOG

Donate with **PayPal**

November 20, 2016 · by Ace of Swords · in #Pizzagate, Global Elite · 143 Comments

FOLLOW ACELOEWGOLD ON FACEBOOK

Some may have noticed the hashtag #Pizzagate around the Internet lately, and aren't sure what it's all about. So, what is #Pizzagate? In the post that follows I will provide a #Pizzagate summary to explain the movement's origin, outline which of its claims have been confirmed as verifiable facts, and offer my own conclusion as to whether or not you should be paying closer attention.

(Note: Was #Pizzagate debunked by the New York Times, Snopes, the Washington Post, and other major outlets? Learn more here.)

Be the first of your friends to like this

First off, forgive the length — quite a bit of context and explanation is required to do an explanation of the "#Pizzagate" phenomenon justice. Also, a disclaimer: In addition to being difficult to digest,

FIGURE 10.1   Screen shot of the website ACELOEWGOLD, taken on November 20, 2016.

Since 2016, there have been numerous websites created with open-source soft-ware that championed stories by supporters of Trump. So when considering the means and media, it is important to trace the origins of a message through its many iterations on social media and open-source websites. Using Internet search engines, web analytics, and the W3 registry, any text can be traced. To demonstrate how student and teacher could examine #Pizzagate as an example. First, use Google or Yahoo to search for the names Clinton, Podesta, and Comet Pizza. Then, find a highly ranked website. One example is the website aceloewgold.com, which published two articles on November 20, 2016, both coinciding with the conversations on social media and Trump's own tweets about the #Pizzagate story.

From there, use a web analytics site to assess the site's traffic. According to the web analytics site Buzzsumo.com, the #Pizzagate article on acelowe-gold.com had almost 7,000 engagements on Facebook and over 200 interactions on Twitter. Further examination reveals how the author of the website wished to challenge to establish media outlets. The sites tagline establishes the ethos of resisting dominant media using a quote from Voltaire reading, "It is dangerous to be right in matters on which established authorities are wrong" (see Figure 10.1). Such activity on social media became the foundation for articles published on several websites sympathetic to conservative causes.

When analyzing the means and media, students can be taught a basic liter-acy in how authors boost their websites' rankings within Google and Yahoo. Students could start by collecting texts they have found on their social media of choice, and then analyzing that text using neo-sophistic criticism in part-nership with online web analytics. Web analytics sites can chart how far the

Most Shared

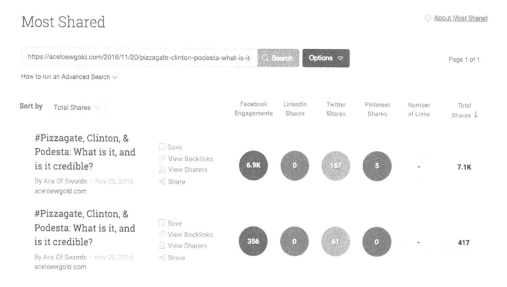

FIGURE 10.2 Screen shot of Buzzsumo's analytics assessing the ACELOEWGOLD site, taken on November 20, 2016.

web text has traveled through Twitter or Facebook. Take, for example, the website aceloewgold.com and their article titled "#Pizzagate, Clinton, and Podesta." Pasting the URL for that article into Buzzsumo.com's search engine reveals that the fake news article received considerable traffic on social media (see Figure 10.2).

Students may then click on the "View Sharers" link and see the top three users who shared the story. For example, as of September 20, 2016, the link's top sharers were Facebook groups called "America's Freedom Fighters" and "USA Patriots for Donald Trump." For a fee, the "View Backlinks" link becomes accessible to determine whether other websites have linked to the article. But even without a fee, web analytics systems like Buzzsumo offer a few free queries per day at no charge.

Next is to determine whether the site is a WordPress installation, which can be done one of the two ways. First, using the URL WHOIS registry on GoDaddy.com, students can see when a website was created and where it is hosted. Take, for example, the website usconservativetribune.com, a website that has proliferated numerous fake news articles. Students can look up the site's registry and see that the website has only existed since December 2017 and that it is inexpensively hosted on NameCheap Inc. The WHOIS registry might also show if a website is hosted on wordpress.com. The second and quickest method for determining whether a site is a WordPress to simply append "/wp-admin" to the end of usconservativetribune.com's URL (usconservativetribune.com/wp-admin). This URL would then navigate the student to the WordPress login page for website, thereby verifying that it is a website composed with WordPress software. Appending "/wp-admin" may not work in every case because the server's administrator may have a rewrite rule in place to redirect users away from the administrative access portal. But thankfully, this security protocol is not in place for most fake news sites, perhaps because the sites are not maintained long enough where such security is necessary.

Worthy of note is that the différend can be embedded within the practice of circumventing traditional media using social networking and open-source tools. Fake news sites often use URLs that either mirror the web URLs of existing media outlets or, more commonly, invoke a particular identity. With many of the sites that proliferated the #Pizzagate story and the story of paid protestors, the URLs of the sites invoked identities and allegiances. Sites such as dailyusaupdate.com, daily-usa.com, usanewsflash.com, and others explicitly invoke an American identity. Sites such as president45donaldtrump.com, swampdrain.com, and hitleryforprison.com invoke allegiance to Donald Trump by echoing his campaign slogans. Sites such as consmovement.com, conservativefighters.com, and conspatriot.com explicitly invoke a conservative identity. This American, conservative identity is constructed in opposition to the liberal différend and as a demonstration of allegiance to Donald Trump. The identity then exists at the confluence of the différend and the available means and media, thereby creating echo chambers that both bypassed traditional media sources and unify users within the common identity. In other words, for there to be an Other, there must be a self and a place to cultivate a shared identity. All these sites played a role in circumventing traditional media channels and boosting the message of Donald Trump, as they provided stable URLs that had the veneer of a news website. As mentioned earlier in this chapter, it is curious how many of these sites are no longer active as of writing this chapter in 2017—vanished, almost like the writings of the Sophists of antiquity. Some of these disappearances can be attributed to increasing competition with sites hosted in Macedonia (Silverman and Alexander 2016), but it is also possible that these sites were created and maintained solely as boosters for Donald Trump and his campaign. If fake news websites have such impermanence, then the need to continually reassess web sources becomes clearer.

The dissoi logoi, the différend, and the means and media comprise a neo-sophistic method for analyzing digital sophistry and identifying an online text as fake news, but only when all three units of analysis are accounted for within online texts. A news article may, for example, rely on anecdotal evidence and still be legitimate. It may exist on social media or a WordPress site and still be credible. It may name a différend and not necessarily be fake, as partisan news can sometimes be credible. But taken in sum, students can assess web texts as potential examples of digital sophistry: does it work to make a weak argument stronger by building evidence for a case? Does it name a différend? Does it bypass traditional news outlets? In order for news to be fake news, all three facets of neo-sophistic critique must be present.

Conclusion

This chapter shows that fake news is distinct from previous forms of misinformation. What makes fake news distinct are the contributions of digital Sophists working within ecosystems of social media networked with open-source websites. Fake news can begin as a rumor on Twitter before taking new life on forums such as Reddit and 4chan. There, the fictitious can become definitive within the minds of social media users working tirelessly to strengthen their arguments in opposition to an Other that is a political and a social opponent. The success of their efforts is measured in likes, shares, and clicks, and within the open-source websites, these interactions can generate substantial profits. Whether motivated by profit or by the need to defend Donald Trump, imagine the power that Trump must feel when he can rely on his supporters to write news stories favorable to him and his administration.

President Trump has seemed willing to embrace fake news in two ways. First is to suit his political aims and in this effort, Twitter is his social media of choice. Leading up to the election, Trump claimed that widespread voter fraud might cost him the election, relying on dubious reports that George Soros and others were paying protestors to attend Trump's campaign functions (Greenburg 2017). This story began when "a little-known conservative activist whose work on the issue has been widely discredited and who has trafficked in conspiracy theories" tweeted about the story (Martin 2017). The story had no factual basis, but it inspired a sort of citizen journalism where users looked for evidence to support the claim. By tweeting, Trump has played a role in legitimizing such activity. The story then becomes 'true,' or at least impactful to the degree with which they earn likes, shares, and upvotes on social media. Instead of factual reporting, the goal seems to be finding a communication product that has resonance with an audience, attracts, followers, and is thus worth selling for more reasons that just affirming their own biases. It would be no wonder why the existence of fake news is so vexing for journalists, pundits, and scholars alike.

Second, Trump is willing to use fake news as a means to discredit any view that does not agree with his own. He has labeled *The New York Times*, CNN, and other news outlets as "fake" as a means to discredit them. If Donald Trump continues to label major news outlets as fake news as a way to frame that all news is merely competing with the President's interests, in lieu of this study, Trump's rise becomes less surprising although no less harrowing. Fake news has created a cacophony of misinformation that blends of truth, half-truth, and fiction that, in the words of Kalev Leetaru (2016), "even the best can no longer tell what's real and what's not." While its persuasive effects are difficult to measure, the effects of fake news extend beyond simply expressing and appeasing bias. Neo-sophistic criticism offers a way for questioning that philosophy of communication to teach the dangers of fake news and the digital Sophists who author it to new generations of writers, communicators, and media consumers.

Sharing information and lively debate are certainly important parts of a democracy, where everyone has a voice in how they are represented and how they are governed. Given this ethos of free exchange of information and the desire to solicit contributions of all, it is no surprise that fake news sites would capitalize on open-source platforms to proliferate their messages. As Mihailidis and Viotty have shown, proliferators of fake news lack trust in traditional media authorities. Digital Sophists are motivated by their distrust and see their new sites as a part of a necessary movement toward further democratizing media and circumventing what they see as corporate-controlled, left-leaning media empires that amass billions of dollars annually. In this context, digital Sophists see crafting a viral story as just beating the media at its own game. Akin to the legacy of Trump's own earning power, if fake news makes money and attracts a loyal following, then it is the demand for alternative facts that reward the effort.

But clearly there are dangers to an Internet that can be used in this way. The most dangerous byproduct is that digital Sophists can anonymously bolster their web presence and share information that is more self-serving and self-affirming than accurate. Journalists working for mainstream news outlets have a reputation to uphold, but digital Sophists can simply abandon one social media presence to assume another, thereby becoming a cacophony of multiple websites and social media accounts that all boost the same misinformation. Through digital sophistry, these authors and users masterfully utilize new technologies to strengthening weaker positions, incite prejudice, and circumvent established media through complex ecologies of social media and open-source websites.

The findings of this study are aligned with scholars who have likewise examined fake news.[3] Mihailidis and Viotty examined #Pizzagate as an example fake news, which they define as a 'spectacle' in the sense that fosters echo chambers out of a shared identity and sense of purpose, and as a form of "spreadable media" in the sense that social media affords use the ability to control their own content, making a digital space for increased interaction among like-minded people outside of conventional media sources. But Mihailidis and Viotty foreground political allegiances and bias as a primary factor within fake news without any explicit reference to issues of identity that are accounted for with neo-sophistic criticism. Similarly, Claire Wardle defines fake news largely by its types of content, the authors' motivations, and the ability to use social media as the primary means of distribution. In addition to Wardle's framework, neo-sophistic critique foregrounds the role of digital Sophists who combine open-source websites with social media to solicit the prejudices of the audience and strengthen a weaker case. Neo-sophistic criticism foregrounds the dissoi logoi, the différend, and the means and media to distinguish fake news from its precursors in tabloid media and to enrich current definitions of fake news beyond simply sensational and partisan stories shared on social media, thereby adding further complexity to how scholars should understand fake news.

Notes

1 Kim LaCapria notes that many of the websites supporting #Pizzagate are no longer available online. Indeed, many of the fake news articles and Reddit threads supporting #Pizzagate have either expired URLs, or they have been banned (https://archive.is/R4lPX). Craig Silverman (cited in this chapter) aggregated some of the Reddit posts, where users authored their arguments that Clinton, Podesta, Weiner, and Alefantis were involved in #Pizzagate. Silverman also notes references to "liberals," "blacks," George Soros, and other consubstantial Others that served as a différend within the forum threads. An archived 4Chan thread discussing #Pizzagate can be found here (http://archive.is/RffAd#selection-1027.0-1032.0). The thread contains references to liberals, as well as racists, sexist, anti-Semitic, anti-Atheist, and homophobic language.
2 The fake news article was possibly written by a Jimmy Rustlying, who claimed to be a reporter for ABC News. The article titled "Donald Trump Protester Speaks Out: 'I Was Paid $3,500 To Protest Trump's Rally'" can be found at http://abcnews.com.co/donald-trump-protester-speaks-out-i-was-paid-to-protest/ as of September 19, 2017. This is the same article tweeted by Corey Lwandowski.
3 Melissa Zimdars, an Associate Professor of communication and media at Merrimack College in Massachusetts, compiled a categorized list of websites that either purposely publish false information or that publish information that generally unreliable. The list includes Zimdars' own rubric for analyzing news sources. (https://docs.google.com/document/d/10eA5-mCZLSS4MQY5QGb5ewC3VAL6pLkT53V_81ZyitM/preview). The International Fact-Checking Network (IFCN) at the Poynter Institute also provides a list of fact-checking websites.

Bibliography

Abramson, Alana. "President Trump Launches Twitter Attack: 'Fake News Is the Enemy.'" *Time.com*, May 28, 2016.

Alefantis, James. "What Happened When 'Pizzagate' Came to My Restaurant." *Washington Post*, WashingtonPost.com, April 20, 2016.

Alexander, Lawrence. "Social Network Analysis Reveals Full Scale of Kremlin's Twitter Bot Campaign." *Global Voices*, GlobalVoices.org, April 2, 2015.

Allcott, Hunt and Mathew Gentzkow. "Social Media and Fake News in the 2016 Election." *Journal of Economic Perspectives* 31, no. 2 (2017): 211–36. American Economic Association.

Bartholomew, Robert E. *Panic Attacks: Media Manipulation and Mass Delusion*. Stroud: Sutton Publishing Ltd, 2004.

Bartholomew, Robert E. and Benjamin Radford. *The Martians Have Landed!: A History of Media-Driven Panics and Hoaxes*, 84–85. Jefferson, NC: McFarland & Company, October 19, 2011.

Bizzell, Patricia and Bruce Herzberg. *The Rhetorical Tradition: Readings from Classical Times to the Present*. Boston, MA: Bedford Books of St. Martin's Press, 1990.

boyd, danah. "The Information War Has Begun." *Apophenia*, Zephoria.org, January 27, 2017.

Carroll, Lauren. "Fact-checking Donald Trump's Tweets about Hillary Clinton and Russia." *Politifact.com*, March 28, 2017.

Chang, JuJu, Jake Lefferman, Claire Pederson, and Geoff Martz. "Fake News Stories Make Real News Headlines." *ABC News*, ABCNews.com, November 29, 2016.

Connery, Thomas B. "A Famous Newspaper Hoax." *Harper's Weekly* 37, no. 1902 (June 3, 1893): 534. Babel.hathitrust.org.

Consigny, Scott. "Edward Schiappa's Reading of the Sophists." *Rhetoric Review* 14, no. 2 (1996): 253–69.

Consigny, Scott. "Nietzsche's Reading of the Sophists." *Rhetoric Review* 13, no. 1 (1994): 5–26.

Dewey, Caitlin. "Facebook Fake-news Writer: 'I Think Donald Trump is in the White House Because of Me.'" *Washington Post*, Washingtonpost.com, November 11, 2016.

Farhi, Paul. "Alex Jones Pizzagate Apology." *The Chicago Tribune Post*, TheChicagoTribune.com, March 24, 2017.

Farley, Robert. "Trump Defends Oswald Claim." *Fact Check.org*, July 22, 2016.

Frankovic, Kathy. "Belief in Conspiracies Largely Depends on Political Identity." *YouGov.com*, December 27, 2016.

Frimer, Jeremy A., Linda Skitka, and Matt Motyl. "Liberals and Conservatives are Similarly Motivated to Avoid Exposure to One Another's Opinions." *Journal of Experimental Social Psychology* 72, no. 1 (2017): 1–12. Print.

Gibson, Walter. "In Praise of the Sophists." *College English* 55, no. 3 (1993): 263–90.

Gillin, Joshua. "How Pizzagate Went from Fake News to a Real Problem for a D.C. Business." *Politifact.com*, December 5, 2016.

Greenburg, Jon. "Pants on Fire Claim that George Soros Money Went to Women's March Protesters." *Politifact.com*, January 25, 2017.

Greenwald, Glenn. "A Clinton Fan Manufactured Fake News that MSNBC Personalities Spread to Discredit Wikileaks." *The Intercept*, December 9, 2016.

Halloway, Kali. "14 Fake News Stories Created or Publicized By Donald Trump." *The National Memo*, TheNationalMemo.com, September 8, 2017.

Hunt, Elle. "What is Fake News? How to Spot it and How to Stop It." *The Guardian*, TheGuardian.com, December 17, 2017.

"International Fact-Checking Network Fact-checkers' Code of Principles." *The Poynter Institute for Media Studies*, Pynter.org, 2018, www.poynter.org/international-fact-checking-network-fact-checkers-code-principles

Kalev, Leetaru. "The Daily Mail Snopes Story and Fact Checking The Fact Checkers," *Forbes*, Forbes.com, December 22, 2016.

LaCapria, Kim. "Chuck E. Sleaze." *Snopes*, Snopes.com, November 4, 2016.

López, Ian Haney. *Dog Whistle Politics: Strategic Racism, Fake Populism, and the Dividing of America*. Oxford: Oxford University Press, 2018.

Maheshwari, Sapna. "How Fake News Goes Viral: A Case Study." *The New York Times*, Newyorktimes.com, November 20, 2016.

Martin, Jonathan. "Dubious Vote-Fraud Claim Gets the Trump Seal of Approval." *The New York Times*, Newyorktimes.com, January 27, 2017.

McCollam, Douglas. "How Chalabi Played the Press." *Columbia Journalism Review*, Archived from the original on 3 July 3, 2004, 31–37.

McHenry, Leemon. "Of Sophists and Spin-Doctors: Industry-Sponsored Ghostwriting and the Crisis of Academic Medicine." *Journalology* 8, no. 1 (2010): 129–45.

McKerns, Joseph Patrick. "The History of American Journalism: A Bibliographical Essay." *American Studies International* 15, no. 1 (1974): 17–34.

McKiharan, Richard D. *Philosophy before Socrates: An Introduction with Text and Commentary*. Indianapolis, IN/Cambridge: Hackett Publishing Company, 1994.

Mihailidis, Paul and Samantha Viotty. "Spreadable Spectacle in Digital Culture: Civic Expression, Fake News, and the Role of Media Literacies in "Post-Fact" Society." *American Behavioral Scientist* 61, no. 4 (2017): 441–54.

Mikkelson, David. "Riot Act." *Snopes*, Snopes.com, January 17, 2015.

Padgett, Lauree. "Filtering Out Fake News: It All Starts with Media Literacy." *Information Today* 34, no. 1 (2017): 6.

Ritchie, Hannah. "Read All About It: The Biggest Fake News Stories of 2016." *CNBC*, CBNBC.com, December 30, 2016.

Rosen, Christopher. *EW Magazine*, EW.com, June 27, 2017.

Schiappa, Edward. "Neo-Sophistic Rhetorical Criticism or the Historical Reconstruction of Sophistic Doctrines?" *Philosophy & Rhetoric* 23, no. 3 (1990): 192–217.

Schiappa, Edward. "Twenty-Five Years after "Did Plato Coin Rhêtorikê?": An Episodic Memoir." *Rhetoric Review* 35, no. 1 (2016): 1–9.

Schlesinger, Robert. "Fake News in Reality." *U.S. News and World Report*, USnews.com, April 14, 2017.

Silverman, Craig and Lawrence Alexander. "How Teens in the Balkans are Duping Trump Supporters with Fake News." *Buzzfeed News*, Buzzfeed.com, November 3, 2016.

Silverman, Craig. "How the Bizarre Conspiracy Theory Behind "Pizzagate" Was Spread." *Buzzfeed News*, Buzzfeed.com, November 4, 2016.

Slotkin, Jason. "'Pizzagate' Gunman Pleads Guilty To Charges." *NPR News*, March 24, 2017.

Struyk, Ryan. "67 Times Donald Trump Tweeted About the 'Birther' Movement." *ABC News*, ABCNews.com, September 16, 2016.

Trump, Donald. Twitter Post. November 10, 2016, 6:19 P.M. https://twitter.com/realdonaldtrump/status/796900183955095552?

Vega, Tanzina. "Decoding the 'dog whistle' Politics of Trump and Clinton." *CNN Money*, CNN.com, October 19, 2016.

Vitanza, Victor. *"The Sophists?" Negation, Subjectivity, and the History of Rhetoric*. Albany, NY: SUNY Press, 1996.

Wade, Peter. "Pizzagate Will Never Die: Here's Why the Conspiracy Theory Has New Life." *Esquire Magazine*, Esquire.com, March 25, 2017.

Wallace, David Rains. *The Bonehunters' Revenge: Dinosaurs, Greed, and the Greatest Scientific Feud of the Gilded Age*, 6–7. Boston, MA: Houghton Mifflin Harcourt. November 16, 2000.

Wardle, Claire. "6 Types of Misinformation Circulated this Election Season." *Columbus Journalism Review*, CJR.org, November 18, 2016.

Wardle, Claire. "Fake News. It's Complicated." *First Draft*. FirstDraftNews.com. Shorenstein Center on Media, Politics and Public Policy. Harvard Kennedy School. February 16, 2017.

Yilek, Caitlin. "Trump Flirts with Suggestion that Scalia was Murdered." *The Hill Blog*, TheHill.com, February 16, 2016.

INDEX

For Product Safety Concerns and Information please contact our EU
representative GPSR@taylorandfrancis.com
Taylor & Francis Verlag GmbH, Kaufingerstraße 24, 80331 München, Germany